Mindreading Animals

Mindreading Animals

The Debate over What Animals Know about Other Minds

Robert W. Lurz

A Bradford Book
The MIT Press
Cambridge, Massachusetts
London, England

For information about special quantity discounts, please email special_sales@ mitpress.mit.edu

This book was set in Stone Sans and Stone Serif by Toppan Best-set Premedia Limited. Printed and bound in the United States of America.

Library of Congress Cataloging-in-Publication Data

Lurz, Robert W., 1968–
Mindreading animals : the debate over what animals know about other minds / Robert W. Lurz.
    p.   cm. — (A bradford book)
Includes bibliographical references and index.
ISBN 978-0-262-01605-6 (hardcover : alk. paper)
1. Extrasensory perception in animals. 2. Cognition in animals. I. Title.
QL785.3.L87   2011
591.5'13—dc22

2011001933

10 9 8 7 6 5 4 3 2 1

For Mary Jane, William, and James

Is this a dagger which I see before me,
The handle toward my hand? Come, let me clutch thee.
I have thee not, and yet I see thee still.
Art thou not, fatal vision, sensible
To feeling as to sight? or art thou but
A dagger of the mind, a false creation,
Proceeding from the heat-oppressed brain?

—Shakespeare, *Macbeth*, act II, scene i

A tactic for embarrassing behaviorists in the laboratory is to set up experiments that deceive the subject: if the deception succeeds, their behavior is predicable from their false beliefs about the environment, not from their actual environment.

—Dan Dennett from "Conditions of Personhood"

Contents

Preface

Many animals live in a world of other minds. They live and interact with offspring, conspecifics, predators, prey, and owners, many of whom feel, see, hear, intend, know, and believe things (to name but a few states of mind). What is more, animals' well-being and survival often depend critically on what is going on in the minds of these other creatures. However, do animals know this about these other creatures? Do they know or even think that these other creatures have minds? Perhaps they simply see them as mindless, self-moving agents that behave in predictable and sometimes unpredictable ways (e.g., much as we might see the behavior of an ant or a toy robotic dog). How would we know? We cannot, after all, ask them to describe how they think about these other creatures.

The question of whether and to what degree animals know something about other minds has been a hotly debated topic in philosophy and cognitive science for over thirty years now. This book is focused on this debate, and it proposes a way to solve one of its long-standing problems.

I was led to the animal mindreading debate some years ago while working on a series of articles on issues related to animal consciousness, and I quickly became engrossed with its content. It became clear to me, after much study, that there were two fundamental issues that defined the debate: (i) how best to conceive of mental state attribution in animals and (ii) how best to test for it empirically. And I soon became dissatisfied with the answers that philosophers and scientists tended to give to (i) and (ii).

Regarding (i), two approaches to understanding mental state attribution in animals dominated the discussion. Many researchers, influenced by functionalist theories of the mind, assumed that if animals attribute mental states to other creatures, then they must attribute functionally defined inner causal states (sometimes referred to as 'intervening variables') to these other creatures (see Whiten 1996; Heyes 1998; Penn & Povinelli

2007). Another group of researchers, with instrumentalist leanings, argued that all there could be to animals' attributing mental states was the fact that their behavior patterns were usefully grouped and predicted by researchers under the assumption ('stance') that they did (Dennett 1987; Bennett 1991).

I was unconvinced by either of these approaches. Functionalist definitions of our own mental state concepts were notoriously problematic (Nagel 1974; Block 1978; Thau 2002), and so I found it difficult to believe they would do any better at capturing what animals meant by their mental state concepts. And the instrumentalist position struck me as too counterintuitive to take seriously (as well as being incompatible with the kinds of causal explanations that empirical researchers sought to provide with their mindreading hypotheses). After all, whether an animal attributes mental states is surely not something that is determined by someone else's stance—not even a researcher's—any more so than whether you attribute mental states is.

And as for (ii), the kind of experimental protocol generally used to test for mental state attribution in animals (principally, apes) was a type of discrimination task in which the animal was required to choose between two objects (typically, containers) depending on whether another agent in the experiment (usually an experimenter) had or lacked a particular mental state (e.g., saw or did not see the object in question placed inside a container). However, this sort of method for testing mental state attribution in animals struck me, as well as others, as problematic. First, these types of protocols simply could not control for the possibility that, in making their choices between the objects, the test animals were merely using the observable cues that were differentially associated with the other agent's mental state and not the agent's mental state itself. And it became clear that simply adding additional controls to such experiments would not solve the problem. The problem was, as Hurley and Nudds (2006) came to remark, "a logical rather than an empirical problem" for such experimental approaches (p. 63). It was a problem that was solvable only by changing the logic of the protocols used to test for mental state attribution in animals, not by adding further controls to the existing type of protocol. For this reason, this methodological problem has come to be called the "logical problem" in the literature (Hurley & Nudds 2006; Lurz 2009a). A principal aim of this book is to show how this problem might be solved.

In addition, I was suspicious of the fact that these discrimination studies were not directly testing an animal's ability to predict or anticipate another agent's behavior, which arguably is what mental state attribution in animals is designed to help animals do (see Santos et al. 2007). And so I came to agree with Gil Harman (1978) that "[t]he fact that the chimpanzee [or any other animal] makes certain distinctions, no matter how complex, does not show that it has the relevant expectations [of the other agent's behavior] and so does not show that it has a theory of mind" (p. 577). The standard experimental protocol used in animal mindreading research, it seemed to me, was the wrong kind of test to use to elicit mental state attributions in animals. The protocols, rather, should directly test an animal's ability to *predict* or *anticipate* another agent's behavior, not its ability to *discriminate* between objects that only distantly have anything to do with the other agent's mental states.

I therefore came to believe that progress could be made in the debate over mental state attribution in animals by making two substantive changes. First, a bottom-up approach to understanding mental state attribution in animals was needed, one which built a conception of mindreading in animals out of already existing cognitive abilities in animals rather than one that appealed to a preconceived view of the mind deemed applicable to mental state attributions in humans. And second, a new type of experimental protocol was needed that was free from the above problems which beset current experimental approaches, a type of protocol that could solve the logical problem. In a series of papers (Lurz 2001, 2007, 2009a), I began to make a case for these changes, and the current book is the culmination of this progress.

Chapter 1 outlines some of the main reasons that the question of mental state attribution in animals is important to topics in philosophy and cognitive science and provides a brief history of the debate within these fields. I show that even within the early years of the debate, a central concern among researchers was how to solve the logical problem.

Chapter 2 clarifies what the logical problem is and is not. In the chapter, I focus on the experimental protocols that have been used to test for cognitive state attribution in animals (e.g., attributions of seeing, hearing, and knowing) and show that none, unfortunately, is capable of solving the logical problem. In general the protocols simply cannot determine whether animals attribute *seeing* to other agents or just the behavioral/environmental cue associated with this mental state in others, *direct line of gaze*. I consider a number of counterarguments to this claim that are designed to show that new experimental protocols are not necessary since the data from the current studies are best explained in terms of these animals' attributing seeing and related cognitive states. I show that these arguments are unpersuasive and argue that only by solving the logical problem in this domain can a sufficiently strong case be made in favor of the hypothesis that animals are capable of attributing cognitive states.

The main objective of chapter 3 is to show how it is possible to overcome the logical problem in tests for cognitive state attribution in animals—specifically, seeing-as attributions. Before doing this, however, I examine a well-known pair of arguments by Povinelli and colleagues that aim to show that mental state attribution in animals is highly unlikely and show that neither argument is particularly convincing. I then outline an abstract framework for how to solve the logical problem and provide a viable, bottom-up account of seeing-as attributions in animals, which I call the appearance–reality mindreading (ARM) theory. The framework and the theory together provide a recipe for designing experiments that test for such mental state attributions in animals which have the potential to overcome the logical problem. Three different types of experimental designs are described and defended.

Chapter 4 is on the vexing question of the possibility of belief attribution in animals. Two well-known philosophical arguments (by Donald Davidson and José Luis Bermúdez, respectively) against belief attribution in animals are discussed and shown to be unconvincing. In response to these arguments, I present and defend a viable, bottom-up account of belief attribution in animals. Having removed these philosophical objections to the possibility of belief attributions in animals, I move on to examine the various empirical studies on belief attributions in apes and dolphins. For those studies that have been interpreted as showing that these animals can attribute beliefs, I argue that this is not the case on the grounds that the protocols used in the studies fail to solve the logical problem. And for those studies that have been taken to show that chimpanzees (in particular) are unable to attribute beliefs, I argue that there is no more reason to draw this conclusion than that these animals simply do not understand the discrimination tasks in the studies as having anything to do with the belief states of the communicator or competitor (i.e., the other agent) involved in them. Thus, the question of belief attribution in animals appears to be empirically wide open. What is needed to move the debate and the field forward is a fundamentally new experimental approach for testing belief attribution in animals, one that is capable of distinguishing genuine belief-attributing subjects from their perceptual-state and complementary behavior-reading counterparts. In the last sections of the chapter, I present three different kinds of experimental protocols to test for belief attribution in animals that can deliver the required evidence.

The various experimental protocols that I propose and defend in the last two chapters have not yet been tested on animals (although I am currently collaborating with a few researchers to run pilot studies using them). Of course, if the protocols had been run, there would be no point in arguing for them. The point of the protocols is not to provide new data but to show how to solve a particular methodological puzzle that has plagued the field since its inception. Thus, the question that this book aims to answer is really a how-to question: How can researchers come to know whether animals attribute mental states (particularly, cognitive states) when there is a viable alternative hypothesis at hand (that animals are behavior readers of a certain sort) for which no type of experimental protocol employed in the field has yet been able to control? The aim of the book is to describe experimental protocols that can control for this alternative hypothesis and show how this question can be answered.

Acknowledgments

In writing this book, I have been aided and influenced by the advice and ideas of a number of philosophers and animal researchers. I am grateful to all of them. Two in particular deserve special thanks, however. Peter Carruthers and Bob Mitchell have provided continuous insightful comments and (needed) encouragement throughout. This book would not have been started or finished without their generous assistance. Others have also played an important role in determining the direction and content of this book. I am particularly indebted for the comments and advice provided by Jonathan Adler, Kristin Andrews, Megan Brabant, Thomas Bugnyar, Dick Byrne, David DeGrazia, Marietta Dindo, Simon Fitzpatrick, Juan Gómez, Uri Grodzinski, Brian Hare, Bill Hopkins, Dan Hutto, Chikako King, Carla Krachun, Elaine Madsen, Jonathan Man, Lori Marino, Chris Petkov, Eric Saidel, Laurie Santos, Amanda Seed, Julie Smith, Francys Subiaul, Jean Reinson, Mike Tomasello, Claudia Uller, Abe Witonsky, and Tad Zawidzki. I wish to thank Whitney Pillsbury for designing some of the figures in chapter 4, to Katherine Almeida and Ellen Tremper for their very helpful editorial advice, and to Phil Laughlin for his unwavering faith in and support for the project throughout. I am grateful to Brooklyn College for a semester's sabbatical which allowed me the opportunity to start writing the book. The bulk of the writing and research was done while I was on an Ethyle Wolfe Fellowship and received a National Endowment for the Humanities Summer Stipend Award. Both awards provided a much needed release from teaching, without which the book would have never been completed. Some of the material in chapters 3 and 4 are derived from "In defense of wordless thoughts about thoughts" *Mind and Language* (2007), "If chimpanzees are mindreaders, could behavioral science tell? Toward a solution of the logical problem" *Philosophical Psychology* (2009a), "Belief attribution in animals: On how to move forward conceptually and empirically" *The Review of Philosophy and Psychology* (2010), and "Can chimps attribute beliefs? A new approach to answering an old nettled question" in R. Mitchell and J. Smith's (eds.) *Minds of Animals*, Columbia University Press (2011). Many thanks to these journals and editors for allowing the use of this material.

1 Mindreading in Animals: Its Importance and History

The question of whether animals read minds may at first sound somewhat comical, evoking images of telepathic pets with paws pressed meditatively to their temples, perhaps. However, the term 'mindreading' used in this book and in cognitive science and philosophy generally departs considerably from its more familiar meaning of direct mind-to-mind communication.[1] Here the term is used to refer to the ability to attribute mental states, such as beliefs, intentions, and perceptual experiences, to others by the decidedly mundane and indirect means of observing their behaviors within environmental contexts.

On this use of the term, ordinary human beings (and not just telepathists) are mindreaders par excellence. We quite readily predict and make sense of other humans' and animals' behaviors by trying to understand what they might be thinking, or seeing, or intending to do. Although we may actually mindread less than we typically think and say we do, as some researchers have argued (Hutto 2008; Bermúdez 2009), there are many everyday cases, as well as countless scientific studies, that quite clearly show that humans have an almost reflexive tendency, beginning early in childhood, to predict, understand, explain, and manipulate the behaviors of others in terms of what we think is going on in their minds (Wellman 1990; Carruthers & Smith 1996; Nichols & Stich 2003; Goldman 2006; Gopnik 2009). Regarding mindreading in humans, there is simply no serious issue.

By contrast, there is a deep and important question in cognitive science and philosophy concerning whether humans are the only living animal capable of mindreading. For over thirty years now, there has been a sustained and heated debate over the question of whether any species of nonhuman animal is capable of attributing mental states. The field is presently divided between those who claim that there is empirical evidence to support the hypothesis that some animals are mindreaders and those who deny this.

In my opinion, the animal mindreading debate has simply stalled, with both sides digging in their heels. This is not to say that empirical research into animal mindreading has stalled—quite the opposite, in fact. In the past eight years or so, there has been an unprecedented flurry of empirical research into mindreading capabilities in a variety of species of animal. Rather, the debate has stalled in that both sides are content with a handful of arguments that, I believe, fail to support the rather strong claims that they are used to make. Contrary to what either side holds, the question of whether animals are mindreaders is in no way a settled matter.[2] I do believe, however, that there is a way to move the debate closer to a settled answer. I shall make the case that what is fundamentally needed to advance the debate is a reconceptualization of what mindreading (specifically, cognitive state attribution) in animals should be understood to encompass and (most important) a solution to an epistemic and methodological problem (dubbed the 'logical problem') that has dogged the field since its inception.

It should be noted at the start that in this debate the mentality of animals as such is not in dispute. It is recognized on all sides, and for good scientific and commonsensible reasons, that many animals have minds, that they perceive, feel, have emotions, perform intentional acts, have beliefs, remember, and (in some instances) engage in various forms of cognition and reasoning (see Griffin 1992; Shettleworth 1998). Thus, it is acknowledged by both sides that animals live in a world with other minded creatures—a world of perceiving, feeling, intending, thinking conspecifics, owners, predators, and prey. And it is equally recognized that animals are adept at predicting the behavior of these other creatures. This is all common ground. The questions that define the debate, rather, are (i) whether animals ever make such predictions by understanding what is (or what they take to be) going on in another creature's mind or simply by being sensitive to the behavioral and environmental cues that indicate (or can be used to infer) what the other creature is likely to do without interpreting them as evidence of the creature's state of mind and (ii) whether behavioral science, with its empirical methods of investigation and testing, has the resources to determine which of these hypotheses is correct.

This book is about this debate, why it is important, and how it can be moved forward. In section 1.1 below, I state some of the reasons the question of animal mindreading is important to cognitive science and philosophy. In section 1.2, I give a concise summary of the history of the debate, its current state of stalemate, and what, in general terms, needs to be done to advance it.

1.1 Why the Question of Animal Mindreading Matters

The question matters for three general types of reasons: those related to our interest in the minds and moral status of animals; those related to our interests in certain philosophical theories about mindreading and the nature of the mind; and those related to various scientific interests in studying mindreading in humans. Below is a representative set of these different concerns.

Relevance to the scientific study of animal minds   Cognition is pervasive in the animal world, and scientists and philosophers have had an abiding interest in studying it, not only for the light it can shed on human cognition, but for what it can tell us about the minds of animals (Walker 1983; Gallistel 1990; Griffin 1992; Shettleworth 1998; Bekoff et al. 2002; Lurz 2009b). Although scientific investigation into animal mentality lay largely dormant during much of the heyday of behaviorism, it has seen a healthy rebirth in the past thirty years or more. Under the auspice of the cognitive revolution in psychology and philosophy, researchers from various fields are now vigorously pursuing questions about animal minds, and one of the more active research programs in the field is the question of mindreading (and social cognition more generally) in animals. Researchers from cognitive and comparative psychology, cognitive ethology, and cognitive neuroscience have been investigating various social cognitive capacities in different animal species (e.g., apes, monkeys, dolphins, dogs, goats, pigs, elephants, and birds) in part for what it can tell us about how these animals understand their social worlds, how this social knowledge may have evolved within a given species, how it compares across different species, and how it may develop within the individual members of the species.

In addition, the question of mindreading in nonhuman primates (hereafter primates) is of particular importance to an influential hypothesis about the evolution of primate intelligence called the 'Machiavellian intelligence hypothesis' or 'social brain hypothesis' (see Jolly 1966; Humphrey 1976; Byrne & Whiten 1988; Whiten & Byrne 1997; Dunbar 1998, 2007). According to the hypothesis, it was a set of demanding social problems resulting from living in large, complex groups that drove the evolution of primates' large neocortex (the seat of higher cognition) relative to their body size and their correspondingly unique intellectual abilities, such as tool use, coalition and alliance formations, mirror self-recognition, and the capacity for transitive inferences, among others. To survive and thrive in their complex social world, according to the hypothesis, primates evolved certain mindreading abilities needed for solving complex social problems, such as anticipating and manipulating conspecifics' behaviors. A number of researchers have now extended the Machiavellian intelligence hypothesis to explain the evolution of similar forms of higher intelligence and brain size found in certain nonprimate animals, such as corvids and dolphins, that also live in large, complex social groups. To date, the Machiavellian intelligence hypothesis (or social brain hypothesis) appears to fit the neurological data—that relative brain size correlates with group size and social complexity—better than any of the alternative ecological hypotheses of the evolution of intelligence (Dunbar 2007). Of course, whether the hypothesis is correct regarding the evolution of mindreading in these social species of animals depends critically upon whether these animals really do have the capacity to attribute mental states.

Relevance to the moral status and welfare of animals Philosophers and ethicists make an important distinction between the biological category of human being, *Homo sapiens*, and the moral/psychological category of persons. *Homo sapiens* are defined by their unique genetic make-up, ability to interbreed, morphology, and evolutionary history, whereas *persons* are defined by a unique set of moral and psychological attributes and capacities, such as the capacity for moral autonomy (roughly, the ability to understand right and wrong and act for moral reasons), self-awareness, and mindreading. Although all (or most) *Homo sapiens* are persons, it does not follow that only *Homo sapiens* are persons, or even legal persons (i.e., entities that are recognized by law as persons).

It has been recently argued by some philosophers and scientists that since the great apes share enough of their DNA, evolutionary history, and psychological capacities with human beings, they deserve to be recognized as persons or (at the very least) as legal persons. Often cited on this list of relevant psychological similarities is the ability of great apes to attribute mental states (or to 'empathize'). And this is no accident. For there is a well-established line of argument in philosophy and cognitive science that holds that of the attributes that define personhood, mindreading is the most central (Dennett 1978b). It is mindreading, the argument runs, upon which empathy and (subsequently) moral autonomy rest, as well as self-awareness, and it is mindreading that should be used as one of the logical grounds for distinguishing animals that should be recognized as (legal or natural) persons from those that should not (see Mitchell 1993). It is important to note that on the basis of such arguments, Spain's parliament recently approved a resolution for the legal recognition and protection of the rights of life, liberty, and freedom from torture for the great apes (Abend 2008). Other countries in Europe seem poised to follow suit.

Independent of the issue of the status of animals as persons, the question of animal mindreading has recently been argued to be relevant to issues of animal welfare (Tschudin 2001). The argument is that if some animals are mindreaders, then they likely have a natural tendency to predict and understand conspecifics' behaviors in terms of the mental states they attribute, and thus they may well be harmed by being placed in conditions that either prevent this natural tendency from being exercised or exercised in ways that induce stress. For example, it has been recently argued by Held et al. (2001) that domestic pigs, which have shown some tentative signs of being capable of understanding the visual perspective of conspecifics, may be adversely affected by the common husbandry practice of mixing these animals in with unfamiliar conspecifics (which would be difficult for them to mindread) or from their being isolated from familiar conspecifics (which would prevent them from exercising their natural tendency to mindread), as well as their being subject to witnessing familiar conspecifics suffering (which may cause them to empathize with the other's pain). It is argued that an improved understanding of mindreading abilities in animals may lead to improvements to their housing conditions and related husbandry practices.

Relevance to philosophical theories on mindreading and the nature of the mind   There are three influential theories in philosophy on the importance of mindreading in shaping a distinctively human mode of cognition. According to the first of these theories, which is traceable through Wittgenstein (1953) and Davidson (1980, 2001), mindreading of a certain type is required for the possession of genuine thought (cognitive states that can be literally true or false, correct or incorrect). The general idea behind the theory is that only through the ascription of thoughts to others can a creature come to grasp a notion of objectivity—the way things really are independently of its own mind—that is required to make sense of how its own cognitive states can be true or false. Defenders of this theory typically go on to argue that mindreading of this sort is only possible for linguistic creatures, such as normal adult human beings, and conclude that only humans are capable of genuine thought and reason. We shall return to this argument and examine it in more detail in chapter 4. For now, it is important to see that the question of animal mindreading is relevant to its plausibility.

A related line of thought, inspired by Peter Strawson (1959), is that mindreading of a certain type is required for possessing thoughts about

particular objects and their characterizing properties. According to this
theory, nothing short of ascribing thoughts (e.g., a belief) and their epistemic grounds (e.g., the perceptual states that justify the belief) to the very
same individual would force a creature to think in terms of re-identifiable
particular objects or individual substances (for a related idea, see Welker
1988; Proust 2009). Deprived of this capacity, the argument runs, creatures
can aspire only to what Strawson describes as a feature-placing mode of
cognition, a way of thinking about the world in terms of repeatable and
projectable kinds of stuff (e.g., rain, snow, gold) but not in terms of recur-
ring individuals (e.g., individual conspecifics or individual objects). The
defenders of this theory typically assume that since animals lack the ability
to mindread, their manner of cognition is relegated to a feature-placing
mode and is thus importantly different from the uniquely human mode
of cognition involving thoughts about re-identifiable individuals and their
characterizing properties (see Burge 2009, 2010 for a recent critical account
of this theory). Again, the question of animal mindreading is relevant to
whether this philosophical theory about a distinctively human mode of
thought is correct.

According to the third theory (which has defenders in both philosophy
and science), mindreading is a necessary condition for self-awareness and
metacognition. The capacity to know or represent the contents of one's
own mind, according to the theory, is dependent upon one's capacity to
know or represent the contents of other minds. Self-awareness and metacognition are understood to be the result of turning one's own mindreading abilities onto oneself (Carruthers 2009). It is sometimes argued that
since most (if not all) animals are incapable of mindreading, they are
thereby incapable of self-awareness and metacognition. One influential
defender of this view (Carruthers 2000) has gone on to argue that since a
type of self-awareness (viz., dispositional higher-order thought) is necessary for phenomenal consciousness (the 'what-it-is-like' or sentient aspect
of experience), animals lacking in any form of mindreading are thereby
lacking in phenomenal consciousness. Obviously, whether some animals
are mindreaders is quite relevant, according to this theory, to whether they
are capable of self-awareness and phenomenal consciousness.

Relevance to human mindreading   The question of animal mindreading is of
particular importance to a branch of evolutionary psychology that seeks
to trace the origins of mindreading in human beings. Researchers in this
field are interested in discovering the place in our evolutionary past
where mindreading first emerged, the selection pressures that led to its

emergence, and how it has evolved from its inception. Various methods of research are used in this field, but a principal method is that of studying the higher primates (e.g., the great apes and monkeys), our closest living evolutionary relatives—for if any of the higher primates demonstrate mindreading capacities, then this would suggest that mindreading in human beings evolved within the primate line due to distinct selection pressures found there (Santos et al. 2007). Conversely, if primates fail to demonstrate any ability to mindread, then this would suggest that mindreading in human beings evolved within the hominid (human) line due to distinct selection pressure found there (Penn et al. 2008).

The scientific pursuit of the question of animal mindreading may also prove useful to scientists studying the mindreading capacities of nonverbal and preverbal humans, as well as those studying the neural basis of mindreading in humans generally. Scientists studying mindreading in aphasic adults and very young infants, for example, are in need of discriminating nonverbal mindreading tests, and, of course, scientists studying animal mindreading are in the business of designing such tests. It is quite possible, therefore, that advances made in the methods used to study mindreading in animals will prove useful for designing more effective or sensitive tests of mindreading in nonverbal and preverbal humans.

Scientific investigation into mindreading in primates may also prove valuable to neuroscientists investigating the neural architecture of mindreading in humans, as well as those interested in developing neuropharmacological treatments for mindreading disorders in humans, such as autism. Both types of investigations are in need of animal subjects to run more invasive and controlled studies that would be otherwise impractical or unethical to run on humans. Of course, the usefulness of such animal models will depend upon whether science is able to demonstrate that these animals are truly mindreaders.[3]

1.2 A Brief History of the Animal Mindreading Debate

Although the question of animal mindreading was a topic of interest in philosophy and science prior to the late 1970s, its official birth date is 1978, the year that David Premack and Guy Woodruff published their landmark paper, "Does the chimpanzee have a theory of mind?" In that paper, Premack and Woodruff described a series of innovative experiments with their chimpanzee, Sarah, the results of which, they argued, indicated that she was capable of attributing mental states to her trainers. In one of these experiments, Sarah was shown a variety of videotapes of a trainer confronting different types of problems (e.g., reaching for a banana suspended from the ceiling or shivering by an unlit heater). The videos were then paused, and Sarah was given the opportunity to select from a pair of still photos. Both photos depicted the trainer engaged in an action, but only one of the photos depicted an action that would have solved the trainer's problem presented in the video. For example, after the suspended banana video, Sarah was presented with one photo showing the trainer stepping onto a chair below the area where the banana was suspended and another photo showing the trainer prone on the floor and reaching to the side with a stick. Sarah consistently chose the photo depicting the solution to the trainer's problem in the video in nearly every test trial. Her stellar performance led Premack and Woodruff to conclude that Sarah understood the trainer's behavior in the videos in terms of the trainer having a particular intention or goal (e.g., to reach the bananas or to be warmed by the heater) and, thus, selected those photos that depicted those types of actions that would lead to the satisfaction of the attributed intention or goal.

In the same paper, Premack and Woodruff described an innovative experimental approach for testing mindreading capacities in animals, subsequently called the knower–guesser protocol, which soon became a standard procedure in the field. In the knower–guesser protocol, a chimpanzee is required to discriminate between two trainers in order to receive or locate food hidden inside one of two containers. The chimpanzee, however, is prevented from observing which container has been baited but is allowed to observe that one of the trainers (the knower) has witnessed the baiting process while the other (the guesser) has not.[4] If the chimpanzee is a mindreader, Premack and Woodruff reasoned, then she ought to favor the knowledgeable trainer over the ignorant one in some way, either by choosing the former to indicate a particular container or by choosing the container indicated by that trainer. When Premack (1988) eventually tested some chimpanzees with the protocol, he discovered that the majority of them (3 out of 4) did in fact show a decided preference, from the very first trial, for choosing the knower over the guesser in selecting the baited container.[5] On the basis of such results, Premack (2007) has come to hold that chimpanzees are capable of attributing simple perceptual states and intentions to others, but not beliefs or knowledge, which he considers too complex for nonhuman animals to comprehend. This has become a rather common view among animal mindreading researchers and will be examined in more detail in chapter 4.

As important as Premack and Woodruff's paper was for initiating and structuring the direction of empirical research into animal mindreading, the critical commentary that accompanied their paper was equally important. A notable series of objections were leveled against Premack and Woodruff's interpretation of Sarah's performance in the video tasks. On closer inspection of the videos and photos, it was pointed out by some researchers (Savage-Rumbaugh et al. 1978; Heyes 1998) that Sarah could have chosen the correct photos simply on the grounds of some formerly learned associations (e.g., choosing a photo with a lit roll of paper because she associated the orange flame with the heater) or by matching items found in the last frame of the videos with the correct photos (e.g., choosing the photo with the horizontal stick since the stick was present in the final frame of the video). But by far some of the most significant commentary came from three philosophers: Gil Harman (1978), Daniel Dennett (1978a), and Jonathan Bennett (1978). All three independently pointed to a critical, underlying problem of empirically testing for mindreading in animals: the problem of experimentally distinguishing genuine mental state attribution in animals from the attribution of the observable cues or facts that serve as the grounds or evidence of such mental states in others. As we shall see, this problem, subsequently dubbed the 'logical problem' (Hurley & Nudds 2006; Lurz 2009a), has come to be held by a number of researchers as the main obstacle to answering the question of mindreading in animals.

The significance of their identifying this problem was matched by these philosophers' innovative proposals to solve it. Each recommended a radically new type of experimental paradigm—the false-belief test. The test was designed to determine whether an animal would anticipate another subject's behavior not simply on the basis of the objective, observable cues or facts regarding the other's behavior and environmental situation, but on the basis of what the other subject erroneously believed to be the case about its behavior/environmental situation. Harman, for example, suggested allowing one chimpanzee (A) to observe while another chimpanzee (B) watched an experimenter place food inside one of two containers. While chimpanzee B was momentarily distracted from the containers (e.g., it had its back to the containers), chimpanzee A would observe the experimenter remove the food from its original hiding place (i.e., the container in which chimpanzee B saw the experimenter place it) and place it in the other container. Harman (1978) reasoned that if chimpanzee A expected chimpanzee B (once it had turned around to face the containers) to look into the container that was originally baited (but was no longer), then "that would seem to show that it has a conception of mere belief" (p. 577).

Although the false-belief test was ignored by animal researchers for many years after Premack and Woodruff's paper, it quickly became the litmus test for mindreading in developmental psychology. Wimmer and Perner (1983) were the first to use a version of the test on children. In their experiment, children from three to five years of age were shown a puppet show in which the main character (Max) had a mistaken belief about the location of his candy. It was discovered that five-year-olds (and some older four-year-olds) were capable of predicting Max's behavior by attributing a mistaken belief to him but that younger children were not. The younger children typically predicted Max's behavior in terms of where the candy actually was, not where Max mistakenly thought it was.[6] Wimmer and Perner's findings were quickly replicated and shown to be robust, and so, not surprisingly, there was a growing sense among some animal researchers that if three- and four-year-old children were incapable of attributing beliefs, animals were unlikely to do any better (see Premack 1988). This suspicion appeared to be borne out later by the negative findings from the first false-belief study on chimpanzees by Call and Tomasello (1999). Such results have, in turn, refueled the view, first held by Premack, that chimpanzees are capable of mindreading for simple states of perception and goal-directed/intentional actions but not for beliefs. However, as we shall see again and again, the road to discovering animal mindreading is anything but a straight line. O'Connell and Dunbar (2003), for example, have recently received positive results from a single chimpanzee on a false-belief test, and Tschudin (2001, 2006) has received even stronger results from three dolphins using a similar test. These studies will be discussed further in chapter 4.

At around the time of Premack and Woodruff's paper, Nicholas Humphrey (1976; see also Jolly 1966) published an important paper in which he argued for what is now called the Machiavellian intelligence hypothesis, which we briefly discussed above. The hypothesis holds that the high level of intelligence and relative brain size observed in primates (particularly, chimpanzees) is best explained as a result of the unique demands that their social living places on them. To survive and thrive in their complex social world, Humphrey argued, primates needed to evolve certain mindreading abilities to solve complex social problems. Inspired by Humphrey's hypothesis, a number of field researchers came forward with reports of anecdotal cases of primate intentional deception (or 'tactical deception') that appeared to show the use of innovative behavioral strategies by these animals for the purpose of inducing false beliefs in conspecifics. Many of these early field observations of intentional deception were collected and discussed in Byrne and Whiten (1988) and Whiten and Byrne (1997).[7] One such case deserves special mention for its subsequent influence in the field.

The American primatologist Emil Menzel (1974) was conducting spatial memory experiments on a group of captive chimpanzees when he observed some rather novel behavior in one of his adult females, called Belle. In the study, Menzel showed Belle the location of some hidden food in the 1-acre field where the chimpanzees lived and then returned Belle to her group mates. The group was then released into the field. On every occasion of their release, Belle made a straight line for the hidden food. The alpha male of the group, Rock, eventually caught on to this pattern of behavior and began to follow Belle to the hiding place of the food, whereupon he would quickly push her aside and consume all the food. On one occasion of the group's release, however, Belle unexpectedly went in the opposite direction from where she saw the food hidden. Rock, quite predictably, followed close behind. However, while Rock was preoccupied with looking in the wrong place, Belle quickly doubled back and consumed the hidden food.

Menzel and others took the novelty and apparent ingenuity of Belle's behavior as evidence of an explicit intention to deceive Rock, an intention to induce a false belief about the location of the food. In the early 1990s, Byrne and Whiten (1990) compiled a large database of similar observations of intentional deception in primates by field researchers. Eighteen of these accounts were identified by the researchers as cases of intentional tactical deception among great apes (Byrne 1995). More recently, researchers have run tests similar to Menzel's with chimpanzees (Hirata & Matsuzawa 2001) and mangabey monkeys (Coussi-Korbel 1994). Both studies report intentional deception in their animals similar to that observed in Belle.

At around the time of the release of Byrne and Whiten's database, Dorothy Cheney and Robert Seyfarth (1990) began to report the results of their experiments on the alarm-calling behaviors of wild vervet monkeys in Africa. Although prior to this, vervets had been known for their repertoire of distinct alarm calls for different types of predators (e.g., calls for eagles, calls for snakes, calls for neighboring troops of vervets, etc.), and for their flexible and appropriate responses to the distinct calls (e.g., looking up in the sky upon hearing an eagle alarm call, looking into the bushes upon hearing a python alarm call, etc.), much was still unknown about the intentional and semantic aspects of their communicative behaviors. Through detailed observations and a series of ingenious playback experiments using hidden speakers, Cheney and Seyfarth discovered that vervets not only appeared to possess some voluntary control over their calls (e.g., calling only when other vervets were known to be nearby) but they appeared to understand the different meanings or semantic information carried by the different alarm calls. From a hidden speaker in the trees, Cheney and Seyfarth played a recorded alarm call (e.g., a martial eagle alarm call) from an individual monkey at a time when the monkey was out of sight from the rest of its troop. Cheney and Seyfarth observed that the other members of the troop quickly habituate (i.e., stop responding) to this individual's alarm call if (after repeated playbacks) it was shown to be unreliable (e.g., when no martial eagle was ever seen). What is more, the researchers discovered that the troop also stopped responding to other semantically related but acoustically distinct alarm calls from this same individual (e.g., other raptor alarm calls). Quite remarkably, though, the troop continued to respond as usual to this individual monkey's semantically unrelated calls (e.g., leopard alarm calls) as well as to the semantically identical calls (e.g., martial eagle calls) from different members of the troop. The monkeys, it seemed, were evaluating the reliability of the individual's calls not on the basis of the calls' brute acoustical properties but in terms of the information the calls carried. Although Cheney and Seyfarth were reluctant to interpret their findings as proof that these vervet monkeys were attributing communicative intentions (a type of mental state) to callers, their findings did suggest to some that the monkeys were engaging in a form of intentional communication that may involve a rudimentary form of (and perhaps an evolutionary precursor to) such mental state attribution (see Gómez 2009).

There were critics of these various field studies, however. Some were skeptical of the data on the grounds of its anecdotal nature (Premack 1988; Povinelli 1996; Heyes 1998), while others were skeptical on more substantive grounds. During the mid and late 1990s, there was a growing skepticism among some researchers about the possibility of mindreading in animals. Chief among these skeptics was Daniel Povinelli and his colleagues. Povinelli and Eddy (1996) ran a series of discrimination tasks with chimpanzees to test their understanding of the mental state of seeing in others, and they received across-the-board negative results from them. In the first phase of the experiment, the chimpanzees were trained to beg for food from a single trainer. They were then tested with two new trainers, one who could see the chimpanzee and one who could not. In some of the test trials, for example, the seeing trainer faced forward while the unseeing trainer faced backward, while in other trials, the seeing trainer wore a blindfold around his neck while the unseeing trainer wore a blindfold over his eyes. The chimpanzees showed no signs of an initial preference for begging from the seeing trainer over the unseeing one. They did, however, show some improvement over time, preferring to beg from the seeing trainer more often than from the unseeing trainer. But the chimpanzees' incremental success, Povinelli and Eddy argued, was best explained in terms of their coming to follow a simple rule of thumb (e.g., pick the trainer whose face is visible) learned during the test trials which had nothing to do with their understanding the psychological state of seeing.[8]

A couple of years later, Cecilia Heyes (1998) published an important critical review of all extant data on primate mindreading and forcefully argued that none of it singly or collectively made a compelling case. Three significant points were made in the article. First, Heyes stressed, as Harman, Dennett, and Bennett had done twenty years earlier, the critical importance of overcoming the logical problem. To make progress on the question of animal mindreading, Heyes argued, researchers needed to design tests that could adequately distinguish genuine mindreading in animals from various plausible behavior-reading capacities in them. Second, Heyes showed in some detail that no experimental approach at that time was capable of solving the logical problem. And finally, and most importantly, she proposed an alternative experimental paradigm, the experience-projection (EP) paradigm, which she argued could effectively discriminate genuine mental state attribution from various forms of behavior reading in animals.

In the version of the EP paradigm that Heyes described in her paper, a chimpanzee is allowed to discover something about its own mental state of seeing while wearing (for the first time) two different kinds of goggles. One pair of goggles (trimmed in blue) was fitted with a clear lens that would allow the chimpanzee to see objects in the environment; the other pair of goggles (trimmed in red), however, was fitted with an opaque lens that would prevent the chimpanzee from seeing objects in the environment. It was speculated that the chimpanzee might learn, through wearing the different googles, that it could see objects in the environment while wearing the blue-trimmed goggles but not while wearing the red-trimmed ones.

After its exposure to the goggles, the chimpanzee would then be tested to see if it would use this knowledge about its own mental states of seeing/

not seeing to discriminate between a seeing trainer (wearing the transparent blue-trimmed goggles) and an nonseeing trainer (wearing the opaque red-trimmed goggles) in a knower–guesser protocol similar to that used by Premack (1988). Heyes reasoned that if the chimpanzee was a mindreader that was capable of introspecting its own states of seeing, it would be expected to choose the container indicated by the trainer with the blue-trimmed goggles on the grounds that that trainer, rather than the one wearing red-trimmed goggles, likely *saw* which container was baited. However, if the chimpanzee were but a behavior reader, and could appeal only to the observable, mind-independent facts presented in the pretest trials, then, Heyes reasoned, it should show no such bias in its choice of containers in the test trials since neither the blue- nor the red-trimmed goggles were ever associated with a container having food inside it.

To this day, Heyes's experimental protocol with goggles has not been run on animals.[9] Inspired by Heyes's protocol, however, Emery and Clayton (2008) recently ran a modified version of it (sans goggles) with scrub jays, the results of which, they argue, show that these birds are capable of projecting their own experience of pilfering caches onto conspecifics who are currently observing them caching. Emery and Clayton's experiment will be discussed in detail in chapter 2. Notwithstanding its infrequent use in animal mindreading research, the EP paradigm has come to be seen by some researchers (Povinelli & Vonk 2006; Lurz 2009a) as the only experimental method that can solve the logical problem. I shall make a strong case for this view in chapter 3.

Research into animal mindreading lay relatively dormant during the late 1990s, perhaps due to the negative findings and critical review discussed above. Then, at the beginning of the new millennium, the tide dramatically changed. Brian Hare and colleagues (2000, 2001) ran a series of unique mindreading experiments on chimpanzees that involved competition rather than cooperation, as in the traditional knower–guesser paradigm. In Hare and colleagues' study, a subordinate chimpanzee and a dominant chimpanzee competed for food placed behind different types of barriers. The researchers discovered that subordinate chimpanzees consistently refrained from taking food that was out in the open or behind clear (transparent) barriers—that is, food that the dominant chimpanzee in the situation could see—but attempted to take food that was behind opaque barriers—that is, food that the dominant chimpanzee in the situation could not see. The researchers argued that the subordinate chimpanzees' performance could not easily be accounted for in terms of learned associations or simple behavioral rules of thumb but was best explained by crediting the chimpanzees with an understanding of the difference between seeing and not seeing in dominant conspecifics. The results have since been replicated and found to be robust (Bräuer et al. 2007; however, see Karin-D'Arcy & Povinelli 2002), leading a number of researchers to believe that chimpanzees are capable of attributing states of seeing to others.

After the negative results from Povinelli and Eddy's experiments involving cooperation between chimpanzee and human trainers, the positive findings from Hare and colleagues' experiments suggested to a number of researchers that the key to unlocking mindreading capacities in chimpanzees and other animals was competition (Hare 2001; Hare & Tomasello 2004; Lyons & Santos 2006; Santos et al. 2007). The competitive paradigm is currently the dominant approach used to test for mindreading in animals. To date, it has been used on monkeys (Flombaum & Santos 2005; Santos et al. 2006), scrub jays (Emery & Clayton 2008), ravens (Bugnyar & Heinrich 2005), bee-eaters (Watve et al. 2002), and goats (Kaminski et al. 2006), all with positive results.

At the same time that Hare and colleagues introduced the competitive protocol to behavioral studies of animal mindreading, a group of scientists and a philosopher were making the case for investigating mindreading in animals at the neuronal level. Back in the mid 1990s, a group of Italian neuroscientists discovered a cluster of neurons (F5 neurons) in the premotor cortex of monkey brains that fired not only when the monkeys were about to perform an intentional action, such as grasping an object, but when they observed another subject (monkey or human) performing the same type of intentional action (Gallese et al. 1996; Rizzolatti et al. 1996). In watching another subject's action, the monkey's own brain appeared to mirror (or resonated with) the observed subject's own premotor intention to act. The monkey, it was argued, in observing the other's action, came to share the intention (though, without acting on it) that it took to be behind the other agent's observed action. Hence the F5 neurons were aptly labeled "mirror neurons." At the same time as this discovery, philosopher Alvin Goldman was defending a radically new theory of mindreading called the simulation theory. The simulation theory viewed mindreading as essentially a process by which a creature uses its own mind as a model or replica of another's mind in order to determine which mental states to attribute, much in the same way that one might use a scaled model to make predictions about or attribute properties to a real object. It did not take long before the two groups came together to advance the view that F5 neurons in monkeys enable these animals to attribute the mental states of goals and intentions to others by a process of mental simulation

(Gallese & Goldman 1998; Gallese et al. 2004; Fogassi et al. 2005; Goldman 2006).

At roughly the same time, researchers in the behavioral tradition were engaged in a number of new studies that probed goal-directed/intentional-action attribution in monkeys and apes. Call et al. (2004) reported evidence that chimpanzees spontaneously (i.e., without prior training) discriminate between a trainer who failed to share food because he was unable but *willing* to share and one who failed because he was *unwilling* but able to share, and Wood et al. (2007) have recently reported evidence that both monkeys and apes discriminate between rationally directed and irrationally directed actions in others.

Despite the positive findings from these new mindreading experiments, some have remained skeptical. Povinelli and colleagues have argued that none of the new experimental approaches fares any better than the old ones at solving the logical problem. All the positive data from these new types of experiments, they maintain, can just as easily be explained in terms of behavior-reading capacities in animals. They argue further that the new experimental approaches cannot even in principle distinguish mindreading from various behavior-reading strategies and are therefore utterly useless for answering the question of whether animals are capable of mindreading. In addition, Povinelli and colleagues (Vonk & Povinelli 2006; Penn et al. 2008) have recently advanced a general theory about the difference between human and animal minds, called the reinterpretation hypothesis. According to this hypothesis, various sorts of cognition in humans, including mindreading, involve reinterpreting first-order perceptual facts and behavioral patterns in terms of nonobservable higher-order causal relations. Animals, Povinelli and colleagues argue, lack concepts for nonobservable higher-order causal relations and are therefore incapable of mindreading. We shall examine this argument and others made by Povinelli and colleagues in chapter 3.

As we saw above, philosophers have made some important contributions to the animal mindreading debate. Some of their views will be explored in more depth in chapter 4. However, two deserve special mention here for their importance in shaping the history of the debate. Arguably the best known and most influential of these philosophers is Daniel Dennett. In a series of papers dating back to the late 1970s (reprinted in Dennett 1987), Dennett proposed and defended the intentional stance strategy. The basic idea behind the intentional stance strategy, as it bears on the question of mindreading in animals, is that there is nothing more to animals' being mindreaders (what Dennett calls "second-order intentional systems") than the fact that researchers find it useful and economical to predict and explain the observed patterns of the animals' behaviors by means of mindreading (second-order intentional) hypotheses. There are no deeper facts about animals' brains or the structure of their internal representations, on this account, that are relevant to whether they attribute mental states. The intentional stance strategy, thus, takes a decidedly instrumentalist (i.e., anti-realist) view of what it is for animals to be mindreaders.

The instrumentalism of the intentional stance strategy is nicely illustrated by the strategy's account of the injured-wing display of piping plovers. These birds, on seeing a likely predator approaching their nest, are known to move away from their nests and then, in full view of the predator, to hop around on the ground with one wing outstretched. This display typically causes the predator to move away from the nest in pursuit of the apparently injured bird. Before being captured, the plover flies off and continues the display until the predator is a safe distance from the nest (Ristau 1991). Regarding this pattern of apparently intelligent and deceptive behavior in piping plovers, Dennett (1978b) writes,

[W]hen we ask why birds evolved with this tropism, we explain it by noting the utility of having a means of deceiving predators, or inducing false beliefs in them; what must be explained is the provenance of the bird's second-order intentions [i.e., the intention to cause in predators the belief that its wing is injured].... [W]hat I want to insist on here is that if one is prepared to adopt the intentional stance without qualms as a tool in predicting and explaining behavior, the bird is as much a second-order intentional system [i.e., a mindreader] as any man. Since this is so, we should be particularly suspicious of the argument I was tempted to use, viz., that representations of second-order intentions would depend somehow on language. For it is far from clear that all or even any of the beliefs and other intentions of an intentional system need be represented "within" the system in any way for us to get a purchase on predicting its behavior by ascribing such intentions to it. (pp. 276–277)

Piping plovers, on the intentional stance strategy, are thus genuine mindreaders—they attribute beliefs to predators—even though there is nothing in their brains, no higher-order representation, that represents predators as having beliefs or any mental state at all.

Unsurprisingly, researchers who take up a more realist interpretation of the mind tend to object to Dennett's account of what mindreading in animals amounts to. To some, the intentional stance strategy, as a result of it rejection of the idea that mental state attributions in animals are or involve higher-order representations in their brains, is destined to make mindreading in the animal kingdom too commonplace to be considered empirically plausible or interesting. Lowly mantis shrimp, after all, are also known for their 'feigned' threat displays while molting (Adams & Caldwell 1990), but few (if any) researchers have ever thought to conclude from this that these stomatopods are as much mindreaders as any human. Their reluctance, undoubtedly, is due to the fact the brains of these animals are just too simple to support such complex, higher-order cognition. In addition, researchers have worried that the intentional stance strategy would unduly rob their mindreading hypotheses from offering causal explanations of animal behavior. As the plover example illustrates, there need be nothing in an individual animal's brain or body that is the animal's belief that another creature has such-and-such mental state for the animal to be said to have such a higher-order belief. Thus, on the intentional stance strategy, the fact that an animal has a belief about another creature's mental state cannot be assumed to be what *caused* the animal to anticipate the creature behaving as if it had such a mental state (on the assumption that the causes of animals' anticipatory behaviors are facts or events that occur within their brains or bodies). For these reasons, some scientists and philosophers have eschewed Dennett's intentional stance strategy for more realist accounts of what mindreading in animals entails.[10]

One such philosopher is José Luis Bermúdez. Bermúdez (2003, 2009) has forcefully argued for just the sort of deeper fact that Dennett's intentional stance strategy denies is relevant to the question of animal mindreading. On Bermúdez's account, mindreading about propositional attitudes (e.g., beliefs and desires) involves processing internal representations that are sentences in the subject's own public language. Without the possession of a public language to think in, Bermúdez argues, animals are incapable of attributing mental states with propositional content and are, thus, restricted to attributing (if at all) simple perceptual and motivational states that lack propositional content. This restriction holds, according to Bermúdez, even if (pace Dennett) researchers find it abundantly useful and economical to interpret animals as attributors of beliefs and desires, or any other propositional attitude. Bermúdez's view will be examined further in chapter 4.

1.3   Conclusion

Obviously much has been left out of this short history of the debate, but enough has been provided, I believe, to reveal in outline the main lines of disagreement. Chief among these is the logical problem—the problem of how to determine by experimental means whether an animal uses a representation of another agent's mental state (e.g., the agent *sees* the food) to anticipate its behavior or just the behavioral/environmental cues associated with the mental state in the other agent (e.g., the agent has a unobstructed line of gaze to the food). In the following chapters, we shall examine the exact nature of this problem more closely, as well as whether it has been, needs to be, or even can be solved.

2 The Logical Problem in Animal Mindreading Research

In this chapter, the logical problem in animal mindreading research is more fully explained. It is argued that no current experimental approach is capable of determining whether animals predict and make sense of other agents' behaviors by attributing simple cognitive states (e.g., seeing, hearing, and knowing) rather than the behavioral/environmental cues that serve as the observable grounds for such attributions. What are needed, it is urged, are more discriminating tests.

2.1 Mindreading in Animal Social Cognition Research: The Issues

Many animals' survival, reproductive fitness, and general well-being depend critically on their being able to predict or anticipate the behavior of other animals (e.g., conspecifics, predators, and prey). Quite generally, animals do this by being sensitive to the behavioral and environmental cues (in some cases quite subtle) that are indicative of an agent's future actions (or the likely consequences of an agent's current actions). Dogs, for instance, seem rather instinctively to anticipate playful, engaging behavior from fellow canines that have their elbows on the ground and their hips and tail in the air (known as 'play bows'; see Bekoff 1977), and subordinate chimpanzees seem to predict (by way of taking evasive actions) aggressive assaults from dominant males that are standing up, pilo-erect, and looking in their direction (Muller & Mitani 2005), and so on. A central issue in animal social cognition research is whether and to what degree animals, in their ability to predict the behaviors of other agents, rely upon an understanding of the mental states in the other agents that are (or might be) responsible for such behaviors.

The emerging consensus among researchers studying social cognition in animals is that some animals—most notably higher primates, corvids, and dogs—are capable of simple forms of mindreading (Call & Tomasello

2008; Bräuer et al. 2004; Hauser & Wood 2010; Emery & Clayton 2009).[1] These animals, according to this hypothesis, are capable of predicting and understanding the actions of others by attributing simple cognitive states, such as seeing and hearing, and states of knowledge and ignorance derived from such perceptual states, as well as simple conative (motivational) states, such as goals and intentions. These cognitive and conative states are considered 'simple' in that they are understood by the attributing animal to be directed at existing objects or events in the environment or events that the attributing animal expects to exist if the agent behaves or continues to behave in the manner predicted.

Such mental state attributions are contrasted with what are generally considered more sophisticated and demanding kinds: attributions of mental states whose contents involve objects or events that the attributing animal does not take to exist or does not think will exist even if the agent acts in the manner predicted by the attributing animal. These mental state attributions, unlike the simple ones adumbrated above, are full-blown intentional state attributions. Paradigm examples of such attributions are those of illusory perceptions (e.g., attributions of seeing or hearing an object/event *as* F when that the attributor himself does not believe that the object/event *is* F) and discrepant beliefs (e.g., attributions of believing that *p* when the attributor himself does not believe that *p*). There is considerable debate within the field regarding whether animals are capable of attributing such full-blown intentional states. This debate will be discussed in chapters 3 and 4.

Diametrically opposed to the animal mindreading hypothesis is the behavior-reading hypothesis. According to this hypothesis, animals have no understanding of other minds but predict and make sense of other agents' behaviors on the basis of what they know or believe (from experience, inference, or in some cases innately) about the contingencies existing between such behaviors and certain observable cues and facts in the environment (Tomasello & Call 1997; Povinelli & Vonk 2006; Vonk & Povinelli 2006; Penn et al. 2007; Penn et al. 2008).

Despite its growing popularity, the animal mindreading hypothesis has not gone unchallenged. The hypothesis's chief opponents, Daniel Povinelli and colleagues, have long argued that the kind of tests that have been used to support the hypothesis are in principle incapable of determining whether animals understand something about the mental states of other subjects rather than just something about the predictive value of the observable cues associated with such mental states in others. In their (2006) paper,

Povinelli and Vonk provide the following succinct (though somewhat technical) expression of the challenge:

The general difficulty is that the design of ... tests [in animal mindreading research] necessarily presupposes that the subject notices, attends to, and/or represents, precisely those observable aspects of the other agent that are being experimentally manipulated. Once this is properly understood, however, it must be conceded that the subject's predictions about the other agent's future behaviour could be made either on the basis of a single step[2] from knowledge about the contingent relationships between the relevant invariant features of the agent and the agent's subsequent behaviour, or on the basis of multiple steps from the invariant features, to the mental states, to the predicted behavior. Without an analytical specification of what additional explanatory work the extra cognitive step is doing in the latter case, there is nothing to implicate the operation of S_{b+ms} [mindreading] over S_b [behavior reading] alone. (p. 393)

In their call for an "analytical specification," Povinelli and Vonk are asking for a description of a test (or tests) in which a mindreading animal would be able to predict the behavior of another agent (S) by attributing a mental state (S_{ms}) on the basis of some observable cue (S_b) but that the animal's behavior-reading counterpart would be unable to make the same prediction on the basis of the same observable cue (S_b) minus the attributed a mental state. Without such tests, Povinelli and Vonk argue, there is no explanatory need to invoke mental state attribution over behavior reading to account for an animal's performance and, thus, no way to tell whether the animal is a mindreader or a behavior reader. The charge, at its roots, is that all current mindreading tests with animals, by virtue of their very design or 'logic,' are liable to produce false positives (i.e., indicating mindreading where behavior reading is actually used by the animal), and that unless more discriminating tests are designed, run, and yield positive results, the case in favor of animal mindreading is far weaker than its proponents claim it to be.

Povinelli's challenge (for the reason just suggested) has come to be called the 'logical problem' in the literature (see Hurely & Nudds 2006; Lurz 2009a).[3] I intend to take it seriously. In particular, I intend to show that the challenge has yet to be met by any of the current studies of simple cognitive state attribution (attributions of seeing, hearing, and knowing) in animals. A similar challenge can be raised for current goal-directed/intentional-action attribution studies with animals, for although some animals (mainly monkeys and apes) appear to be capable of understanding others' actions as directed toward external goals or future states of affairs

(Wood et al. 2008), as well as being able to distinguish intentional and accidental actions in others (Call & Tomasello 1998; Call et al. 2004), it can be (and has been) questioned whether such capacities require these animals to attribute motivational or conative mental states, such as the state of *having a goal in mind*, or *willing*, *desiring*, or *intending* to do something (see Gergely & Csibra 2003; Lurz & Krachun under review). However, these studies may be in a better position to overcome the logical problem than the various cognitive state attribution studies with animals. It is possible, as some have argued (Call & Tomasello 2008 and Hauser & Wood 2010), that the data from the various goal-directed/intentional-action attribution studies are not as easily accounted for by a general behavior-reading hypothesis as they are by a general mindreading hypothesis that credits animals with the ability to understand simple conative mental states in others. And yet, I shall argue, this has not been convincingly shown to be the case for the various cognitive state attribution studies. Therefore, I concede, for the sake of argument, that for all the current mindreading studies have shown, animals may well be incapable of attributing simple cognitive mental states despite their being capable of attributing simple conative mental states.[4] A challenge to this possibility will be address in section 2.10 below. For now, the focus will be on the question of simple cognitive state attribution in animals.

Although I do not see the acceptability of the hypothesis that animals are capable of attributing simple cognitive states as hanging solely on solving the logical problem—there are, after all, other relevant criteria of theory choice to be considered (e.g., simplicity, coherence with surrounding theories, and predictive fruitfulness)—I believe that, all things being equal, a much stronger case can be made in favor of the hypothesis, and the field of animal social cognition much advanced, by doing so. I take the importance of solving the logical problem to be akin to the importance of a recent solution to a similar dispute over the possibility of discrepant (or 'false') belief attribution in infants. Prior to the innovative false-belief tests by Baillargeon and others, developmental psychologists were generally quite skeptical about the possibility of belief attribution in infants. Although a few early nonverbal belief-attribution tests with young children (Clements & Perner 1994; Onishi & Baillargeon 2005) yielded positive results, the findings were susceptible to deflationary interpretations (Perner & Ruffman 2005; Ruffman & Perner 2005). With the recent invention and use of more discriminating tests, which have now yielded rather robust findings (particularly, Song & Baillageon 2008 and Scott & Baillargeon 2009), the case for belief attribution in infants and young children has become considerably stronger, and the field as a whole has benefited. It is my hope, and it is the objective of this book, to make a case for a similar course of development in animal social cognition research.

In the remainder of this chapter, I extend Povinelli's general line of argument and show that current experimental approaches to test for simple perceptual states and knowledge/ignorance attributions fall short of solving the logical problem. The tests alone cannot determine whether animals are mindreaders rather than behavior readers. What are needed are more discriminating tests. In the following chapters of the book, I go on to show how the logical problem can be solved for cognitive state attributions. For reasons that will emerge in due course, the solution, I argue, can be achieved only with tests for attributions of full-blown intentional states, such as misleading appearances and discrepant beliefs. Clean tests for cognitive state attributions in animals, I argue, need to focus on these more demanding mental state attributions. Of course, if animals pass these tests, then perforce they will be capable of attributing the simpler sorts of cognitive states. In this way, I hope to show how both debates—the debate between simple cognitive state attribution versus behavior reading in animals and the debate between simple cognitive state versus full-blown intentional state attribution in animals—can be resolved positively.

2.2   The Logical Problem

According to the behavior-reading hypothesis, animals predict the behaviors of other agents without understanding anything about the underlying mental states of the agents. Despite what its name might suggest, the hypothesis does not assume that animals make such predictions only on the basis of brute associations or learned behavior rules. Of course, an animal may come to anticipate an agent's performing a certain type of action (B) in a perceived behavioral/environmental condition (S) as a result of having observed this sort of behavior in other agents (perhaps even in itself) in similar environmental conditions and coming to learn the behavior rule that condition S generally leads to behavior B. However, in some cases, the anticipated behavior might be a stereotypical motor pattern in the animal's species that is triggered by a certain class of behavioral/ environmental conditions (e.g., playful behavior in dogs in the presence of play bows from conspecifics). In such cases, the animal might be credited with anticipating the behavior (playful behavior) in a perceptual condition (presence of a play bow) on the basis of knowing innately that conspecifics tend to behave in such ways in such conditions. And in still other cases, an animal may be credited with reasoning out the predicted behavior of the other agent from the observed or inferred behavioral/ environmental conditions obtaining by means of a process of embodied or radical simulation (see Gallese 2005; Gordon 1995, 1996). In such a case, the animal could be credited with anticipating an agent's behavior by reasoning from something like the initial query 'what have I done (or what would I do) in such behavioral/environmental circumstances in which the agent is currently?' The output of this simulation routine—'I did/would do X'—can be used by the animal to predict what the other agent is likely to do—'he will likely do X.'

Thus, the behavior-reading hypothesis allows that animals may anticipate other agents' behaviors by a variety of cognitive strategies, not simply by means of brute association or behavior rules (Povinelli & Vonk 2006; Penn & Povinelli 2007). Only empirical investigation, of course, can determine which behavior-reading strategy animals use and when they are likely to use it.

Povinelli's challenge to the animal mindreading hypothesis is that since mental state attribution in animals will (if extant) be based on observable features of other agents' behaviors and environment—for the minds of others are not open to direct inspection—every mindreading hypothesis has (what might be called) a *complementary behavior-reading hypothesis*. Such a hypothesis proposes that the animal relies upon certain behavioral/ environmental cues to predict another agent's behavior (by associative learning, innate knowledge, or simulation-/analogical-like inference based on its own behavioral repertoire) that, on the mindreading hypothesis, the animal is hypothesized to use as its observable grounds for attributing the mental state in question. Where a mindreading hypothesis might explain an animal's ability to anticipate another agent's behavior, B, in behavioral/ environmental condition, S, by crediting the animal with an understanding of the underlying, behavior-eliciting mental state (M) that condition S indicates the agent is in (see figure 2.1a), the complementary behavior-reading hypothesis would explain the animal's anticipatory behavior by crediting it with an understanding of the likelihood of the agent's doing B because that is what it has observed similar agents doing in S-like conditions, or perhaps because that is what the animal itself has done (or would do) in a S-like condition, or perhaps even because the animal knows instinctively that such agents stereotypically do B in S-like conditions (see figure 2.1b).

According to Povinelli, no experimental protocol used in animal mindreading research is capable of distinguishing the mindreading hypothesis

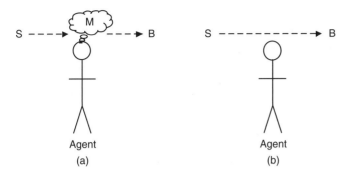

Figure 2.1
Schematic representation of the method of predicting an agent's behavior, B, under a behavioral/environmental condition, S, according to (a) the mindreading hypothesis and according to (b) the complementary behavior-reading hypothesis.

that is being tested from its complementary behavior-reading hypothesis. For all the current studies show, animals are either mindreaders (figure 2.1a) or complementary behavior readers (figure 2.1b).

   If asked why an animals might come to use a behavioral/environmental cue S to anticipate a type of behavior B in another agent (either through associative learning, or inference, or innate knowledge) without any appreciation of the intermediary, behavior-producing mental state of which S is evidence, the answer, according to the behavior-reading hypothesis, is simply that the strategy of doing so generally works (or works well enough).[5] A similar question, of course, can be posed for the mindreading hypothesis: Why might an animal come to use a representation of an intermediate mental state of another agent to predict its behavior B instead of just using the representation of the behavioral/environmental cue S that serves as evidence of this mental state in the agent? Answer: because whatever reasoning or learning process the animal uses that takes it from the premise that the agent is in such-and-such mental state to the conclusion that the agent will do B is generally reliable (enough). As Laurie Santos et al. (2007) state, writing on behalf of the animal mindreading hypothesis,

[i]dentifying and then analyzing exactly the [behavioral/environmental] variables that best predict future behavior [of other agents] (because they constrain mental states [in these agents]) is, functionally, what a system that is specialized for ToM [theory of mind, i.e., mindreading] does.... (p. 446)

The behavior-reading hypothesis, of course, says much the same, save the material that the authors place in parentheses. Thus, on the behavior-reading hypothesis,

Identifying and then analyzing exactly the behavioral/environmental variables that best predict future behavior of other agents because they reliably constrain the future behavior of these agents, is, functionally, what a system that is specialized for behavior reading does.

And so the question that constitutes the logical problem is whether any current experimental approach can determine whether animals use the first kind of system to predict the future behaviors of other agents rather than the latter kind.

Since the logical problem is liable to be confused with other methodological issues in the field, it is helpful to state what it is not. To this end, it is important to make clear that not all behavior-reading hypotheses are complementary behavior-reading hypotheses. All behavior-reading hypotheses—whether complementary or otherwise—have one thing in common: They hold that animals lack mental state concepts and predict or respond to another agent's actions by knowing (either from past experience, or by inference, or perhaps even innately) that certain observable features of the other agent or its environment are reliable indicators of its future behavior. These observable features, however, may or may not be the ones that, on some mindreading hypothesis, the animal is hypothesized to use as its observable grounds for attributing a mental state. If they are, then the behavior-reading hypothesis is said to be complementary to the mindreading hypothesis in question. If they are not, then the hypothesis is said to be a *minimal* behavior-reading hypothesis. Only complementary behavior-reading hypotheses create the logical problem.

To illustrate the difference between these two kinds of behavior-reading hypotheses, let us consider one of the earlier mindreading experiments by Povinelli and Eddy (1996). As discussed briefly in chapter 1, Povinelli and Eddy tested chimpanzees on a discrimination task that required them to choose between two experimenters from whom to beg food. The experimenters were otherwise identical except that one of them could not see the chimpanzee (e.g., the experimenter was wearing a blindfold over her eyes, a bucket over her head, or was looking away from the animal, etc.) while the other could see the chimpanzee (e.g., the experimenter had a direct line of gaze to the chimpanzee while wearing the blindfold around her neck, or while resting the bucket on her shoulder, etc.). Povinelli and Eddy hypothesized that if chimpanzees possess the mental state concept *see*, then they should prefer to beg from the experimenter who can see them.

One competing behavior-reading hypothesis that the researchers pitted against this mindreading hypothesis was the front-versus-back hypothesis.

This hypothesis proposed that the chimpanzees really had no understanding of the mental state concept *see* but simply preferred to beg from humans whose fronts (i.e., torso and legs) were facing toward them, irrespective of whether the human could see them. The researchers tested this hypothesis by having both experimenters sit with their backs to the chimpanzee while one of the experimenters looked over her shoulder so that she could clearly see the animal. The front-versus-back hypothesis predicted that the chimpanzees should show no preference toward the seeing human over the nonseeing one, which incidentally is what the researchers discovered. We shall discuss the results of this study in the next chapter. For now, what is important to note is that the front-versus-back hypothesis is not a complementary behavior-reading hypothesis but a minimal behavior-reading hypothesis, for the mere fact that a human's torso and legs are facing forward, irrespective of where the individual is looking or whether the individual's line of gaze is occluded, is clearly not the grounds that the mindreading hypothesis in question assumed the chimpanzees would use to attribute the mental state of seeing to the experimenters. The observable ground that the mindreading hypothesis assumed that the chimpanzees would use to determine whether an experimenter could see them or not was whether the experimenter possessed a direct (nonoccluded) line of gaze to the animal. It was, after all, this observable cue that the researchers manipulated in the various trials to test whether their chimpanzees understood something about seeing.

As can be seen from this description of Povinelli and Eddy's experiment, there is no deep methodological puzzle about how to distinguish a mindreading hypothesis from a competing minimal behavior-reading hypothesis. To distinguish these hypotheses, one need only run controls that split the confounding variables (e.g., torso and leg position versus direct line of gaze). The reason the logical problem is so difficult to solve is that one cannot use the same split-stimulus control to pit the mindreading hypothesis against its complementary behavior-reading hypothesis since the postulated observable cues (e.g., direct line of gaze) that the animal is hypothesized to use are the same for each hypothesis. The vexing empirical question that constitutes the logical problem is how an experimental protocol might distinguish these two hypotheses given that the confounding observable cues involved cannot, in principle, be distinguished.

It is also important to note that the logical problem is not a search for a 'decisive' test, for there are no such tests in empirical science. Empirical theories are always underdetermined by evidence, and hypotheses always require auxiliary assumptions to make predictions (Duhem 1906;

Quine 1953). Solving the logical problem does not involve or require designing a test (or tests) the positive results of which would conclusively *prove* that an animal is a mindreader. There are no such tests. Solving the logical problem, rather, involves designing a test (or tests) the positive results of which are more plausibly explained or predicted by a mindreading hypothesis than by its complementary behavior-reading hypothesis, or the other way around. As we shall see in this chapter, some researchers have claimed to have already provided such results with their existing tests for cognitive state attribution in animals. I intend to show that this is not the case.

It is also worth mentioning that the logical problem is not a methodological conundrum on which little empirical importance hangs—quite the contrary, in fact. Solving the problem is relevant for testing theories concerning the evolution of human mindreading, as noted in chapter 1. There are a number of theories in evolutionary psychology and anthropology that claim or imply that mindreading in humans evolved well after our split from the great apes some six million years ago (see, e.g., Mameli 2001; Sterelny 2003; Corballis 2003, 2007). According to one well-known theory in this class, *the reinterpretation hypothesis*, advanced by Povinelli and colleagues, mindreading in humans developed on the back of various complementary behavior-reading capacities that we inherited from our great ape ancestors. These inherited behavior-reading capacities, according to this theory, allowed early humans to observe patterns of environmental cues and behavioral actions in others which they then reinterpreted in terms of common, underlying causes (see Vonk and Povinelli 2006; Penn et al. 2008). On this theory, complementary behavior reading without mindreading is all but expected in the great apes. Of course, to test this theory, as well as the others in the same class, requires designing and running tests on apes that can successfully discriminate mindreading subjects from their supposed complementary behavior-reading counterparts. It requires solving the logical problem.

Finally, it is important to note as well that the logical problem is not a general problem for human mindreading research as it is for mindreading research in animals. Thus, one cannot undermine the singular importance of solving the problem in the animal case by pointing out that it is a problem even for mindreading research in humans. Our ability to understand language rich in psychological expressions enables us to attribute mental states to others on the basis of third-party communication that, in some instances, does not provide us with any information regarding the observable facts or cues of the other agent or the environment that might warrant such attributions. We can come to think that someone sees, believes, or knows something, for example, simply by being told by a reliable third party that he does. As a result, not every mindreading hypothesis in human mindreading research has a complementary behavior-reading hypothesis. This is undoubtedly true for research on normal adult human beings, but it is also true for some research on children. Some rather nice illustrations of this can be found in the early studies of mindreading by Bartsch and Wellman (1989; see also Wellman 1990). In one such study, for instance, children were told by a third party (the experimenter) that a protagonist in a story wanted to find an object (e.g., a kitten), that the object was in fact hidden in the kitchen, but that the protagonist thought that it was hidden in the playroom. The children were then asked to predict where the protagonist would look for the object. Children as young as 4 perform extraordinarily well on this task, predicting that the protagonist would search in the location where he or she incorrectly thought the object was. The mindreading hypothesis that the researchers put forward was that these children predicted the protagonist's behavior on the basis of the distinct beliefs and desires that they attributed to the protagonist. However, the children in these studies were not informed of any behavioral or environmental facts about the protagonist on which they might have based their belief and desire attributions. They simply attributed these states on the basis of what the experimenter had said. In such experiments, therefore, there is simply no complementary behavior-reading hypothesis to be had, and thus no logical problem to be solved.

The same, of course, cannot be said for the various nonverbal mental state attribution studies that have been run on infants and aphasic adults since these studies explicitly provide the subjects with the relevant behavioral and environmental cues (e.g., Onishi & Baillargeon 2005; Apperly et al. 2006; Southgate et al. 2007). Nevertheless, some of the experiments, I believe, do appear to solve logical problem, either because they test for deceptive appearance or discrepant belief attribution in a manner that, I shall argue, is capable of solving the logical problem for cognitive state attribution research in animals, or because the mindreading hypothesis provides a more unified account of the various data than the complementary behavior-reading hypothesis. Either way, the logical problem, if it is a problem for human nonverbal mindreading research, is at most a local problem for some types of nonverbal tests. With cognitive state attribution studies in animals, the problem is global—or so I shall argue.

2.3 Current Protocols to Test for Cognitive State Attribution in Animals

The various types of experiments used to test for cognitive state attribution in animals can be (somewhat arbitrarily) divided into three main groups by virtue of the type of cognitive state attribution they are designed to test. In the first group are those that test for perceptual state attribution (e.g., attribution of seeing and hearing). In the second group are those that test for attributions of knowledge and ignorance based upon such attributions of seeing or hearing. And in the third group are those that test for belief attribution. It is well beyond the scope of this chapter (or book) to examine all of the experiments that have been run in each of these groups. Thankfully, this is not necessary since many of the experiments employ the same general methodology and only a few come close to solving the logical problem. The objective of the chapter, recall, is to examine whether any type of experimental protocol used in cognitive attribution research is capable of solving the logical problem. In the remainder of this chapter, I examine just a handful of recent experiments in the first two groups that have yielded positive results and have been taken by some as the flagships in the empirical case for mental state attribution in animals. I shall show that none of them is capable of distinguishing the mindreading hypothesis under consideration from its complementary behavior-reading hypothesis. Experiments on belief attribution in animals deserve special attention, however. I shall examine these in chapter 4. Unfortunately, they too will be shown to have a similar fate.

2.4 Hare and Colleagues' Competitive Paradigm Experiment

No experimental protocol in animal mindreading research is better known than Brian Hare and colleagues' (2000), and none has done more to convince researchers that, at least in the case of chimpanzees, animals are capable of attributing simple perceptual states. In their experiment, a subordinate and a dominant chimpanzee competed for food placed at various locations in their rooms or in a middle area between their rooms. During the pretesting phase of the experiment, the subordinate chimpanzee was shown, by the placement of food in different locations, that it was able to retrieve the food that was both visibly and physically inaccessible to the dominant chimpanzee (e.g., food placed inside the subordinate's room while the dominant chimpanzee was in its own room), but that the dominant chimpanzee would invariably retrieve the food that was visible and accessible to it (e.g., food placed in the middle area or in its own room).

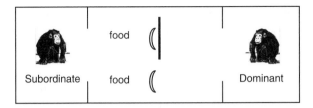

Figure 2.2
Setup for Hare and colleagues' competitive paradigm experiment.

The researchers then ran a series of tests. In one of them, a piece of food was placed out in the open of the middle area while another piece was placed on the subordinate's side of an opaque barrier in the middle area (see figure 2.2).

After the placement of the food, the doors of the chimpanzees' rooms were raised enough so that both animals could see into the middle area. The chimpanzees could also see each other and the food that was out in the open, but only the subordinate could see the food on its side of the opaque barrier. The subordinate's door was then opened fully, allowing it a slight head start into the middle area. The dominant's door was then fully opened, allowing it to enter the middle area.

By far the most revealing test that the researchers ran, and the one that they took to be the best measure of whether their chimpanzees "truly understood something of the mechanics of visual perception," was the transparent barrier test. In this test, the researchers placed one piece of food on the subordinate's side of a clear transparent barrier (a clear plastic bottle) and another out in the open. After the placement of the food, the animals' doors were raised enough so that they could see into the middle area. The test was then run just like the opaque-barrier test described above.

Hare and colleagues' reasoned that if their subordinate chimpanzees understood the mental state of seeing in dominant conspecifics, then they would be expected to use this knowledge to anticipate their rival's behavior in the test trials. Thus, in the opaque barrier test, the subordinate chimpanzees were expected to understand that their rivals could see the food out in the open but *not* the food behind the opaque barrier and, as a result, to take the food behind the opaque barrier. However, on the transparent barrier test, the subordinate chimpanzees were expected to understand that their rivals could see the food out in the open *and* the food behind the transparent barrier and, as a result, to refrain from taking either piece of food.

Thus, on Hare and colleagues' mindreading hypothesis, the subordinate chimpanzees are taken to reason something like the following:

(a) In the past, the dominant chimpanzee has always eaten food that it can *see* but not food that it cannot *see*.
(b) In the test trials, the dominant can *see* the food out in the open and behind the transparent barrier, and so those pieces of food are off limits. However, the dominant cannot *see* the food behind the opaque barrier, so that food can be retrieved.

The researchers discovered subordinate chimpanzees behaving as (a) and (b) above predict. Subordinate chimpanzees typically tried to take and eat the food behind the opaque barrier but not the food out in the open or behind the transparent barrier. What is more, subordinate chimpanzees treated the food behind the transparent barrier and the food out in the open much in the same way: as off limits. From these results, as well as those from similar test trials, the researchers concluded that chimpanzees have the capacity to understand the mental state of seeing in conspecifics.[6]

It is important to note as well that the researchers discovered no evidence that subordinate chimpanzees had learned to anticipate their rivals' reactions to food behind the barriers as a result of repeated exposure to test trials. The performance of subordinate chimpanzees was largely the same on the first and subsequent test trials. Apparently, subordinate chimpanzees recognized the competitive nature of the test situation at the very beginning of the trials and knew in advance how to anticipate their rivals' actions in such settings. This is most strongly evident in the transparent-barrier trials since the chimpanzees had little or no exposure to such barriers prior to the experiment. Subordinate chimpanzees, it seem, quickly assessed from their very first encounter with the transparent barrier that, as far as their rivals' response was concerned, the food placed behind the barrier was analogous to food placed out in the open.

2.5 A Complementary Behavior-Reading Hypothesis: Direct Line of Gaze

Unfortunately, Hare and colleagues' experiment does not solve the logical problem. Showing this, though, requires a little background discussion regarding the observable ground that the hypothesized mindreading chimpanzees are thought to use in attributing seeing to their rivals.

Although one can see another subject looking at an object, one cannot see his or her seeing the object. That is because seeing (as opposed to merely looking) is a mental state and is not accessible to direct observation by another subject. Attributions of seeing to others, then, must rest upon certain observable behavioral or environmental cues. Intuitively, a principal part of the observable basis for thinking that another subject sees an object is that there is a certain observable relation between the object and the subject's open eyes, a relation that Heyes (1994, 1998) calls "eye-object line," Penn and Povinelli (2007) call "uninterrupted visual access," and I, following others (e.g., Okamoto-Barth et al. 2007), shall call *direct line of gaze*. Whatever this observable relation is called, the idea is that in order to judge that another subject sees an object, one must base one's judgment on one's observation or judgment that there is "an unobstructed, notional, straight line between [the subject's open] eyes" and the object seen (Heyes, 1998, p. 113). Of course, not all lines of gaze are direct or unobstructed; some may be blocked (more or less) by intersecting opaque barriers or media.[7] Therefore, to judge that another creature has a direct line of gaze to an object is to judge that there is no opaque barrier/medium intersecting the line between the creature's eyes or face and the object itself.[8]

Thus, on the hypothesis that the subordinate chimpanzees in Hare and colleagues' study attribute seeing/not seeing the food to their rivals, it must be assumed that they base their attributions on their observations of whether their rivals have/lack a direct line of gaze to the food—on whether there was an opaque barrier intersecting the line between the dominant chimpanzee's eyes or face and the food. Hence, the grounds on which these mindreading chimpanzees are hypothesized to understand (a) above would be something like the following:

(a′) In the past, the dominant chimpanzee has always eaten food to which it has had a direct line of gaze but not food to which it did not.

And the observable grounds on which the subordinate chimpanzees are hypothesized to understand (b) above would be something like:

(b′) In the test trials, the dominant chimpanzee has a direct line of gaze to the food out in the open and behind the transparent barrier, and so those pieces of food are off limits. However, the dominant does not have a direct line of gaze to the food behind the opaque barrier, so that food can be retrieved.

It should be clear that (a′) and (b′) here constitute a complementary behavior-reading hypothesis. And as one can see, the hypothesis predicts the same performance from the subordinate chimpanzees as Hare and colleagues' mindreading hypothesis. Thus, Hare and colleagues' competitive paradigm protocol simply cannot determine whether chimpanzees understand seeing or the observable grounds used to attribute seeing—direct line of gaze.

It might be thought that the complementary behavior-reading hypothesis here is actually incoherent. After all, it might be argued, judgments about whether another has a direct line of gaze to an object are judgments about whether there is an *opaque* barrier/medium intersecting the line between the other's eyes or face and the object, and the concept of opacity is (presumably) that of something which prevents one from *seeing* an object behind/within it. Thus, it would appear that any animal capable of making judgments about another's direct line of gaze would need to understand what opacity is and hence what seeing is, and, thus, such an animal would *not* be a complementary behavior reader.

It is quite true, of course, that opaque barriers/media prevent one from seeing the objects behind/within them, but this in no way entails that a chimpanzee capable of judging whether a conspecific has or lacks a direct line of gaze to an object behind/within a barrier/medium must possess the concept see—or any mental state concept, for that matter. A chimpanzee that is able to determine whether another has or lacks a direct line of gaze to an object needs some way of understanding opaque barriers/media, of course, but it need not understand them as barriers/media that prevent one from seeing the objects behind/within them. It is quite plausible that the concept of opacity that chimpanzees (as well as other animals) use to distinguish opaque from transparent barriers/media are primitive (i.e., nondefinable), much in the way that color concepts are generally taken to be. Thus, for example, a chimpanzee's concept of opacity might simply be the concept C^* such that if it sees (or seems to see) an object O behind/within a barrier/medium Y, then, ceteris paribus, it is disposed to believes that Y is not C^*,[9] and if it sees (or seems to see) a barrier/medium Y but does not see (or seem to see) object O but nevertheless believes (based upon the contents of its working memory of the environment) that O is behind/within Y, then, ceteris paribus, it believes that Y is C^*.

This would, of course, require chimpanzees to have an understanding that objects (e.g., the floor or wall) continue to exist behind or within such barriers or media, but many animals, chimpanzees included, appear to have this rather low-level understanding of object permanence (see Call 2001; Collier-Baker et al. 2006; Salwiczek et al. 2009). In addition, the many amodal completion experiments (which will be discussed in some depth in the following chapters) clearly show that a variety of animals, from fish to monkeys to great apes, perceive certain types of occluded objects as having unseen parts behind the occluder (see Sato et al. 1997; Vallortigara 2006; Matsuno & Fujita 2009). A chimpanzee in possession of such a concept (C*) of opacity could then learn to group certain kinds of barriers and media, such walls and darkness, as 'opaque' (as C*) and others, such as clear glass or water, as 'transparent' (as not-C*). Thus, all that is required for a chimpanzee to determine whether another has a direct line of gaze to an object is for it to judge whether there is a C*-type barrier/medium intersecting the line between the object and the other's eyes or face. A complementary behavior-reading chimpanzee, therefore, can clearly possess and employ the concept direct line of gaze without being taken to possess and employ the mental state concept see (or any mental state concept).

It deserves emphasizing that the point being made in this section is not that the complementary behavior-reading hypothesis of Hare and colleagues' study is necessarily true. For what has been shown, it may well be that there is an even more plausible minimal behavior-reading explanation of the data (such as the 'evil-eye' hypothesis; see Povinelli & Vonk 2006). The point, rather, is that the kind of experimental approach used by Hare and colleagues is unable to distinguish the mindreading hypothesis under consideration from its complementary behavior-reading hypothesis. And this is so, in large part, because the mental state attribution being tested, the attribution of seeing, and its observable grounds, direct line of gaze, are necessarily confounded across the test trials.

Since their findings were published, Hare and colleagues' competitive paradigm protocol has inspired a bounty of additional visual perspective-taking studies with animals, and many of these studies have produced positive results (see, e.g., Hare et al. 2003; Flombaum & Santos 2005; Hare et al. 2006; Melis et al. 2006; Kaminski et al. 2006). Unfortunately, since the studies use the same general experimental procedure as Hare and colleagues' study—manipulating the other agent's direct line of gaze to an object to determine whether the animal understands that the agent sees the object—they do not solve the logical problem. There are, however, a number of mindreading studies with animals that deserve special examination, either because they employ a somewhat different experimental methodology from Hare et al. (2000, 2001) or because they test for cognitive state attributions other than seeing. These studies will be examined in sections 2.8 and 2.9 below. However, before moving on to examine these studies, a slight digression is in order to address the charge of ad hocness and unnecessary complexity that is occasionally made against behavior-reading hypotheses.

2.6   Are Complementary Behavior-Reading Hypotheses Necessarily Ad Hoc?

Let me address a concern that is sometimes voiced against such apparently post hoc behavior-reading explanations, such as the one given above to Hare and colleagues' study. Such explanations are sometimes accused of being "just theoretical possibilities" that are undeserving of any serious acceptance. Tomasello and Call (2006), for example, argue that, given the novelty of the transparent barrier used in Hare and colleagues' study, a behavior-reading explanation of the subordinate chimpanzees' performance in the transparent-barrier trials would be quite ad hoc indeed. They write,

> Learning that transparent barriers do not block the visual access of others would require [the subordinate chimpanzees to have had] a series of experiences in which each subject approached food behind a barrier, took it while the dominant was looking, and was punished by the dominant when the barrier was transparent but not when the barrier was opaque.... And it is important that there is no evidence for any of these hypothesized learning experiences. They are just raised by scoffers [proponents of the behavior-reading hypothesis] as theoretical possibilities to account for certain results. (p. 382)

Tomasello and Call's objection is clearly aimed at a behavior-reading hypothesis that seeks to provide a brute associative or otherwise noncognitive account of the subordinate chimpanzees' performance. However, as noted above, this is not an essential element of behavior-reading hypotheses. There is no reason why a behavior-reading hypothesis cannot appeal to the very same kinds of cognitive processes, though operating on different data structures, as the mindreading hypothesis in question.

It is also surprising that Tomasello and Call do not see that their objection cuts both ways since even mindreading hypotheses must appeal to merely theoretical possibilities regarding the mode of acquisition and underlying cognitive processing involved in mental state attribution in animals. A case in point is Hare and colleagues' own mindreading hypothesis. One can ask how on this hypothesis the subordinate chimpanzees are thought to have figured out that their rivals can see through the transparent barrier but not through opaque ones, given that they have never encountered transparent barriers before. The researchers themselves never say. I take it that that is not a way out of the objection. To be told that the chimpanzees come to know by some means or other that their rivals can see through the transparent barrier but not through the opaque ones is as much a theoretical possibility for which there is no direct independent empirical support as being told that they simply learn from past experience or other means to retrieve food behind opaque barriers but avoid doing so for food behind transparent barriers when a dominant chimpanzee is watching. What Tomasello and Call's objection must establish is that the possibilities on which the complementary behavior-reading hypothesis rests are (on the whole) not supported by any independent grounds while those on which Hare and colleagues' mindreading hypothesis rests (on the whole) are. Tomasello and Call certainly do not show this.

It may be suggested, however, that at least on Hare and colleagues' mindreading hypothesis, the subordinate chimpanzees can be credited with an analogical-like inference to the effect that since they themselves see objects (e.g., the floor) on the far side of the transparent barrier, so too do their rivals with respect to objects (e.g., the food) on the far side of the barrier to them, and that they can use the outcome of this inference to predict that their rivals will attempt to retrieve the food behind the barrier.[10] But, of course, there is no independent evidence to support this suggestion; it is just as much a theoretical possibility as the brute-associative behavior-reading hypothesis that Tomasello and Call consider. More important, though, is the fact that the complementary behavior-reading hypothesis can provide nearly the same kind of possible explanation: The subordinate chimpanzees reason analogically to the effect that since they themselves have a direct line of gaze to objects (the floor) on the far side of the barrier, their rivals also have a direct line of gaze to objects (the food) on the far side of the barrier to them. Such an inference, like the one credited to the mindreading subordinates above, would allow the complementary behavior-reading chimpanzees to make the same predictions regarding the dominant chimpanzees' reaction to the food (i.e., that they will try to retrieve it) without having to suppose that the subordinate chimpanzees have somehow undergone a series of past experiences with food located in front of transparent barriers in the presence of dominant rivals.

Cecilia Heyes (2001) once objected that it was simply implausible to suppose that chimpanzees could know in their own case that they have or lack a direct line of gaze to a distal object, such as the floor behind the transparent barrier, since this would require, as if from some impossible first- and third-person perspectives, their seeing themselves seeing the object.[11] However, this is not so. Chimpanzees can know that they have such a spatial relation to a distal object, as we undoubtedly do, simply through the contents of their own visual perception. Visual perception, after all, does not merely represent intrinsic features of distal objects; it also represents various spatial relations existing between distal objects and the subject having the perception (Harman 1990). In seeing a tree, one sees it as being in a certain direction and distance on a straight line from here, where 'here' is roughly where one's eyes or face is located. Direct line of gaze is a spatial relation represented *in* visual perception. As a result, the subordinate chimpanzees in Hare and colleagues' study can easily know via the contents of their own visual perception of the transparent barrier that they have a direct line of gaze to the floor on the far side of the barrier—no impossible first- and third-person perspective is required.

Finally, it is worth mentioning that there is some independent evidence showing that chimpanzees, as well as many other types of animals, are attuned to other agents' line of gaze.[12] Chimpanzees, for instance, have been shown to follow the line of gaze of conspecifics and humans to distant objects, even past detractors and around opaque barriers, in effect projecting the other agent's line of gaze to a place in space which the animal itself cannot, at the moment, observe (Itakura 2004; Anderson & Vick 2008; Rosati & Hare 2009). And Krachun and Call (2009) have recently shown that chimpanzees appear to know in advance where they need to position themselves in space so as to get an unobstructed, direct line of gaze to an otherwise occluded object, suggesting that chimpanzees are able to project their *own* line of gaze into different possible spatial settings. Hence, quite independent of the results of Hare and colleagues' study, there is abundant evidence that indicates that chimpanzees and other animals can represent the line of gaze of others as well as their own.

Gaze following and gaze projecting in animals is undoubtedly a remarkable cognitive ability. At a minimum, it requires the deployment of a representation of an imaginary line between another agent's or the subject's own eyes or face and a distal object. As abstract and sophisticated as the representation is, however, it is not a representation of a mental state. An agent cannot have, or be thought to have, a line of gaze to an object, for example, unless the object exists or is thought to exist by the attributing animal. The relation is an extensional relation, not an intentional one.[13] And neither can an animal tell by introspection alone whether it has an unobstructed line of gaze to an object since it cannot tell by introspection alone whether the object which appears to be in its line of gaze actually exists.[14] Thus, by the traditional marks of the mental—intentionality and introspectability—the concept of direct line of gaze is not a concept of a mental state. What is more to the point, however, is that it is not the concept seeing. Blind folk quite often have objects positioned directly within their line of gaze; it is just that they cannot see these objects. Even normal sighted individuals at times have objects in their direct line of gaze and yet do not see them (e.g., the proverbial white elephant against a white background, a needle in a haystack, an imperceptible speck of dust, objects flashed on a screen below the visible threshold, etc.).[15] To see an object is to be conscious of it (or at least to register it, if below consciousness), and having a direct line of gaze is neither a type of consciousness nor a type of registration. It is, rather, an objective, mind-independent relation that holds between a subject's face or eyes and a distal object. Metaphysically speaking, direct line of gaze is of a piece with other objective, mind-independent, spatial relations between agents and distal objects, such as the relation of facing an object, standing next to an object, being to the left or right of an object, and so on. However, unlike these spatial relations, direct line of gaze serves as the principal grounds for ascribing a type of awareness (or registration) to an agent, that of seeing.

It is sometimes argued that if one refuses to interpret animals' attunement to others' line of gaze in terms of their understanding the mental state of seeing, then one is forced to say the same thing regarding infants' and young children's analogous abilities involving others' line of gaze. Infants as young as twelve months have been shown to follow the line of gaze of an adult, even around opaque barriers (Brooks & Meltzoff 2002; Moll & Tomasello 2004), and two-year-olds have been shown to give an object to a requesting adult as a result of whether the adult had or failed to have a direct line of gaze to the object (Moll & Tomasello 2006). These studies are often (though not always; see Ruffman & Perner 2005) interpreted as showing that infants and young children understand the psychological state of seeing in others. Thus, the charge is that if we are justified in giving this mentalistic interpretation of the data from the infant and children gaze-following studies, we should do the same for the data drawn from analogous gaze-following studies with animals. Arguing along these lines, Call and Tomasello (2008) write,

[I]f one were to use the behavioral rules critique rigorously and fairly across the board, one would have to conclude that human infants and young children also have no understanding of the perception or knowledge of others because many of the studies correspond rather closely to studies conducted with infants. (p. 190)

However, there are two important reasons that one might use to support the mentalistic interpretation of the infant/children data that are not (yet) available to do the same for the animal data. First, not too long after their showing an ability to be attuned to others' line of gaze, young children begin to use and understand the mental state term 'see' (as well as 'know' based upon seeing) in describing and explaining others' and their own behaviors (Shatz et al. 1983; Booth et al. 1997). Since the comprehension of concepts in infants and young children sometimes predates their linguistic mastery of the concepts, it is not implausible to suppose that infants' and young children's gaze-following/predicting abilities represent an early understanding of seeing in others.

Second, infants as young as 14.5 months have been shown to be able to predict an adult's behavior not merely on the basis of what object the adult has a direct line of gaze to but on the basis of how the object to which the adult has a direct line of gaze *visually appears* to the adult (Song & Baillargeon 2008). Attributions of visual appearances—attributions of seeing-as—presuppose attributions of simple seeing. One cannot understand that another sees an object *x as* F unless one understands that the other *sees* the object *x*. Thus, it is plausible to suppose that if infants can attribute seeing-as, then they can understand simple seeing in others, as well.

Neither of these points, however, can be said of animals (at least not yet). Therefore, contrary to what Call and Tomasello's parity of reason argument above maintains, there are justifiable grounds for accepting a mentalistic interpretation of the data from the infant/children line of gaze studies while refraining to do the same for the data from the animal line of gaze studies.

2.7   The Issue of Simplicity

We also need to address the question of simplicity, which is often invoked in debates over Hare and colleagues' mindreading hypothesis, as well as in the animal mindreading debate generally. Premack and Woodruff (1978) famously claimed that chimpanzees had to be mindreaders since they were not smart enough to be behavior readers. Their argument, roughly, was that since mindreading is a simpler, less demanding, cognitive process than behavior reading, mindreading explanations of chimpanzee (as well as other animals') social behaviors are to be preferred to more complex behavior-reading explanations, all things being equal. To be sure, there is something intuitively appealing about Premack and Woodruff's argument, at least as it is applied to Hare and colleagues' (2000) study. When one compares the complementary behavior-reading hypothesis above, along with its corresponding concept of direct line of gaze, with Hare and colleagues' mindreading hypothesis, along with its corresponding concept of seeing, it certainly feels as if the latter hypothesis and its concept are simpler than the former. After all, I spent much more ink trying to say what the concept of direct line of gaze is than what the concept seeing is. Should we then conclude, as Premack and Woodruff suggest, that, on these grounds of simplicity, Hare and colleagues' hypothesis is preferable to the complementary behavior-reading hypothesis? I do not believe so.

First, many uses of 'simplicity' in the debate over animal mindreading are too vague and subjective to support the weight of the substantive conclusions that are drawn from them. The fact that a concept or skill seems simpler or easier to us compared to another is not a stable ground from which to conclude that it really is simpler or easier than another or that we are thereby justified in choosing between competing hypotheses on the basis of whether they appeal to such concepts and skills. As is well known, we quite naturally find those concepts and skills of which we are experts intuitively simpler and easier than those (even in the same domain) of which we are not, though there may be no objective difference in simplicity between the concepts and skill sets. Most of us, for example, are quite skilled in basic decimal counting and arithmetic but find it exceedingly difficult to count or do arithmetic in any other base. This subjective fact about us does not show that there is something objectively simpler or easier about decimal counting and arithmetic, or that we should take it as justifiable grounds to conclude, for example, that animals that can count and do simple arithmetic must do so in base ten—that they are somehow not smart enough to do it in some other base (for recent research on counting in animals, see Uller 2008). For similar reasons, we should be cautious in concluding that chimpanzees are more likely to be mindreaders than complementary behavior readers simply because we find the skills and concepts used in the former strategy of predicting others' actions easier and simpler than those used in the latter.[16]

Not all notions of simplicity are so vague and subjective, however, and there may be some behavior-reading hypotheses that credit animals with psychological states and processes that are objectively more sophisticated and complex than those credited to them by the alternative mindreading hypothesis. This may be the case, for example, with some of the brute associative hypotheses that Tomasello and Call (2006) discuss in their article, hypotheses that appear to credit animals with the capacity to keep track of an inordinately large number of past contingencies between different behaviors in other agents in different environmental settings. However, this cannot be so easily said of complementary behavior-reading hypotheses, for a complementary behavior-reading animal is hypothesized to represent the very same behavioral and environmental cues that its mindreading counterpart is hypothesized to represent in attributing mental states. In terms of counting kinds of representations, then, the complementary behavior-reading animal is taken to employ one fewer kind than its mindreading counterpart. Thus, if what the mindreading animal is thought to do is somehow simpler, then it must be in terms of the cognitive processes it employs, not in terms of the types of representations the processes range over. However, as we saw above, the cognitive processes a complementary behavior-reading animal might conceivably employ need not be different in kind from those its mindreading counterpart employs (see Penn & Povinelli 2007). Both types of animals may reason by analogy, or by simulation, or by following/applying a general rule (learned or innately known) to a particular situation, for example. There is no reason, then, to think that Hare and colleagues' mindreading hypothesis (or the mindreading hypotheses in general) will credit chimpanzees with cognitive states and processes that are objectively simpler in kind than those credited to the animals by the complementary behavior-reading hypothesis.

The oldest and most widely used simplicity argument in the animal mindreading debate is undoubtedly the unifying hypothesis strategy. This type of argument can be traced back to Premack and Woodruff (1978), and versions of it can be found in Bennett (1990), Whiten (1996), Sober (1998), and Fitzpatrick (2009), among others. The basic idea and motivation behind the strategy is that the logical problem, although unsolvable at the local level of individual experiments, is solvable at the global level of many experiments. More formally, the argument can be represented as follows. Suppose that (1) an animal performs behaviors (e.g., predictive, exploratory, discriminatory) under a wide range of behavioral/environmental conditions $S_1, S_2, S_3, ..., S_n$ in different experiments, $E_1, E_2, E_3, ..., E_n$. And suppose that (2) these various conditions $S_1, S_2, S_3, ..., S_n$ across the experiments do not possess any common nonmental feature that might plausibly explain or predict the animal's performance in the different experiments, but that they do possess a common mental feature M that can do so—namely, that in each experiment, the animal does what it does because it understands something about the mental state M in another agent or itself. If (1) and (2) are satisfied by a series of experiments with the same animal (or group of animals), then it appears as if a mindreading hypothesis is in a position to offer a more unified, simpler, and, thus, preferable account of the data than any behavior-reading hypothesis, for a mindreading hypothesis would be in a position to predict and explain the data as follows:

Mindreading hypothesis: The animal performs in the way it does in the various experiments because it understands something about the mental state M.

A behavior-reading hypothesis, on the other hand, would appear to be constrained to provide separate predictions and explanation for each of the different experiments:

Behavior-reading hypothesis: In experiment E_1, the animal performs in the way it does because it understands something about the behavioral/environmental condition S_1, in E_2, the animals performs in the way it does because it understands something about the behavioral/environment condition S_2, and so on for the other experiments and conditions.

Clearly, there is something intuitively less economical and less acceptable about the behavior-reading hypothesis here. Of course, this is a matter of degree: It depends on the actual number of distinct types of observable conditions involved. If there are only two (e.g., S_1 and S_2), then the behavior-reading hypothesis is not as uneconomical as it would be if there were, say, four (S_1–S_4). How much less economical a behavior-reading hypothesis must be before we should prefer the mindreading hypothesis, the unifying hypothesis strategy does not say. The idea is that the less economical it is, the more we should prefer the mindreading hypothesis, all things being equal, of course.

A limitation of the unifying hypothesis strategy, however, is that it does not work well for mental state attributions, such as attributions of simple cognitive states, that possess a fairly circumscribed range of observable grounds. As shown above, the attributions of seeing are done in large part on the observable grounds of direct line of gaze. As a result, there is reason to think that wherever an animal's performance is explainable or predictable in terms of saying that it understands that another agent sees/fails to see an object or state of affairs, it is explainable or predictable in terms of saying that it understands that the other agent has/lacks a direct line of gaze to the object or state of affairs. The unifying hypothesis strategy, therefore, would seem to have a much greater chance of working for mental state attributions that have a wider, more heterogeneous range of observable grounds (e.g., attributions of goal-directed/intentional actions or attributions of belief) than attributions of simple cognitive states, such as attributions of seeing.

Yet despite this apparent limitation to the strategy, Tomasello and Call (2006) have recently argued that the data from Hare et al. (2000), plus those from a number of other studies, can be given a unified explanation by the general hypothesis that "chimpanzees understand seeing" (p. 381) but not by any alternative behavior-reading hypothesis. The authors examine only low-level associative behavior-reading hypotheses, however. Thus, even if they are correct, it does not follow that there is no complementary behavior-reading hypothesis that can provide an equally plausible unified explanation of the data. There is no substitute for examining the data, however, so let us take a look.

Some of the data to which the authors refer come from studies on gaze following in chimpanzees that I briefly described in the previous section. In addition, the authors refer to data from a study by Kaminski, Call, and Tomasello (2004) that found that chimpanzees tend to produce more begging gestures from an experimenter who was bodily facing and looking at the chimpanzees than from an experimenter who was bodily facing but not looking at them.[17] In another such study, Melis et al. (2006) discovered that chimpanzees will steal food from an experimenter if they observe the experimenter looking away from the food (even though the experimenter's body may be oriented toward the food) or, if the experimenter is looking in the direction of the food, her line of gaze to the food is blocked by an opaque barrier. The chimpanzees were not inclined to steal the food, however, if they saw that the experimenter was seated behind an opaque barrier with an open section (a window) allowing the experimenter an unobstructed line of gaze to the chimpanzees' approach to the food or if the chimpanzees observed the experimenter looking directly at the food from behind a transparent barrier. In addition, the researchers observed that when the chimpanzees attempted to steal the food, they tended to take paths that allowed them to keep an opaque barrier between their bodies and the experimenter's line of gaze.

All of the data mentioned above attest to the genuine ingenuity, cleverness, and insightfulness of chimpanzees. They are truly intelligent animals. However, their being smart in these ways does not mean that they understand anything about seeing over and above direct line of gaze. All of the tests above, like Hare et al.'s (2000) competitive tests, involve manipulating what the other agent can see by manipulating the agent's direct line of gaze. The results, therefore, can just as plausibly be explained by the general complementary behavior-reading hypothesis that chimpanzees understand direct line of gaze as they can by the general mindreading hypothesis that chimpanzees understand seeing.

This may not seem so clearly the case regarding the last study that Tomasello and Call discuss, however. In this study by Call and Carpenter

(2001), an ape (either a chimpanzee or an orangutan) watched while an experimenter baited one of two tubes. The ape was then allowed to choose a tube and was given the food if it chose the baited tube. In the 'hidden' test trial, the ape's view of the baiting process was partially blocked by a screen. However, from its experience in the training trials, the ape had reason to believe that the experimenter was baiting a tube from behind the screen, though the screen prevented the animal from seeing which tube the experimenter had baited. The screen was then removed, and the ape was allowed to choose a tube. What the researchers discovered was that in the 'hidden' test trials, some of their apes (both chimpanzees and orangutans) on the very first trial looked inside the tubes before choosing a tube more often than they did in the 'visible' trials in which they were allowed to see the experimenter bait a particular tube. In the 'visible' test trials, the apes nearly always chose the tube that they saw being baited by the experimenter without looking into the tubes first (but only if the apes were allowed to choose immediately; their look-before-choosing behavior increased the longer they had to wait to choose a tube).[18]

The researchers took the results as indicating that chimpanzees and orangutans (as well as all great apes; see Call 2005) understand seeing *in their own case*, that the apes looked inside the tubes before choosing in the 'hidden' trials because they knew that they did not see the baiting process and (presumably) wanted to gain specific information regarding which tube was baited, and that they did not look inside the tubes before choosing in the 'visible' trials because they knew that they had seen the baiting process and, thus, already had information regarding which tube was baited. The apes are, thus, credited with having introspective access to their own mental state of seeing. On this interpretation of the apes' performance, the data from Call and Carpenter's study may seem to fall more easily under Tomasello and Call's hypothesis that chimpanzees understand something about the mental state of seeing than under the complementary behavior-reading hypothesis that chimpanzees understand something about direct line of gaze.

However, the complementary behavior-reading hypothesis also provides a credible account of the data from Call and Carpenter's study.[19] I should think that the data would seem to resist falling under this hypothesis only by those holding the mistaken assumption that animals are incapable of knowing in their own case whether they have or had a direct line of gaze to objects and events in their environment. However, as we saw in section 2.6 above, there is every reason to think that higher animals, such as chimpanzees, can know such a fact about themselves and their environment mainly through the contents of their own visual states and working memory. Call and Carpenter's study manipulates the events that the apes can and cannot see by manipulating their direct line of gaze to these events. Thus, we have just as much reason to say that the apes looked inside the tubes before choosing in the 'hidden' trials because they knew that they did not have a direct line of gaze to the baiting process and (presumably) wanted to gain specific information regarding which tube was baited, and that they did not look before choosing in the 'visible' trials because they knew that they did have a direct line of gaze to the baiting process and, thus, already had information regarding which tube was baited. On this interpretation, what the apes are credited with having access to in order to determine whether looking before choosing is necessary is *not* their past states of *seeing* the baiting process but their past environmental relation of *having a direct line of gaze* to the baiting process. This is not to suggest that the apes' performance was guided by some fixed and rigid behavior rule, such as continue searching for food until it is seen, or whenever a barrier is presented during baiting, always bend down and look into the tubes (see Call 2005, p. 334). Quite the contrary, it is to suggest, as Call and Carpenter's own metacognitive hypothesis does for seeing (see Call 2005, p. 336), that the apes have access to what they have or have not had a direct line of gaze to and use this information flexibly and intelligently to determine whether future searching behavior is necessary. Obviously some chimpanzees will be more adept at using this information in new situations than others, as the data from Call and Carpenter's study appear to show. There is no reason to suppose that apes' access to what they have or have not had a direct line of gaze to must be controlled by a rigid program or learned after trial and error—at least, no more reason than there is to make a similar assumption regarding their putative access to their own states of vision. Thus, the complementary behavior-reading hypothesis which holds that chimpanzees understand direct line of gaze can account for the data from Call and Carpenter's study just as well as the mindreading hypothesis that chimpanzees understand seeing.

There are, of course, numerous studies on metacognition in animals in addition to Call and Carpenter's that have also yielded positive results (see, e.g., Smith et al. 2009 and Hampton 2009). Most of these studies, however, are not on meta-awareness of seeing. Rather, they are on meta-memory capabilities in animals (i.e., on whether animals are aware of the strength of their memory traces of past events) or meta-confidence judgments in animals (whether animals are aware of the level of certainty regarding earlier choices in a problem task).[20] Therefore, they do not lend support to

Tomasello and Call's hypothesis that chimpanzees have a metacognitive understanding of their own states of seeing. Furthermore, in my opinion, Carruthers (2008) and Crystal and Foote (2009) have rather persuasively shown how the results from these additional metacognitive studies can be explained in terms of first-order/low-level (i.e., nonmetacognitive) processes in the animals. However, I wholeheartedly agree with Crystal and Foote that as far as testing metacognition in animals, "new, innovative methods" are needed to distinguish first-order/low-level explanations from genuine higher-order/metacognitive ones. As will be seen in the following chapters, the types of experimental protocols that I advocate using to test for cognitive state attributions in animals are indirect ways of testing for genuine meta-awareness of perceptual states (seeing and hearing) in animals. Thus, in my criticism of Tomasello and Call's unifying hypothesis argument, I am not denying that animals are capable of having meta-cognitive access to their own states of seeing, only that Call and Carpenter's study demonstrates that they are.

I also do not deny that there may be a better general account of the data from all the above studies which appeals neither to the hypothesis that chimpanzees understand direct line of gaze nor the hypothesis that they understanding seeing. However, if there is, that would not help Tomasello and Call's unifying hypothesis argument. The point being made here is simply that if the data can be unified by Tomasello and Call's hypothesis that chimpanzees understand seeing, it can be unified just as well by the complementary behavior-reading hypothesis that chimpanzees understand direct line of gaze. In the end, the unifying hypothesis strategy is, I believe, the wrong approach to take toward solving the logical problem for perceptual state attribution in animals.

2.8   Knowledge/Ignorance Attribution in Primates

There have been a handful of studies with primates to test for attributions of knowledge and ignorance. Attributions of knowledge in these studies are generally understood in terms of attributions of *past* states of seeing. An animal is interpreted as attributing to an agent a state of *knowing* the location of a hidden object, for example, if the animal is taken to understand that the agent *saw* the object hidden. Correspondingly attributions of *ignorance* are generally understood as attributions of the *absence* of past states of seeing. Thus, an animal is interpreted as attributing to an agent a state of ignorance (or lack of knowledge) of the location of a hidden object, for example, if the animal is taken to understand that the agent *did not see* the object hidden. Since judgments of whether an agent *saw/did not see* an event rest upon judgments of whether the agent *had/ lacked* a direct line of gaze to the event, all knowledge/ignorance attribution studies are amenable to a complementary behavior-reading explanation in terms of the animal predicting another agent's behavior by understanding what the agent had or did not have a direct line of gaze to in the past. To see this, let us consider a few of the more influential knowledge/ignorance studies to date.

In 2001, Hare and colleagues published a competitive experiment with chimpanzees similar to their 2000 study (see above). In this experiment, a subordinate chimpanzee competed with a dominant chimpanzee for food that was hidden inside one of two opaque objects (cloth bags) that were placed in the middle area between their facing rooms. Some time prior to the actual competition, the subordinate chimpanzee either observed the dominant (from its respective room across the way) watching the experimenter hiding the food inside a bag or observed that its rival's door was closed and, thus, that the dominant chimpanzee could not witness the experimenter hiding the food. The researchers discovered that their subordinate chimpanzees, at the time of the competition, were less likely to try to take food from the hiding place if they had earlier observed the dominant chimpanzee witnessing the hiding of the food than if they had not. The researchers took these results to imply that the subordinate chimpanzees were capable of attributing the state of knowledge (i.e., having seen the hiding of the food) and the state of ignorance (i.e., having not seen the hiding of the food) to their dominant rivals.

However, since the knowledge/ignorance attributions here are based upon (or are equivalent to) attributions of having seen/having not seen the hiding of the food, and since these, in turn, are based upon the subordinate chimpanzees' judgments of whether the dominant had or did not have a direct line of gaze to the hiding of the food, an equally plausible complementary behavior-reading hypothesis of the data are presentable. On this hypothesis, the subordinate is understood merely to understand that the dominant chimpanzee will attempt to retrieve the food from where it was hidden if and only if it *had* a direct line of gaze to the hiding of the food in that location. There is no more of a mystery of how the subordinate might come to know this about the dominant chimpanzee's behavior than there is about how the subordinate is expected to know that the dominant chimpanzee will attempt to retrieve the food from where it was hidden if and only if it had seen the food hidden in that location.

In a more recent set of knowledge/ignorance studies, Kuroshima and colleagues (2002, 2003) had capuchin monkeys watch while a trainer hid a piece of food inside one of three opaque containers behind an occluding screen. The screen was positioned in front of the containers so that the monkeys could not tell which container was baited, but based upon their earlier training experience, the monkeys had reason to believe that the experimenter was baiting a container behind the screen. After the baiting, the trainer removed the screen and one experimenter (the knower) looked inside each container and then placer her hand on top of the container that contained the food, while another experimenter (the guesser) simply placed her hand on one of the remaining (empty) containers without ever looking inside. The experimenters then removed their hands and the containers were moved toward the monkey so that it could make a choice. It was discovered that some of the monkeys eventually learned to prefer the container that was touched by the knower rather than the one touched by the guesser; and in one control test where the knower's and guesser's behaviors were made to be as similar as possible, save that the former looked inside the containers while the latter did not, one monkey (Kiki) preferentially selected the container indicated by the knower over the one indicated by the guesser. The researchers interpreted their results as showing that their monkeys learned to recognize the relationship between seeing and knowledge, that they understood that the knower had seen (and thus knew) which container was baited while the guesser did not.

Again, even if this were true, the monkeys' past-tense attributions of seeing/not seeing the food must be based upon their judgments about whether they thought the experimenter had or lacked a direct line of gaze to the food inside the container. Undoubtedly the reason that the monkeys purportedly thought that the knower saw which container was baited was that, as a result of her looking inside each container, the knower was able to get an unobstructed, direct line of gaze to the food inside the container. And undoubtedly the reason the monkeys purportedly thought that the guesser did not see which container was baited was that the experimenter never came to have an unobstructed, direct line of gaze to anything inside the container. But now we can account for the monkeys' preferential selection of containers merely on the basis of whether they thought the experimenter had or lacked a direct line of gaze to the contents of the containers. The monkeys came to learn that the experimenter that did have such an unobstructed line of gaze to the contents of the containers was the experimenter that touched the container that had food inside.

Perhaps the most innovative knowledge/ignorance study to date is the 'key' experiment, first conducted by Gómez and Teixidor (1992). The logic behind the 'key' experiment is quite elegant indeed. In the pretesting stage of the experiment, the test animal watches while an experimenter (the hider) places a desirable object (e.g., food or toy) inside one of two cabinets. The hider then locks the cabinets with a key, places the key in a designated box, and then leaves the room. Moments later, another experimenter (the helper) enters the room, sits down facing the animal, and prompts the animal to choose a cabinet. The animal is trained (if training is needed) to point to the baited cabinet upon being prompted. Once the animal points to a cabinet, the helper retrieves the key from its usual location, unlocks the indicated cabinet, and gives the animal the desirable object inside (provided that the animal chose the baited cabinet; otherwise, the animal is not rewarded).

Once the animal reaches criterion on this stage of the experiment, it is given two types of test trials. In one (the ignorant helper test), the helper is absent while the hider places the key in a new location in the room—usually in a location out of sight of the incoming helper. In the other test trial (the knowledgeable helper test), the helper is present and watches while the key is placed in its new location. The general idea behind the tests is that if the animal understands that the helper needs the key to open the cabinet, and that the helper in the former type of trial is ignorant of the key's new location but is knowledgeable of its new location in the latter type of trial, then the animal is expected to reason and behave along the following lines:

> Reasoning in the ignorant helper test trials: The helper didn't see the placement of the key in its new location, so he doesn't know it's there and won't retrieve it unless I point to it. Therefore, I had better point to it.

> Reasoning in the knowledgeable helper test trials: The helper saw the placement of the key in its new location, so he knows it's there and will retrieve it. Therefore, there's no need to point to the key.

Thus, the hypothesis that the test animal understands the helper's state of knowledge/ignorance in the test trials predicts that the animal will point to the key's new location in the ignorant helper trials but not in the knowledgeable helper trials.

Most of the animals that have been tested (great apes and canines) on this experimental paradigm tend to point to the key's new location in the ignorant helper trials but only *after* they first see the helper searching for and failing to find the key in its old location (see Zimmermann et al. 2009; Topál et al. 2006). This behavior, Gómez (2004) notes, "does not demonstrate an ability to understand the state of ignorance of the [helper]. Pointing to the key is not a reaction to the wrong knowledge of the human, but to his wrong behavior—his failure to get the key. It therefore does not imply a theory-of-mind ability" (p. 231). However, two subjects—the orangutan Dona (in Gómez & Teixidor 1992) and the chimpanzee Panzee (in Whiten 2000)—did succeed in pointing to the key's new location in versions of the ignorant helper test from the very first trial, though they generally refrained from pointing to the key in the knowledgeable helper trials.[21] The researchers took these results as indicating that Dona and Panzee understood the helper's respective states of knowledge and ignorance regarding the key's new location, and that they used their communicative pointing gestures to direct the helper to the key's new location in those cases where the experimenter was interpreted by the animals as being ignorant of the key's location.

However, since an animal's attributions of knowledge/ignorance in the 'key' experiment will be based upon its judgment of whether the helper had or lacked a direct line of gaze to the placement of the key in its new location, any animal that is credited with understanding that (a) the helper will retrieve the key if but only if he saw it (and hence knows that it is) placed in the new location should also be credited with understanding that (b) the helper will retrieve the key if but only if he had a direct line of gaze with its placement in the new location. If Dona and Panzee had absolutely no reason to think (b), it would be exceedingly difficult to understand how they might have come to think (a). For not implausibly the very reason these apes think that the helper will locate the key (an object) placed in a new location if but only if the helper saw it placed there is that this is how humans (and apes) generally behave with respect to objects (e.g., food or tools for getting food) depending upon whether they had or lacked a direct line of gaze to these objects while they were moved to a new location. Thus, if Dona and Panzee are credited with knowing (a), as the knowledge/ignorance hypothesis assumes that they are, then they are likely to know (b) as well. However, if Dona and Panzee understand (b), then a complementary behavior-reading account of their respective performances can be provided. On this hypothesis, Dona and Panzee reason along the following lines:

> Reasoning in the ignorant helper test trials: The helper was absent while the key was placed in its new location, so he didn't have a direct line

of gaze with its placement in its new location, so he won't retrieve it there unless I point to it. Therefore, I had better point to it.

Reasoning in the knowledgeable helper test trials: The helper had a direct line of gaze to the placement of the key in its new location and will retrieve it there. Therefore, pointing to the key is unnecessary.

I can't see how the complementary behavior-reading explanation of Dona's and Panzee's performance is any less plausible than the knowledge/ignorance explanation. Thus, as innovative as the 'key' experiment is, I do not see that it solves the logical problem.[22]

2.9   Those Amazing Scrub Jays

In the past five years or so, some of the most interesting and innovative experiments in animal mindreading research have been done with birds, specifically corvids (see Bugnyar & Heinrich 2005; Emery & Clayton 2008). Of these, the experiments that come closest to solving the logical problem have been with scrub jays. Scrub jays, as well as other corvids, are known for their sophisticated cache-protection strategies. They prefer to cache food in private or behind opaque barriers if other scrub jays (who are known pilferers) are around; they have been observed making 'false' caches of objects, such as stones, that look like acorns in the presence of conspecifics, and studies show that they have a strong tendency to return to cache sites and to recache the food in new locations if (and generally only if) they observed another scrub jay watching them at the time of the initial caching (Clayton et al. 1994; Emery & Clayton 2001; Emery et al. 2004; Grodzinski & Clayton 2010). It has been argued that these caching/recaching strategies function to reduce pilfering of food by conspecifics (and perhaps other thieving animals, as well). The behaviors themselves undoubtedly require the birds to be able to observe the difference between the presence and the absence of a competing conspecific during caching, the difference between a conspecific having and lacking a direct line of gaze to the caching, as well as the ability to remember these differences at later times in order to determine whether recaching is required.

As intelligent as these cache-protection behaviors are, none of them, unfortunately, determines whether scrub jays understand seeing rather than direct line of gaze. In all of the cases mentioned above, the birds have just as much reason to expect theft from a conspecific that they think sees them caching as from a conspecific that they think has a direct line of gaze to the caching. After all, a jay that has a direct line of gaze to a caching event is (unless blind) a jay that *sees* the event, and vice versa. It is, therefore, rather unlikely for there to be any projectable difference in the pilfering behaviors between conspecifics that jays believe *see* their caching and those conspecifics that the jays believe have a *direct line of gaze* to their caching.

However in the past five years or so, Nicky Clayton, Nathan Emery, and Joanna Dally have run a series of very clever experiments with scrub jays designed to test whether these birds are capable of mindreading or just some variety of behavior reading. Two studies in particular deserve special comment because I believe they, of all the mindreading studies to date, come closest to solving the logical problem. The general strategy behind both studies was to keep the observing jay's direct line of gaze to the storer jay's caching event constant while varying the observer jay's visual acuity of the event. The mindreading hypothesis that scrub jays understand seeing and use it to anticipate conspecifics' pilfering behaviors would predict that the storer jay's caching and recaching behaviors should vary according to the level of visual acuity that it had reason to believe the observer jay had during the initial caching. The behavior-reading hypothesis that scrub jays understand direct line of gaze only, on the other hand, would putatively predict no variation in the caching and recaching behaviors since, by hypothesis, the observer jay's direct line of gaze is held constant across the test trials.

The first of these studies was by Dally et al. (2004). In this study, the subject jays (storer jays) were selected from those jays that had some previous experience with raiding other jays' caches after observing the initial caching. These storer jays were then given a bowl full of pine nuts and allowed to cache them in either a tray placed in a well-lit area of their cage or in a tray placed in a shaded area. What the researchers discovered was that if the storer jays were allowed to cache in private, they showed no preference for either type of tray, but they showed a decided preference toward caching in the shaded tray if they saw another jay observing them from an adjacent cage. After a 3-hour wait, the trays were returned to the storers' cages and the birds were allowed to recache in private. Although they recached very few nuts in total (perhaps because pine nuts are not their preferred food), the storer jays showed no preference for recaching from either tray if their initial caching was done in private, but they showed a clear preference for recaching from the well-lit tray if their initial caching had been observed by another jay.

The researchers took the results as strongly supporting the hypothesis that scrub jays understand the differential effects that light and shade have on "the quality of visual information available to pilferers ... and ... the accuracy of [their] observational spatial memory" (Emery & Clayton 2008, p. 73). Scrub jays, according to the researchers, understand that conspecifics see better in the light than in the shade and (as a result) are more likely to remember and steal food that they have seen cached in the light than in the shade.

The question is whether the data are inconsistent with a complementary behavior-reading hypothesis in terms of direct line of gaze. Now, the data would be inconsistent with this hypothesis if the degree to which an agent has a direct line of gaze to an object inside or behind a medium/barrier did not vary proportionally to the agent's degree of visual acuity of the object inside or behind the medium/barrier. However, this is not the case. Since opacity comes in degrees, so too does direct line of gaze. Absolutely opaque barriers (e.g., wooden doors) and media (e.g., pitch darkness) block an agent's line of gaze to objects absolutely; less opaque barriers (e.g., dark tinted glass) and media (e.g., thick fog) block it less. In the current studies, the storer jays can plainly perceive that in some conditions, the observer jay is looking at/facing a tray that is covered by a semi-opaque medium—shade—and in other conditions, the observer jay is looking at/facing a tray that is not so covered. Arguably this perceived difference is the very basis on which the storer jays putatively know to attribute low visual acuity to the observer in the former condition and high visual acuity to the observer in the latter condition. Thus, whether scrub jays are mindreaders or complementary behavior readers, the storer jays must be understood as observing the difference in the degree to which the observer jays have a direct line of gaze to the different trays.

But now it seems rather plain that the storer jays could just as well have predicted the likelihood of future theft by the observer jays simply on the grounds of how direct they thought the observers' line of gaze was to the initial caching event. It is not implausible to suppose that the storer jays know, either from reflecting on their own acts of pilfering caches or from observing similar behaviors in conspecifics, that the more opaque the medium or barrier between the caching event and an observer jay's eyes/head the less likely the cache will be pilfered by the jay. Anyway, such a supposition is surely no less plausible than the one that Dally and colleagues must make—namely, that storer jays know, either from their own case or from observing others, that conspecifics are more likely to steal from those sites of which they had a greater visual acuity (as a result of the degree of opacity of the intervening medium or barrier) at the time of the initial caching. Thus, I do not see that the sun–shade study solves the logical problem.

In the near–far study by Dally and colleagues, as with the former study, the storer jays were selected from those jays that had previous experience with observing and stealing from other jays' caches. In this study, however, two trays were placed at opposite ends of the storer jay's cage. The 'near' tray was placed on the side of the storer's cage that was closest to an adjacent cage containing an observer jay, while the 'far' tray was placed on the opposite side of the storer's cage (i.e., the side farthest from the observer jay's cage). The storer was then given wax worms to cache under two conditions. In the private condition, a screen was placed between the adjacent cages, blocking the observer jay's view and allowing the storer to cache in private. In the observer condition, the screen was removed, and the storer jay cached under the watchful eye of the observer jay. The researchers observed that the storer jays cached equal amounts of worms in both trays in the private condition but cached more worms in the 'far' tray in the observer condition. The storer jays were then allowed to recache in private. The jays showed no preference for recaching from either tray if their initial caching was done in private but showed a decided preference for recaching from the 'near' tray if their initial caching was observed.

In line with their previous interpretation, the researchers took the results as strongly indicating that scrub jays understand the differential effects of distance on visual acuity. Scrub jays, according to the researchers, tend to cache in sites farthest from an observing conspecific because they understand that these site are harder for the observer to see and thus harder for the observer to remember and pilfer later, and that they tend to recache from those sites that were closest to the observer because such sites are easier for the observer to see and thus more likely to be remembered and pilfered later.

Although this interpretation is consistent with the data, the complementary behavior-reading hypothesis in terms of direct line of gaze is also consistent. As with the previous study, it is a mistake to think that the observer jay's line of gaze to the different trays does not vary proportionally with its visual acuity of the trays. As we saw above, line of gaze can vary according to its directness—that is, according to the degree of opacity of the intervening barrier or medium. However, it can also vary in terms of its length. Some lines of gaze to an object are longer than others. Hence, in the present study, the jays can perceive that the observer's line of gaze to the 'far' tray is longer than it is to the 'near' tray.[23] And, similar to the point made above, this is arguably the very grounds that, on Dally and colleagues' mindreading hypothesis, the storer jays use to determine the level of visual acuity of the observer. Thus, it is not at all implausible to suppose that the jays know, either from reflecting on their own past acts of stealing or from observing like behaviors in conspecifics, that scrub jays are more likely to steal from sites to which they had, at the time of the initial caching, the shortest line of gaze. Anyway, such a supposition is no less plausible than the one that Dally and colleagues must make: that the jays know, either from their own case or from observing conspecifics, that scrub jays are more likely to steal from sites of which, at the time of the initial caching, they had the greatest visual acuity (because of the distance between the site and the conspecific's eyes/face). The near–far study, then, fares no better in solving the logical problem than the sun–shade study.

For those familiar with their work, two additional studies by Clayton, Emery, and colleagues might seem better equipped to solve the logical problem than the ones I have just discussed. Although I do not believe this to be the case, we should, so as to leave no stone unturned, take a look at these studies as well. The first of these (Emery & Clayton 2001) was a private/observed cache protocol, similar to the ones described above, that was run with three different groups of scrub jays. In the first group, the naive group, the subjects had the experience of caching food and recovering it later, as well as having seen other jays caching food, but had never had the opportunity to pilfer from other jays' caches. In the experienced group, however, the subjects had observed other jays caching and had later stolen the food from those caches. And in the control group, the subjects had experience with pilfering other jays' caches but had not observed the initial caching of these sites. The results from the study were remarkable. The experienced jays and the control jays—those that had the experience of stealing other jays' caches—preferred to recache their food in new locations if, during their initial caching of the food, they had been observed by another jay. However, the naive jays—those that had no experience with stealing other jays' caches—showed no such preference; they simply recached roughly the same amount of food (and very little at that) in new sites whether they had been watched during their initial caching or not.

Emery and Clayton (2008) interpret these findings as supportive of the hypothesis that "storers with the specific experience of stealing another's caches (even when they had not seen the caches being made), project this experience onto another bird, namely one which is observing their caching, and so is a potential thief" (p. 85). Since experiences are naturally thought to be mental states, the researchers quite understandably conclude that their hypothesis entails that scrub jays attribute mental states to conspecifics.[24]

However, the "experience" that Clayton and Emery take the storers to project onto the observer jay is not a mental state. The researchers are most certainly not maintaining, for example, that the jays project the kinds of proprioceptive or tactile sensations that they have while stealing food from another jay's caches. For how would the projection of such sensory experiences onto the observer give the jays any reason to think that the observer "is a potential thief"? After all, every jay, whether thief or not, has these types of sensations while recovering food from caches. Arguably, what the jays project, and what the researchers actually say they project, is not a mental state but the behavioral disposition to take food from another jay's cache. The problem here is that Emery and Clayton's argument, from the premise that jays project their experience of stealing onto others to the conclusion that jays attribute mental states to others, trades on a confusion regarding two uses of the word 'experience.' The word 'experience' has both a mental and a nonmental reading. The expression 'the experience of pain' or 'the "aha!" experience of discovery,' for example, clearly describes a type of mental state, a kind of noxious bodily sensation in the one case and a type of conscious occurrent thought in the other. However, the expression 'the experience of stealing another's cache,' much like the expression 'the experience of running a multinational corporation,' does not, and is not intended to, describe a type of mental state; it is intended to describe a type of behavior or skill. To be experienced in stealing other jays' caches, which the experienced and control jays are, is simply to have stolen other jays' caches. What the jays purportedly project onto the observer is not a mental state but the tendency to steal another jay's caches. Thus, what on the surface may look to be a test for mental state attribution in scrub jays is really a test of behavior projection—not something to sneeze at, of course, but not mindreading either.

More recently, Stulp, Emery, Verhulst, and Clayton (2009) gave scrub jays two kinds of trays in which to cache wax worms, one filled with small pebbles that made noise when the birds cached in it, and the other filled with sand that made very little noise. The researchers ran the birds through three different caching conditions. In the hear–blind condition, the storer jays were allowed to cache in the presence of a conspecific in an adjacent cage that could hear the storers' caching but could *not* see it (due to a screen's blocking its view). In the hear-and-see condition, the storer jays were allowed to cache in the presence of another jay with the screen removed, allowing the observer to see *and* hear the storers' caching.

And in the private condition, the storer jays were allowed to cache in private.

It was discovered that the storer jays showed a decided preference for caching in the quiet tray only in the hear–blind condition. In the other two conditions, they cached equal amounts in both trays. The researchers took the results as evidence that the birds attribute the mental states of hearing and seeing to conspecifics. They maintained that the scrub jays favored the quiet tray in the hear–blind condition because they understood that, although the observer jay could not see the trays, it could still hear the caching of food in the noisy tray and would, as a result of hearing the caching in that tray, pilfer from it later. In the other conditions, according to the researchers, the storer jays did not favor one tray over the other because they understood that the observer could see both trays equally well (and so both were equally vulnerable to pilfering) or because the observer was not present (and so both trays were equally invulnerable to pilfering).

The results are, quite simply, fascinating. Scrub jays are cognitively sophisticated animals, of this there is little doubt. Unfortunately, the experiment does not solve the logical problem. One might have thought otherwise, however, since the results do not lend themselves to being explained simply in terms of the jays understanding direct line of gaze. But not every complementary behavior-reading hypothesis is a direct line of gaze hypothesis, of course. The specific content of the complementary behavior-reading hypothesis largely depends upon the content of the mindreading hypothesis being tested. Thus, we need to consider the behavior-reading hypothesis that is complementary to Stulp and colleagues' mindreading hypothesis.

Scrub jays cannot directly observe another's hearing any more than they can directly observe another's seeing, and so if they attribute hearing to conspecifics, then they do so on the basis of some observable feature of the other agent and its environment. Arguably, the most likely candidate in this case is the different volume of sound produced by an event in spatial proximity to the other agent. Unfortunately, there is not a simple word or phrase in English to describe this relation as there is in the case of direct line of gaze. However, that does not mean that the relation is not used by jays to attribute hearing to conspecifics. For ease of discussion, we could call this relation 'direct line of sound.' Thus, it must be assumed on Stulp and colleagues' mindreading hypothesis that the storer jays understand that the observer jay is more likely to hear the noisy tray during caching than the quieter tray because the former emits a higher volume of sound in proximity to the observer than the latter.

The question, then, is whether we could explain the storer jays' performance just as well in terms of their observing the difference in the volume of sound produced by the trays in equal proximity to the observer jays—in terms of their understanding direct line of sound. It seems rather clear that we can. The jays, after all, could easily have come to know, from observing either their own behavior or that of other jays in response to sound volume (in general) or the volume of sound produced by caching (in particular), that jays that are present tend to be attracted to the source of a sound the higher the sound's volume—especially, if the source of the sound is a caching event. In fact, it is difficult to understand how the jays in the hear–blind condition could even be thought to understand that the observer is more likely to pilfer from the noisy tray if they did not understand the differential effects of sound volume on conspecifics' behaviors. Thus, on the complementary behavior-reading hypothesis, the scrub jays' preferential choice for caching in the hear–blind condition can be explained in terms of their understanding that, although the observer jay lacks a direct line of gaze to the caching in either tray, the noisy tray by virtue of its production of a higher volume of sound in relative close proximity to the observer jay is more likely to attract (and thus more likely to lead to pilfering by) the observer jay than the quieter tray.[25]

2.10   Remarks on Goal-Directed/Intentional-Action Attribution in Animals

I have argued that none of the current experimental approaches used in animal social cognition research is capable of determining whether animals predict or make sense of others' behaviors by attributing simple cognitive states rather than the behavioral/environmental cues used as the grounds for attributing such states. For all the current studies show, animals may be incapable of attributing such states of mind.

It may be wondered, however, how an animal might be capable of attributing goal-directed/intentional actions to an agent, which I am allowing is possible, without being able to attribute simple cognitive states, such as seeing and knowing. Call and Tomasello (2008) voice this concern, writing that "[t]o understand how another works as a goal-directed agent, an observer *must* [my emphasis] understand not only his goals but also his perceptions because what he sees and knows help to determine what he does" (p. 189). So is it really possible for animals to attribute simple conative states (e.g., states of having a goal, willing, intending, etc.) without their being able to attribute simple cognitive states, such as seeing and knowing? I believe so—at least, Call and Tomasello's argument here gives little reason to think otherwise.

In reply, it is relevant to note that what an agent believes and remembers at the time of his intentional action, as well as what the agent's prior intentions and plans were before the execution of the action, also help to determine what he does. And yet no researcher in the field, and certainly not Call and Tomasello, thinks that because of this, goal-directed/ intentional-action attribution in animals requires belief or memory attribution, or attribution of prior intentions and plans. Thus, it is widely agreed in the field (at least implicitly) that even if goal-directed/intentional actions are determined by a host of mental states in addition to the agent's goals and intentions, this alone does not mean that the attributing animal "must" represent these additional states in order for it to use its representation of the agent's goal or intention to predict and make sense of the agent's behavior—not unless, that is, these other mental states are somehow shown to be part of the very idea of what it is for an agent to engage in goal-directed/intentional action. But that does not appear to be the case for the mental states of seeing and knowing. Agents quite often search for objects (goal-directed/intentional action) for which they have never seen nor have ever known as a result of having seen them. People grope in the dark for the lights (goal-directed actions), all without seeing the switch and, hence, without knowing where it is and, in some cases, even without knowing whether there is a switch. And, of course, animals often search for food and mates (goal-directed actions) without first seeing these items or knowing their location based upon having seen them. In such cases, it could be said, what an agent does not see and does not know (as a result of what it has seen) about the existence or location of an object is what determines what he or she does or will do. Hence, it does not appear to be part of what it is to understand an agent as engaging in goal-directed/ intentional actions that the agent must be represented as seeing or as having knowledge of the objects toward which his or her goal-directed/ intentional actions are understood to be directed.

It may be argued, however, that although the concepts of seeing and knowing are not part of what it means for an agent to engage in goal-directed/intentional actions, the concept of believing is (Grice 1971; Harman 1976). If an agent does A (e.g., puts the key in the ignition) with the goal/intention to x (e.g., to start the car), then he or she must be thought to *believe* (to some degree) that his or her doing A stands some chance of leading to x —otherwise, we would be rather reluctant to say that the agent did A with the goal/intention to x. Thus, according to such an understanding of goal-directed/intentional action, it would appear that were animals capable of understanding others as engaging in goal-directed/ intentional actions, they must be capable of understanding others as having beliefs, and, of course, beliefs are cognitive states (albeit not simple ones). Thus, attributions of conative states by animals, on this account, would require their having the ability to attribute cognitive states.

Such an account of goal-directed/intentional-action attribution in animals is not, of course, the one endorsed by Call and Tomasello. What is more, if it were endorsed by animal researchers, it would make the idea of genuine goal-directed/intentional-action attribution in animals much less certain than it is, given the considerable controversy over the possibility of belief attribution in animals (which will be discussed in chapter 4).[26] However, as noted above, researchers are far more confident about the possibility of goal-directed/intentional-action attribution in animals than the possibility of belief attribution in animals. Hence it is unlikely that any researcher would be willing to endorse the above belief-based account of goal-directed/intentional action as a way to understand the nature of the attributions of goal-directed/intentional actions in animals. Is there an alternative? I believe so. Animals may simply understand that if an agent does action A with the goal/intention to x, then the agent's doing A is expected (to some degree) *by the animal* to lead to x—not that the animal thinks that the agent believes that his doing A will likely lead to x.

Admittedly, such an account does not reflect our full-blown intentional understanding of goal-directed/intentional actions in others since we can make sense of an agent doing A with the goal/intention to x, even though we know flat out that there is no chance of his doing A leading to x, provided that we think that the agent believes (again, to some degree) that his doing A will lead to x. However, even if animals are incapable of attributing goal-directed/intentional actions under conditions that would require them to attribute such incongruent beliefs to agents (and there is no evidence from the empirical literature that suggests that they can attribute such incongruent beliefs), there is no reason why they could not attribute goal-directed/intentional actions to agents under conditions in which they believe the agent's action will likely lead to its intended goal. Such goal-directed/intentional-action attributions would, then, be simple—that is, not full-blown intentional attributions. And that, I should think, is enough to say that animals can attribute goal-directed/intentional actions without their having the capacity to attribute beliefs, that they have an understanding of goal-directed/intentional actions in others—though, not our full-blown intentional understanding.[27]

That goal-directed/intentional-action attribution in animals does not *require* attribution of simple cognitive states, such as seeing and knowing, is further reflected in the fact that the two main theoretical accounts of goal/intentional-action attribution in nonhuman primates—the *embodied simulation account* (Gallese 2007) and the *teleological account* (Gergely & Csibra 2003)—do not require that animals attribute such cognitive states to agents (see Wood & Hauser 2008 for a review). On the embodied simulation account, primates are understood to predict and make sense of another agent's actions by mapping (via their mirror neural systems) the observed behavior patterns of the agent onto their own motor capacities; and on the teleological account, primates are understood to assign a goal to an agent's action by assessing the efficiency of the action within the current constraints observed in the environment. On both accounts, of course, the attributing animal may take various contextual and behavioral cues of the agent into consideration in determining what goals/intentions to attribute, such as the agent's past or present direction of gaze to an object, but this alone, as argued above, does not show that they take into consideration what the other agent sees or knows.

It is also relevant to add that some studies that have been taken as indicating goal-directed/intentional-action attribution in primates cannot plausibly be interpreted in terms of the animals' attributing seeing (or knowing based upon having seen) to the agent, either because the facts relevant to what (if anything) the agent sees or saw are simply blocked to the attributing animal, or the agent does not manifest any relevant cues that might allow the animal to attribute such simple cognitive states to it. Kohler et al. (2002), for example, discovered that a certain class of F5 mirror neurons in the macaque monkey's brain fire both when the monkey itself executes a particular hand action (e.g., tearing a piece of paper) and when it sees this very type of action in other subjects. What is more, these very same premotor neurons fire when the monkey hears but cannot see a subject tearing a piece of paper behind a screen. The researchers interpreted the neural data as evidence that the monkeys, upon hearing the tearing sound, comprehended what the subject was intentionally doing behind the screen—namely, manually tearing a piece of paper. It is exceedingly unlikely, however, that the monkeys' comprehension of what the subject was doing behind the screen rested upon their understanding what the subject was currently seeing (or knowing based upon what they were currently seeing) since the monkeys were blocked from observing any cues that might have been relevant for ascribing such cognitive states to the subject.

Goal detection in chimpanzees

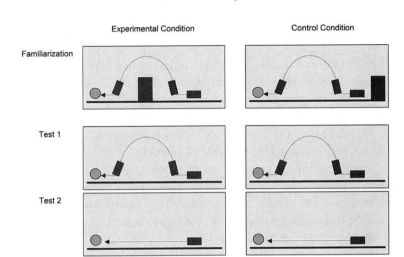

Figure 2.3
Habituation and test videos from Uller (2004).

And in 2004, Claudia Uller used an innovative violation-of-expectancy looking-time method (inspired by Csibra et al. 1999) to test for goal attribution in chimpanzees. In the study, four infant chimpanzees were familiarized (habituated) to one of two video displays in which a block moved toward and finally made contact with a ball, at which point the block stopped moving (see figure 2.3).

In the experimental video, the block was shown making a parabolic 'jump' over a barrier before making contact with the ball on the other side. In the control video, the barrier was off to the side and the block was shown making the same parabolic 'jump' in the air before making contact with the ball. The experimental video, of course, was designed to make it look as if the block had the goal to make contact with the ball by the most direct path possible (in the circumstance, by jumping over the barrier); whereas, the control video was designed to make it looks as if the block either had no goal at all or the goal of making contact with the ball by jumping in the air first. After the habituation phase, the chimpanzees were then shown two videos with the barrier removed. In one of the videos (old action test), the block performed the same movements as before, a parabolic 'jump' and then contact with the ball; in the other video (new action test), the block moved in a straight line toward the ball.

Uller hypothesized that if the chimpanzees that were habituated to the experimental video interpreted the block as having the goal of contacting the ball in the most direct way possible, then they should find the old action test surprising and look longer at it than the new action test, and if those chimpanzees that were habituated to the control video interpreted the block as having no goal or the goal of contacting the ball by jumping, then they should find the new action test surprising and look longer at it than the old action test. And these are precisely the results that Uller received. What is more, these results are routinely interpreted in the field as showing that chimpanzees are capable of anticipating an object's future movements by attributing simple goals/intentions. Nevertheless, there is vanishing little (if any) reason to think that the infant chimpanzees made such predictions of the block's future movements, not only by attributing a particular goal/intention to the block, but by attributing states of seeing (or knowing derived from having seen) to the block as well. The block, after all, possessed nothing that even remotely resembled eyes or perceptual organs, or even a head that might have enabled the chimpanzees to make such attributions.

2.11   Conclusion

Thus, there appears to be little reason to think that if animals are capable of attributing simple conative states, they must be capable of attributing simple cognitive states, such as seeing and knowing, or even the more complex cognitive state of believing. Rather, the question of cognitive state attribution in animals is something that will need to be tested directly, and ideally the tests should overcome the logical problem, if possible. In the next chapter, I begin to show how this can be done.

3   Solving the Logical Problem for Perceptual State Attribution

In the previous chapter, it was argued that none of the experimental approaches currently used to test for simple cognitive state attribution in animals is capable of solving the logical problem. In this chapter, we begin by examining the pessimists' thesis that solving the logical problem is pointless since there are sufficiently strong empirical and theoretical grounds against animal mindreading of any kind. One of the best-developed arguments for this thesis is shown to be unconvincing. This, together with the argument from the previous chapter, provides the motivation to solve the logical problem for cognitive state attribution in animals. An abstract framework for how to solve the problem is outlined along with a viable evolutionary theory of perceptual state attribution in animals. The framework and the theory together provide a recipe for designing experiments that test for perceptual state attribution in animals which overcome the logical problem. Three types of experimental designs are described.

3.1   The Case against Animal Mindreading of Any Kind

The objective of the previous chapter was to demonstrate that presently we lack any clear empirical grounds for thinking that animals understand simple cognitive states (e.g., seeing, hearing, knowing) in others rather than just the behavioral/environmental cues that serve as the observable grounds for ascribing such states. Of course, showing that there is a lack of evidence of mental state attribution in animals is not the same as showing that there is evidence that animals actually lack the capacity to attribute mental states. Some researchers, however, have argued for the actual absence of mindreading in animals. Although many in this camp argue for the more modest thesis that animals are incapable of attributing beliefs and other full-blown intentional states (and their arguments will be examined in the next chapter), some have argued for the bolder thesis that animals are incapable of attributing any type of mental state. Their argument will be examined here.

The best-developed argument for this strong pessimist thesis comes from Povinelli and colleagues (see Povinelli 2000; Vonk & Povinelli 2006; Povinelli & Vonk 2006; Penn & Povinelli 2007; Penn et al. 2008). The argument itself is made up of two parts or smaller arguments, both of which rest on the assumption (argued for in the previous chapter) that there are currently no empirical data that unequivocally show that animals are capable of attributing simple cognitive states. On the basis of this assumption, the first part of Povinelli and colleagues' argument mounts a direct empirical case against mindreading of any kind in chimpanzees. The empirical evidence used here comes from a series of discrimination studies by Povinelli and Eddy (1996) and later by Theall and Povinelli (1999). Since some aspects of these studies have been discussed in earlier chapters, a brief description is given here. In Povinelli and Eddy (1996), chimpanzees were trained to beg for food from an experimenter. In the test trials, the chimpanzees were presented with two experimenters who were otherwise identical except that one could not see the chimpanzee while the other could. In some of these trials, for instance, the nonseeing experimenter wore a blindfold over her eyes or a bucket over her head while the seeing experimenter wore a blindfold around her neck or a bucket on her shoulders. In Theall and Povinelli (1999), the task was simplified by having the chimpanzee beg from only one experimenter. In some of the test trials, the experimenter looked directly at the chimpanzee, while in others the experimenter closed her eyes or looked at the ceiling (see Reaux et al. 1999, as well). The researchers hypothesized that if chimpanzees had any understanding of the mental state of seeing, then they should prefer to beg from the experimenter who can see them. The chimpanzees, however, showed no such preference in either study. In fact, where they showed any preference at all, it was toward the experimenter whose body was facing forward, irrespective of whether she could see the chimpanzee.

Povinelli and colleagues interpret these findings as providing strong, empirical evidence for the absence of any understanding of seeing in the chimpanzee. Such an interpretation of these findings, if true, could also be taken (though Povinelli and colleagues do not do so explicitly) as providing indirect support for the more general hypothesis that chimpanzees are unlikely to be capable of attributing *any kind* of mental state. The reasoning for this more general hypothesis is that if, as Povinelli and colleagues maintain, chimpanzees really do not understand the concept seeing—a relatively simple but nevertheless central mental state concept—

then it is unlikely that they would be capable of understanding other mental state concepts, such as *belief* or *knowledge*, that are more complex in various ways and dependent on an understanding of the concept seeing. And if one were to accept this general hypothesis regarding the absence of mindreading in chimpanzees, then it seems reasonable to draw a similar conclusion about *all* animals. If the chimpanzee—the animal most likely to be capable of mindreading given its high degree of intelligence and relatively close evolutionary ancestry with human beings—is incapable of attributing mental states, then it is difficult to understand how any other species of animal would do any better.

There are various places in this argument that one might take issue, of course. One might, for example, object to the argument's inference to the general conclusion about chimpanzees by pointing out that even if chimpanzees are incapable of attributing seeing, they may well be capable of other types of mental state attribution that arguably do not depend upon their understanding the mental state of seeing (e.g., attributions of hearing or goal-directed/intentional actions).[1] Or one might object that even if chimpanzees are incapable of mindreading, it does not necessarily follow that all species of intelligent, social animals are equally unlikely to be mindreaders. It is quite possible that mindreading evolved in the animal kingdom on separate occasions in different species, much like wings, vision, territoriality, and other analogous traits. As discussed in previous chapters, a number of researchers now claim to have found some evidence (though equivocal) of mental state attribution in species as diverse as dolphins (Tschudin 2001), birds (Watve et al. 2002; Bugnyar & Heinrich 2005; Emery & Clayton 2008), canines (Topál et al. 2006), pigs (Held et al. 2001), goats (Kaminski et al. 2006), and elephants (Nissani 2004). Thus, failure to mindread in the chimpanzee may not be a particularly strong reason by itself to conclude that there is likely to be a similar failure in other species of intelligent, social animal.

Or one might follow the lead of some researchers and object to the design of Povinelli and colleagues' studies. Chimpanzees, it is largely believed, are not naturally disposed to cooperative acts of food sharing, and so it is likely that their mindreading abilities (if extant) did not evolve to be deployed in such cooperative food-sharing contexts. Thus, it is possible, some have argued, that Povinelli and colleagues' studies, which explicitly use communicative–cooperative acts of food sharing, fail to engage the chimpanzees' mindreading abilities, causing the animals to use a nonmindreading strategy to solve the task problem (e.g., learning to associate food distribution with a particular body orientation of the experimenter). Proponents of this line of criticism often point to the successes of chimpanzees on more ecologically naturalistic mindreading tasks involving *competition* for food (Hare et al. 2000, 2001; Hare 2001; Hare & Tomasello 2004; Lyons & Santos 2006; Santos et al. 2007).

On the other hand, one might argue that the results of Povinelli and colleagues' studies are not, in fact, inconsistent with chimpanzees' understanding seeing. On the basis of a study similar to that of Povinelli and Eddy (1996), for example, Kaminski, Call, and Tomasello (2004) hypothesize that chimpanzees may attribute the mental state of seeing to others primarily on the basis of the direction of the other agent's face rather than, as we humans do, on the basis of the other agent's eyes (e.g., whether the eyes are open or closed), using the agent's body posture instead as their primary grounds for attributing certain behavioral capacities to the agent, such as the capacity to deliver food (see Gómez 2004 for similar arguments along this line).[2]

Each of these objections has its merits. However, by far the most serious problem for Povinelli and colleagues' empirical argument here is the fact that their studies have failed to replicate with other chimpanzees. Bulloch et al. (2008) recently ran essentially the same series of experiments as Povinelli and Eddy (1996) and found that the majority of their chimpanzees actually showed a decided preference, from the very first set of trials, for begging from the experimenter who could see them. Bulloch and colleagues speculate that the difference in performance between the two groups of chimpanzees may be due to a difference in the length and depth of exposure that they had with humans. The chimpanzees in Bulloch and colleagues' study appear to have had a significantly longer and richer history of social interaction with human caregivers and trainers than those that participated in Povinelli and colleagues' studies, which may have afforded the animals with more opportunity to understand the significance of eye gaze in humans for the purpose of predicting their behaviors during food sharing tasks. Whatever the exact reason for the difference, the results from Bulloch and colleagues' study undermine Povinelli and colleagues' argument that chimpanzees as a species lack the capacity to attribute seeing to others. This does not mean, however, that Bulloch and colleagues' study solves the logical problem. There is just as much reason to think that their chimpanzees, as a result of their long, rich social interactions with humans, have come to understand the mental state of seeing in humans as there is to think that they have come to understand the importance of direct line of gaze in humans. The importance of the study is that it undermines the strength of Povinelli and colleagues' empirical argument, not that it proves their conclusion is false.

The second part of Povinelli and colleagues' overall argument makes a more indirect case against animal mindreading. This part of their argument is based on their *reinterpretation hypothesis*. According to this hypothesis (discussed briefly in chapters 1 and 2), mindreading evolved for the purpose of enabling subjects to reinterpret the behavior patterns observed in others (the very types of behavior patterns that complementary behavior-reading animals are sensitive to) in terms of superordinate causal patterns. On this hypothesis, mindreading evolved out of complementary behavior reading. The rationale behind the hypothesis, I believe, is not too difficult to see. Mental states, after all, are quite commonly understood on many scientific and functionalist models of the mind to be states that are literally hidden inside a subject's brain or body which are apt to cause patterns of overt behavior. Thus, on such a model of the mind, it stands to reason that attributing mental states to others should be understood as involving the attribution of such hidden internal causes of overt behavior.

In addition, proponents of the reinterpretation hypothesis often point to the fact that the same type of mental state (e.g., knowledge or belief) can sometimes be caused by various different types of environmental stimuli and can, in turn, produce various different types of behaviors in an agent. As a result, these researchers quite frequently stress that the capacity to attribute mental states involves not only the attribution of internal causes but the capacity to "encode" a wide range of perceptually distinct behavior patterns as belonging to a single type of superordinate causal class of behaviors—behaviors, that is, that all have a common type of hidden, internal cause (Penn et al. 2008, p. 119).[3] As a way of an illustration, Povinelli and colleagues contend that a mindreading animal that had the capacity to comprehends that an agent, X, knows that food is in bin A ought to be capable of "encoding" the perceptually distinct behavior patterns of X (as well as perhaps other agents) which have this type of knowledge state as their common inner cause as belonging to the same abstract class of behaviors. Thus, the animal is expected to be able to

encode the observable patterns "X saw Y [a third animal] put food in bin A," "X hid food in bin A," and "X sees Y glancing at bin A" as members of the same abstract equivalence class [i.e., as behavior patterns having the same type of inner causal state—the state of knowing that food is in bin A]. (p. 119)

And so the reinterpretation hypothesis holds that mindreading in animals (if it exists) would necessarily involve the deployment of two cognitive abilities: the ability to attribute hidden, internal causes and the ability to group perceptually distinct stimuli according to higher-order (abstract) properties or classes (specifically, superordinate causal classes). If animals can attribute mental states, Povinelli and colleagues reason, then they should exhibit these skills in nonsocial domains, as well. And yet, the researchers argue, animals routinely fail experimental tasks designed to test their understanding of nonobservable internal causes as well as those designed to test their ability to understand higher-order (abstract) properties and classes (Penn & Povinelli 2007; Penn et al. 2008).

One of the clearest examples of this routine failure, the researchers contend, is the poor performance of animals on various trap-tube experiments designed to test their understanding of nonobservable causal properties, such as gravity and support. In these studies, animals are presented with the problem of extracting food from a clear tube by pushing or pulling the food (by means of a stick or string) away from a strategically placed trap hole on the tube's underside. Pushing or pulling the food over the hole naturally causes the food to drop into the hold, rendering it inaccessible to the animal. Some animals have been shown to be able to solve the problem after some training, but the vast majority of these, Povinelli and colleagues point out, show rather clear signs of being oblivious to the causally relevant properties of the trap hole. For example, after learning to dislodged the food from the tube by pushing or pulling it away from the trap hole, most animals simply continue to behave in the same way when the trap hole is conspicuously rotated upward, making it causally impotent to trap the food (see Visalberghi & Limongelli 1994; Povinelli 2000). And in transfer tests, those subjects that were able to solve the normal trap-tube test were unable to solve a novel trap-hole test using an analogous but perceptually distinct apparatus (see Seed et al. 2006; Tebbich et al. 2007; Martin-Ordas et al. 2008). Povinelli and colleagues interpret these findings as strong evidence that animals lack the ability to represent nonobservable causal factors, such as support and gravity, as well as to classify distinct perceptual stimuli (in this case, different trap apparatuses) in terms of a common underlying (internal) causal mechanisms. Nonhuman animals, Povinelli and colleagues claim, simply

do not understand 'unobservable causal properties' such as gravity and support; nor do they reason about the higher-order relation between causal relations in an analogical or theory-like fashion. Instead, [animals] appear to solve tool-use problems based on evolved, domain-specific expectations about what perceptual features are likely to be most salient in a given context and a general ability to reason about the causal relation between observable contingencies in a flexible, goal-directed but task-specific fashion. (Penn et al. 2008, p. 119)

The researchers conclude that if animals are not able to exercise these cognitive abilities in a nonsocial domain with which they have some skill (all the animals that were tested have a natural talent for using sticks to dislodge food from trees, anthills, etc.), then they are unlikely to exercise them in the social domain where they are needed to attribute mental states.

As with the first part of their argument, there are various places one might wish to object to here. One may join those in arguing that some animals have in fact passed tests that demonstrate their understanding of nonobservable causes (e.g., Call 2004; Hauser & Spaulding 2006; Hanus & Call 2008; Taylor et al. 2009) as well as tests that demonstrate their capacity to categorize observably distinct stimuli into higher-order classes (e.g., Thompson & Oden 2000; Bovet & Vauclair 2001; Thompson & Flemming 2008; Haun & Call 2009). Or one may object, as some modularists undoubtedly would, to Povinelli and colleagues' assumption that the cognitive skills necessary for mindreading should be thought transferable to solving problems in nonsocial domains (see, e.g., Lyons & Santos 2006; Santos et al. 2007; Carruthers 2006).

Again, I believe all of these objections have merit. Yet it strikes me that the most serious problem with Povinelli and colleagues' argument by far is the reinterpretation hypothesis on which it rests. The researchers simply fail to provide any convincing grounds for thinking that mental state attribution in animals must be thought to involve the attribution of hidden, internal causes of behavior or the capacity to "encode" perceptually disparate patterns of behavior into superordinate causal classes. And convincing grounds are needed, for there is a serious question of whether such skills are even required for many ordinary cases of mental state attribution in humans.

Most ordinary folk, of course, think that mental states have something to do with what is physically going on inside the body and brain of a subject, but this does not mean that they view mental states themselves as literally inside (like a proper part of) the subject's body or brain. Quite the contrary it would seem, since most folk find it rather odd to say that their beliefs or thoughts or desires, for example, are literally inside their skull—say, in a region of their brain behind their nasal cavity, and they are quite surprised to hear that their visual experiences are nothing more than physical events happening at the back of their brains in the dark! In addition, close examination of our own ordinary mental state attributions reveals that many of them describe *relations* (not internal states or proper parts of a subject) that the subject bears to various external items, such as propositions, states of affairs, or intentional objects. And even when it comes to our ordinary attributions of sensation, which are more closely associated with certain bodily locations, it is anything but clear that ordinary folk view them as spatially inside the body. If one has a pain in one's finger, for example, and one places one's finger in a glove, no one thinks that there is a pain in the glove (at least, not in the same sense in which there is a pain in one's finger). However, we would accept such an inference were we to think of the pain as being spatially inside the finger in the same way we think of the finger as being spatially inside the glove (or as a brain state as being spatially inside the brain). Thus, there is some doubt regarding whether all or even most of our own ordinary mental state attributions are taken as ascribing states that are literally hidden inside a subject's body or brain. This alone should make us wary of any account of mindreading in animals that requires that mental state attributions in animals be understood as attributions of states that are literally hidden inside other agents' bodies.

And for similar reasons it is equally inadvisable to define mental state attributions in animals as attributions of inner causes of overt behaviors. Of course the term 'cause' is polysemous, and can mean just about anything to anyone, but the authors of the reinterpretation hypothesis take the term to stand for a nondirectly observable, nomologically necessary relation between observable events, to be contrasted with mere spatiotemporally contingent associations among such events (see Povinelli 2000). However, as we just saw above, there is at the moment a deep debate in comparative psychology about whether animals are capable of understanding physical events as being causally related in this way, as opposed to being merely spatiotemporally associated. Given the current state of controversy regarding causal cognition in animals, it is surely unjustified to define mental state attribution in animals as involving attributions of inner causes if there is no compelling reason to do so and if there is an alternative account that does not make this requirement (to be given in section 3.3 below).

What is more, it seems rather clear that attribution of inner causes of overt behavior, although a common feature of some of our own mental state attributions, is not an essential feature of mental state attributions. Some of our own mental state attributions, after all, have been shown to fail to attribute inner causes of behavior, and yet this realization has in no way stopped our practice of attributing such mental states, as would be expected if it were essential to our mental state attributions that they attribute inner causes of behavior. Upon seeing someone place his hand on a hot stove, for instance, we intuitively attribute the state of pain and expect the subject to jerk his hand away from the stove. We now know that the subject's hand-removing behavior in such cases is not caused by the subject's feeling of pain but is the result of a simple reflex arc in the spinal cord. Yet the knowledge of this fact has not undermined our continued practice of attributing pain to such subjects for the purpose of predicting their hand-removing behavior. We do not, therefore, seem to require that our attributions of pain attribute the cause of the subjects' hand-removing behavior. And what goes for the attribution of pain goes for many other mental state attributions.

It is also important to note that there are quite a large number of substantive theories of mind in philosophy and psychology that explicitly deny that mental states cause behavior. Although these theories may be false, they are undoubtedly coherent theories of the mind. Thus, if the likes of Leibniz, Hume, Kant, Huxley, Wundt, and Jackson (to name but a few) can be credited with attributing mental states to others, despite their explicit refusal to take such attributions as ascribing inner causes of overt behavior (on par with the physical causes of events due to gravity and physical forces), then it seems unlikely (to say the least) that mental state attributions *must* be thought to involve attributions of causes of behavior. Hence if humans can be mindreaders without attributing inner causes of overt behavior, there is no reason to think that animals cannot as well—at least no reason that the proponents of the reinterpretation hypothesis have given. And if animals do not need to attribute inner causes in order to attribute mental states, then they do not need to encode perceptually disparate behavior patterns as belonging to the same superordinate causal class.

My points here are not meant to deny that mental states may in fact be physical states that are literally inside a subject's brain or body, or that they are causes of overt behavior in the same way that gravity and physical forces cause objects to fall or move. This may be a true ontological theory of what mental states really are, but it is a fallacy to assume that a theory about the true nature of the mind must be reflected in the way ordinary folk or animals (who have no explicit commitment to such a theory) understand mental states in others.

It is surprising that Povinelli and colleagues appear to acknowledge this as a problem for their view. In Penn and Povinelli (2007), for example, the researchers admit that mental state concepts on the reinterpretation hypothesis bear little "resemblance to the mental state concepts putatively posited by our commonsense folk psychology" (p. 732). Yet despite this admission, the researchers go on to assert that mental state attribution in animals "boils down to" whether animals treat other agents as if their behaviors were caused by nonobservable internal states that are defined by their abstract causal roles (p. 733). One wonders why, if the reinterpretation hypothesis fails to capture what *we* mean by our mental state concepts, it should be thought to do any better at capturing what *animals* mean by theirs.

A much more plausible approach to understanding what mental state attribution (in particular, simple cognitive state attribution) in animals is is to start with what we know animals are capable of—namely, using the line of gaze of others to predict and make sense of their behaviors—and incrementally adding to this capacity, in an evolutionary and psychologically plausible fashion, elements that would enable animals to come to attribute something approximately close to states of consciousness and/or intentionality—the traditional marks of the mental. This is the approach that I shall pursue in section 3.3 below. As we shall see, the resulting theory does not require animals to understand anything about hidden inner causes or superordinate causal classes.

3.2 A General Framework for Solving the Logical Problem

If the argument above is sound, then the best-developed case against animal mindreading of any kind is unconvincing. And if the argument in the preceding chapter is also sound, the best attempts to date to demonstrate that animals are capable of attributing simple cognitive states are equally unconvincing. Thus, the question of cognitive state attribution in animals, it would appear, is empirically wide open. What is needed to answer it is a solution to the logical problem. And to this we now turn.

As we noted in the previous chapter, the main reason why Povinelli's challenge has been described as a logical problem is that some researchers have thought that it is, in principle, empirically unsolvable given the logic behind current experimental protocols. Although it is rarely stated explicitly, the general argument for its insolubility can be expressed in the following steps.

Step 1 Consider a mindreading hypothesis (MRH) for an animal A. According to this MRH, A anticipates that another agent B will perform behavior *r* on the grounds that B is in some mental state *m*, and that B's being in *m* is likely to lead him to do *r*.

Step 2 Since mental state concepts applied to others are based on observable facts or cues about the other agent's behavior or environment, A must apply the mental state concept *m* to B on the grounds of some such fact or cue, *s*, about B's behavior or environment.

Step 3   Now generate the complementary behavior-reading hypothesis (CBRH) by replacing A's mental state attributions of *m* to B with A's observable grounds for this attribution—that is, A's judgment that *s* obtains. According to this CBRH, A anticipates that B will do *r* on the grounds that *s* obtains.

Step 4   If it is plausible to suppose that prior to its anticipation of B's behavior, A has experienced *s*-type conditions followed by *r*-type behaviors in other animals or in itself,[4] then it is plausible (perhaps, even more so) to suppose (as the CBRH does) that A anticipates B doing *r* on the grounds that *s* obtains, as opposed to supposing (as the MRH does) that A anticipates B's behavior on the grounds that *s* is evidence of (or is followed by) B being in mental state *m*.

Step 5   No experimental protocol is able to eliminate the plausible supposition stated in step 4.

Conclusion   No experimental protocol can distinguish an MRH from its CBRH.

The conclusion follows, of course, only if step 5 is true. And although it was argued in the preceding chapter that no current experimental protocol to date has eliminated the supposition made in step 5, at least for cognitive state attributions, it does not follow that no experimental protocol can. In fact, we can see, in very general terms, what an experimental protocol would have to do in order to eliminate such a supposition. What is needed is an experimental protocol in which the animal, A, is tested on whether it will anticipate the agent, B, doing *r* on the basis of some observable fact *s* such that from the setup of the experiment it is plausible to suppose (on the assumption that A is a mindreader that possesses the mental state concept *m*) that

(i) A has reason to believe that the observable fact *s* is evidence of mental state *m* in B;

(ii) A has reason to believe that mental state *m* in B will lead to B doing *r*; but

(iii) prior to his anticipation of B's behavior, A has no independent reason to believe—independent, that is, from what can be inferred from (i) and (ii) alone—that *s*-type conditions will lead to *r*-type behavior in other animals or in himself (e.g., A has never observed *s*-type conditions followed by *r*-type behaviors in itself or others, nor is *r*-type behavior a stereotypical type of behavior in A's species that is triggered by *s*-type conditions).

In such an experimental situation, a complementary behavior reader is unlikely to have the right sorts of belief to make the prediction that B will do *r* when *s* obtains since it has no reason to believe that *s* is likely to lead to B doing *r*. A mindreader, on the other hand, has the potential to acquire the right sort of belief, for it need only combine its beliefs identified in (i) and (ii) to arrive at the belief that B is likely to do *r* when *s* obtains.

Recall that Povinelli and colleagues (Povinelli & Vonk 2006; Penn & Povinelli 2007) have challenged those in support of the possibility of mind-reading in animals to specify the "unique causal work" that mindreading might provide animals over and above complementary behavior reading. Their belief, based upon their reinterpretation hypothesis, is that no such specification will be readily forthcoming since on the reinterpretation hypothesis, mindreading does not aim to afford a subject a better way of predicting other agents' behaviors, just a different way of interpreting them (i.e., in terms of hidden inner causes and/or superordinate causal classes). The above experimental framework, however, provides a formal answer to Povinelli and colleagues' challenge. If conditions (i)–(iii) obtain, then the mindreading animal has the capacity to predict behaviors in agents that its complementary behavior-reading counterpart cannot. That, in a word, is the unique advantage that mindreading provides over complementary behavior reading.

The behaviors in question, it is important to note, are not novel in the sense that the attributing animal has never before observed them. They are novel in the sense that the attributing animal has never observed their occurrence having been preceded by a type of observable (objective) fact or cue *s* that it supposedly uses to attribute the mental state *m* that is being tested. More precisely, call a type of behavior *r* 'strongly novel' relative to some observable (objective) fact or cue *s* used to attribute mental state *m* for attributing animal A just in case A has no independent reason—again, independent from what can be inferred from the types of beliefs described in (i) and (ii) above—to believe that *s*-type conditions will lead to *r*-type behavior. What the above experimental framework identifies, at least in the abstract, are the types of conditions in which a mindreading subject would be in the position to predict others' behaviors that are strongly novel (relative to observable fact or cue *s*) on the basis of *s* but in which a complementary behavior reader would not.

In 1998, Cecilia Heyes proposed one of the first experimental tests for cognitive state attribution in chimpanzees that was aimed to solve the logical problem by satisfying conditions (i)–(iii) above.[5] The experimental paradigm has subsequently come to be called the experience-projection (EP) paradigm. (In the previous chapter, we saw an attempt by Emery and Clayton 2001 to use an EP paradigm with scrub jays.) Although I believe that the EP paradigm can solve the logical problem for cognitive state attributions in animals, I do not believe that Heyes's version of it can. The reason, as will become clear below, is that Heyes uses the EP paradigm to test for attributions of simple seeing, whereas the logical problem can only be solved by using the paradigm, I shall argue, by testing for attributions of seeing-as (or attributions of states of perceptual appearing more generally).[6]

The general idea behind Heyes's EP protocol is to allow an animal, in this case a chimpanzee, the opportunity to learn something about its own mental state of seeing in relation to a novel stimulus and then to test whether the animal will use this knowledge about the mind to anticipate the behavior of another agent (e.g., an experimenter) when the agent is presented with the novel stimulus. Heyes describes her protocol in three stages. In the pretraining phase, the chimpanzee is trained to wear different kinds of goggles over its eyes. Red-trimmed goggles are equipped with an opaque lens that prevents the chimpanzee from seeing anything in its environment; blue-trimmed goggles are equipped with a clear transparent lens that allows the chimpanzee to see things in its environment. From a distance, the only discernible difference between the goggles is their distinct colored trim. In the training phase, the chimpanzee watches while one of four containers is baited by an experimenter behind a screen while a second experimenter (the knower) watches the baiting process and a third experimenter (the guesser) does not (e.g., he may have his back turned or be out of the room). The knower and the guesser (upon his return) then point to different containers. The chimpanzee is rewarded for choosing the container indicated by the knower. The test trials are just like the training trials except that the knower, while watching the baiting process, wears the blue-trimmed (transparent) goggles and the guesser, who is present and whose head is directed toward the baiting process just like the knower's, wears the red-trimmed (opaque) goggles.

Heyes reasoned that "if chimpanzees have the concept 'see,' then on [test] trials one would expect them to choose the [container indicated by the] knower, wearing transparent goggles, more often than the [container indicated by the] guesser, wearing opaque goggles" (1998, p. 113). Thus, the mindreading chimpanzee is expected to learn through reasoning about its own capacity to see items in the environment while wearing the different goggles that

(a) red-trimmed goggles prevent one from *seeing* objects/events in the environment, while blue-trimmed goggles do not.

And from its experiences in the training phase, the mindreading chimpanzee is also expected to have learned that

(b) food is under the container indicated by the trainer that *saw* the baiting process.

And finally from his knowledge of (a) and (b), the mindreading chimpanzee in the test trials is expected to predict that

(c) food will be under the container indicated by the trainer with the blue-trimmed goggles who *saw* the baiting process.

The idea behind the protocol, and its aim to satisfy conditions (i)–(iii) above, are as follows. The chimpanzee, from its experiences of wearing the goggles in the pretraining phase, is provided with a reason to believe that wearing blue-trimmed goggles (*s*) allows seeing (*m*) objects/events in the environment, which satisfies condition (i). From its observation of the knower's behavior in the training phase, the chimpanzee is provided with a reason to believe that the experimenter that saw (*m*) the baiting process is the one that indicates the baited container (*r*), which satisfies condition (ii). However, due to the novelty of the goggles (chimpanzees typically do not wear such goggles), the chimpanzee is apparently stripped of having any independent reason—save what it can infer from its beliefs expressed in (a) and (b) above—to think that the experimenter who wears the blue-trimmed goggles (*s*) is the one who will indicate the baited container (*r*). Thus, it would appear, a complementary behavior-reading chimpanzee, having *no* reason to think that the environmental cue *s* (wearing blue-trimmed goggles) will lead to behavior *r* (indicating baited container), is not in a position to infer that the baited container is the one indicated by the blue-trimmed goggle wearing experimenter. However, a chimpanzee that understands the mental state concept seeing would be in such a position, for it need only conjoin its beliefs expressed by (a) and (b) to infer (c) above. Hence, the experimental protocol appears to be capable of distinguishing a perceptual state attributing animal from its complementary behavior-reading counterpart.

Unfortunately, this is not the case. This should be somewhat apparent, I should think, given that the protocol (though not competitive) is nearly identical to Hare et al.'s (2000) experiment save that the opaque/transparent barriers in this case are worn by the other agents (the experimenters) rather than (as in the Hare and colleagues' study) placed out in the middle area. What is not considered is the fact that in Heyes's protocol, the complementary behavior-reading chimpanzee could learn about its own capacity to have a *direct line of gaze* to objects/events in the environment while wearing the different colored goggles. It could learn, for example, that

(a') red-trimmed goggles prevent one from having a direct line of gaze to objects/events in the environment, while blue-trimmed goggles do not.

And from his experiences in the training phase, the complementary behavior-reading chimpanzee could have learned that

(b') food is located under the container indicated by the trainer who had a direct line of gaze to the baiting process.

And from its knowledge of (a') and (b'), the chimpanzee could predict in the test trial that

(c') food will be located under the container indicated by the trainer wearing blue-trimmed goggles who had a direct line of gaze to the baiting process.

Hence, Heyes's EP test for perceptual state attribution seems to fare no better than Hare et al.'s (2000) at discriminating between genuine mindreading animals and their complementary behavior-reading counterparts.[7]

In response to an earlier criticism along these lines (see Lurz 2001), Heyes (2001) responded by challenging the assumption that in the pretraining phase of the experiment, the chimpanzee could learn in its own case that red-trimmed goggles, but not blue-trimmed goggles, prevent direct line of gaze to objects in the environment. Her reasoning for saying this was as follows:

When I, or a chimpanzee, put on the [blue-trimmed], translucent goggles, I see what is before me; I do not, as if from a combination of first and third person perspectives, see myself wearing the [blue-trimmed] goggles, the object before my eyes, and myself seeing that object. (p. 1144)

However, given what we said in chapter 2, Heyes's objection here can be seen to miss its mark. As shown there, to know (or to be justified in believing) that one has a direct line of gaze to an object or event does not rest upon seeing oneself seeing the object or event (whatever that might involve), and neither does it rest upon any introspective judgments about oneself seeing the object or event; rather, it rests upon the content of one's own visual experience and working memory of the environment. What one sees when one sees an object is (in part) that the object bears a certain spatial relation to oneself—namely, a direct, unobstructed line. Heyes seems to assume that in seeing "what is before me," one does not see the object as being in a particular direction and at a particular distance from oneself. But, again, visual experiences do not simply represent intrinsic features of objects but certain relational features, such as direct line of gaze, as well.

Thus, when the chimpanzee dons the blue-trimmed goggles, it has visual experiences of objects in the environment as being directly before it (or its eyes). While wearing the red-trimmed goggles, it does not have visual experiences of objects in the environment but visual experiences of the back of the opaque lens of the goggles. What it sees (in part) is the opaque lens being directly before it (or its eyes). However, based on its working memory of the objects in the environment, the chimpanzee has reason to believe the objects are where they were before it donned the red-trimmed goggles and, hence, reason to believe that it now no longer has a direct line of gaze to these objects that are still before it (or its eyes).

Moreover, as we saw in chapter 2 in our discussion of Call and Carpenter's (2001) metacognition study, an animal's putative introspective judgments about its capacity to *see* objects are confounded with its perceptual judgments about its having a *direct line of gaze* to these objects. Thus, in Heyes's protocol, the complementary behavior-reading chimpanzee would have access to the same direct line of gaze information that a perceptual state attributing chimpanzee has, and vice versa. And this is precisely what Heyes sought to avoid in her experimental protocol and what prevents it from solving the logical problem. Although the behavior (r) of indicating the baited container by the knower was strongly novel relative to the environment condition (s) of his wearing blue-trimmed goggles during the baiting process, it was not strongly novel relative to (s') his having a direct line of gaze to the baiting process, which is the observable grounds that the mindreading chimpanzee supposedly must use to attribute the mental state (m) of seeing to the knower in the test trials. Thus, the complementary behavior-reading chimpanzee could just as well use s' (direct line of gaze) to deduce behavior r (indicating baited container) as the mindreading chimpanzee is thought to use s' to infer the mental state (m) of seeing in the experimenter to deduce behavior r. And that is just another instance of the logical problem.

What is needed, as I hope is becoming clear, is an experimental protocol in which the predicted behavior r of the other agent is strongly novel relative to the environmental cue s that the mindreading animal is hypothesized to use to attribute the mental state m that is being tested. As noted, I do not think that this can be done for the mental state of simple seeing and its observable basis for ascription, direct line of gaze, but it can be done for simple seeing's more sophisticated cousin, the concept seeing-as (or perceptual appearing more generally), as I shall argue below. Of course, if animals are capable of attributing seeing-as, then they are, perforce, capable of attributing simple seeing.

3.3   The Appearance–Reality Mindreading (ARM) Theory

In this section, I make a case for a plausible 'just-so' evolutionary story about the likely adaptive advantages that perceptual appearing (particularly, seeing-as) attributions might have provided animals. The story will serve as a theoretical foundation for the experimental protocols described in later sections that I argue can solve the logical problem. For reasons that will become clear shortly, I call this evolutionary story the *appearance-reality mindreading* (ARM) theory.

To begin, let us suppose that some animals have evolved the ability to attribute states of perceptual appearing—specifically, states of seeing-as—to other agnets. Why should they have evolved such a skill? What adaptive advantage would such attributions bring them? Of course, simply knowing that other agents see objects or states of affairs in the environment *as* being certain ways, or that these objects or states of affairs visually *appear* to these agents in certain ways, would be of little value to animals unless they could use this knowledge to increase their own chances of survival and reproduction. One thing that perceptual appearing attributions would allow an animal to do, of course, is to predict other agents' behavior, and this would undoubtedly increase the animal's chances of survival and reproduction in those cases where the other agents involved were conspecifics, predators, or prey. Thus, it is unsurprising that the most widely accepted view of the evolution of mindreading in the animal kingdom, the *Machiavellian intelligence hypothesis*, takes the adaptive value of mindreading in animals to be its enhancement of the predictability of other agents' (specifically, conspecifics') behavior.[8] Thus, on this hypothesis, the capacity to attribute states of perceptual appearing to other agents evolved in the animal kingdom (insofar as it did) for the express purpose of enabling animals to predict the behavior of other agents in environmental settings where the animal's competing behavior-reading counterparts (such as other conspecifics) could not.[9]

The ARM theory and the Machiavellian intelligence hypothesis are in agreement on this point. What is not so clear on the Machiavellian intelligence hypothesis, however, and what the ARM theory aims to clarify, are the kinds of environmental settings that would give animals capable of attributing states of perceptual appearing to other agents this advantage in predicting the behavior of these agents. In what sorts of environmental settings would such a mindreading animal be expected to be better at predicting an agent's behavior than a similarly placed complementary behavior reader? The answer, I submit, is illusory environmental settings.

The natural environments in which most animals evolved and currently live are far from perceptually transparent—quite the contrary, in fact. On the whole, they tend to be rather ambiguous places. Objects often appear to have properties that they do not have. Camouflaged prey and food, for example, may appear absent or different from what they really are; competitors and suitors may behave in ways that make them look healthier, larger, or stronger than they really are; partially occluded objects and sounds may appear to have shapes or continuities that they in fact lack; distinctive colors of predators, prey, or conspecifics may look different from what they really are when viewed at dusk or dark, at a distance, or in the water, and so on. As a result of such persistent perceptual ambiguities, the visual and auditory systems of many animals have evolved strategies for resolving some of them in ways that typically lead to accurate perception and adaptive behavior—yet as good as these strategies are, they are far from perfect. Animals are frequently subject to perceptual illusions, seeing and hearing things in ways that are different from what they really are. And what is more, they are often fooled by these illusions: A naive animal, ignorant of being in an illusory setting, will act on the way things perceptually appear to it rather than on the way things really are. This is an immutable truth regarding the mind and actions of naive subjects in illusory settings. Understanding this psychological fact would clearly enhance an animal's ability to predict (and perhaps even manipulate) the behavior of naive agents in such illusory settings.

Understanding that a dominant conspecific, for example, does not see the camouflaged insect before it as an edible insect but *as a leaf* would enable a subordinate mindreading conspecific to predict that the dominant conspecific in this setting will not try to eat the insect—perhaps providing the subordinate the opportunity at some later time to consume the insect for itself without fear of reprisal. Were a complementary behavior-reading subordinate placed in the very same situation as this mindreading one, it would be capable of understanding only that the dominant conspecific is looking directly at an edible insect. Knowing this, however, would be of no help to the animal in predicting that the dominant conspecific will *not* try to eat the insect. If anything, it is more likely that the animal would wrongly predict that the dominant conspecific *will* try to eat the insect since quite probably that is how dominant conspecifics typically behave when they are looking directly at such edible insects.

This and similar examples can be used to illustrate the general point that animals capable of attributing states of perceptual appearing to other agents have a distinct advantage over their complementary behavior-reading counterparts in predicting the actions of naive agents in illusory environmental settings. The reason for this is not difficult to see, I believe. In illusory environmental settings, the observable, objective facts—which are all that the behavior-reading animal has to go on—are not the facts on which the naive agent, benighted to the illusion, will act. The agent will act on the subjective facts—on the way things perceptually appear to it—in the situation, for those are the facts that stand before its mind (as it were) and which, being naive to the illusory nature of the setting, it has no reason to doubt. And these are precisely the sorts of subjective facts that an animal capable of attributing states of perceptual appearing can appreciate. Thus, if perceptual appearing attribution evolved in the animal kingdom, it quite plausibly did so for the express purpose of enabling animals to predict the actions of naive agents in illusory settings better than their similarly placed behavior-reading counterparts could.

This would not be the case, however, if the only way that an animal capable of attributing states of perceptual appearing could come to predict the behavior of an agent in such settings was by first observing such behaviors in such agents or in itself in response to the objective features presented in the setting—for under such conditions, a similarly situated behavior-reading animal, having observed the same pattern of behaviors in response to the same type of objective features, would be just as well placed to predict the agent's behavior by appealing to these past contingencies. For example, if the only way for the subordinate mindreading animal (in the case above) to predict the dominant's noneating behavior by understanding that the dominant doesn't see the insect as such but as a leaf was by first observing similar noneating behaviors in other agents or in itself in the presence of such edible insects (or food) on similarly colored/patterned backgrounds, then a behavior-reading animal, who has also observed these past behavior patterns, could simply appeal to them to predict that the dominant in this case will likely not try to eat the insect. Thus, in order for animals capable of attributing states of perceptual appearing to have an advantage over their similarly situated behavior-reading counterparts in predicting the behaviors of naive agents in illusory settings, they must have the ability to detect the illusory effect in the setting and use it to predict the other agent's behavior *without* having to first observe a correlation between the objective facts in the setting that produce the illusory effect and the type of behavior that is predicted in the agent.

The only way for an animal to do this, as far as I can see, is if it possessed the ability to introspect its own perceptual states. With introspection, the animal would be able to represent its own perceptual states directly, without having to rely upon known or believed external environmental facts—specifically, facts regarding its own behavior or that of others' past behaviors.[10] With introspection, for example, the animal could know that an object or state of affairs before it perceptually appears a certain way (as F) even if the animal were unsure whether the object/state of affairs really is an F, or even how it or others have behaved in the past when objects/states of affairs were F. Just as important as enabling an animal to represent its own perceptual states directly in this way, introspection would also provide the animal with the capacity to distinguish perceptual appearances from reality. It would give the animal the capacity to know simultaneously that things perceptually appear a certain way to it but are not really that way at all. And this, in fact, is quite plausibly the reason that the introspection of perceptual states evolved in the animal kingdom (assuming it did) in the first place (see McGinn 1989).[11]

In providing the means to distinguish appearances from reality, introspection gives animals a powerful new tool for adaptively responding to illusory environmental situations. Nature, after all, designed perception to be the main driving cognitive force in the minds of animals, immediately fixing their world-directed beliefs and actions. Consequently, where there is a conflict between what an animal perceives and what it has reason to think is really the case, as is the case in perceptual illusions, perception is designed to win out by default. (In this respect, animals are naturally disposed empiricists.) Thus, without the ability to introspect their own perceptual states, the only way for animals to respond adaptively to an illusory situation—the only way for them to overcome their natural tendency to take their percepts at face value—is through something like a process of psychological extinction. Through the process of extinction, an animal's illusory percept eventually loses its force to fix its world-directed beliefs and action in the illusory setting after repeated failure to produce a desirable or anticipated outcome for the animal in the setting. However, this process of adaptive behavior by extinction takes time. The singular advantage of introspection is that an animal, by virtue of being aware of its own perceptual states, is put in the position of being able to refrain from believing or acting on them and can do so from its very first encounter with an illusory situation. An animal that sees an insect land on a similarly colored/ patterned background may have good reason to think that the object before it is an insect despite its looking like a leaf. Without introspection, the animal would be naturally disposed to take its percept at face value and believe and act as if the object before it were a leaf. With introspection, it is in a position to put its percept in neutral, as it were, and to believe and act on what it has good reasons to—namely, that the object is an insect.

Thus, with these two features of introspection—its role in enabling an animal to make an appearance–reality distinction and its power to represent perceptual states directly—an animal can come to know that an object/state of affairs before it appears one way (as F) but is really another (is G), and it can know this even if this is its first encounter with an object/ state of affairs being G, and (thus) even if it has no knowledge of how it or others might have behaved in the past toward objects/states of affairs that were G.[12] Upon seeing an insect land on similarly colored/patterned foliage for the first time (to recycle the example from above), an animal with the power to introspect its own perceptual states would be able to know that the object before it looks to be a leaf but is in fact an edible insect. What is more, it can know both of these things quite independently of knowing how it or others might have behaved in the past toward insects (or food) placed on similarly colored/patterned backgrounds. In fact, it is quite possible that given the surprising effect of the camouflaged insect, the animal might even try to reach out and grasp the insect as a way of verifying that it was still there. Either way, the important point is that the animal would have no grounds in this case—independent of what it could infer from its own mind—for thinking that a dominant conspecific who has just come upon the scene and is currently looking in the direction of the insect will not try to eat it. The animal may have observed this or other dominant conspecifics in the past, or even itself, gazing at such edible insects (or food) on contrasting backgrounds, but on those occasions, most plausibly, the dominant conspecific, or the animal itself, ate the insects (food). Observation of such past behavior patterns, therefore, would not enable the subordinate in this case, where the insect is on a similarly colored/patterned background, to predict that the dominant conspecific will not try to eat it. But, of course, that is precisely how the dominant conspecific in this case is likely to behave, being naive to the illusion. And it is exactly what an animal capable of attributing states of perceptual appearing with introspective abilities would be capable of understanding and predicting.

This is not so for an analogously placed behavior reader—a behavior reader that, like the mindreading animal above, has never until this moment observed an insect (food) placed on a similarly colored/patterned background. The behavior reader in this case would be able to comprehend only that the dominant conspecific has just come on the scene and is now looking in the direction of the edible insect which is on a similarly colored/pattern background. These are the objective facts on the ground, as it were. With this understanding of the objective facts, the behavior reader would either not know what the dominant conspecific will do or (perhaps more likely) predict that it will try to eat the insect (since, not implausibly, that is what dominant conspecifics typically do with such insects or food on contrasting backgrounds). The only way that the behavior reader in this situation could correctly predict that the dominant conspecific will not eat the insect is if it had observed such noneating behavior in others or itself when in the direct presences of edible insects (or food) on similarly colored/pattern backgrounds. The beauty of the mindreading animal with introspective abilities is that it does not have to wait to observe such past patterns of behavior in order to correctly predict the dominant conspecific's behavior in such a setting. It can use what it knows about its own mind, the way things appear to it, in such settings as a way of understanding the mind and future behavior of the other agent.

This, then, completes my sketch of a prima facie plausible account of the adaptive value of perceptual appearing attribution in the animal kingdom (on the assumption that it exists). Although I have illustrated the account with a case of attributing seeing-as, similar reasoning can be given for attributions of hearing-as, as well. To recap, the ARM theory maintains that

1. Perceptual appearing attribution evolved in animals (insofar as it did) for the purpose of predicting other agents' behaviors in those environmental situations in which their behavior-reading counterparts could not,

2. these environmental situations are illusory perceptual settings, and

3. 1 and 2 are possible only if such mindreading animals have the capacity to introspect their own perceptual states and use their introspective ability to distinguish appearance from reality.

3.4 How Animals Might Attribute States of Perceptual Appearing

Thus far, I have said little about the nature of the cognitive processes that might underlie a mindreading animal's predictions of another agent's behavior in an illusory setting. By what cognitive steps, for example, is the animal thought to move from its knowledge of how things perceptually appear to it to its attribution that that is how things perceptually appear to another agent and, from here, to its prediction of the agent's behavior? And, more fundamentally, how might the animal come to have its mental state concept of perceptual appearing in the first place? It is disappointing to hear, I am sure, that the short answer to these questions is that we simply do not know at present. The ARM account sketched above is consistent with a range of possible answers to these questions, but unfortunately there are simply not enough empirical data at the moment to say in any meaningful way which answers to these questions are more or less probable. However, despite our failing to have any concrete answers at the moment to these important questions, it will be helpful in understanding the experimental designs described in the following sections if we can provide an (at least) prima facie plausible answer to them.

Let us, then, start with the question of concept acquisition—undoubtedly the more difficult. How might an animal come to possess concepts of perceptual appearing, such as *seems* or *appears*, which it can apply to itself in introspection and others in mindreading? An intuitively plausible answer, I believe, is that the concept is acquired as a result of the animal's coming to affix a qualifier to the subject–object spatial relations represented *in* its perceptual beliefs. As we noted in the preceding chapter, perception does not merely represent intrinsic properties of distal objects and states of affairs. It also represents the objects' or states of affairs' spatial relation to the subject. In seeing a tree, for example, one sees the tree as being in a certain direction and at a certain distance from the front part of one's face or eyes. In hearing a sound, one hears it as happening in a certain direction and at a certain distance from one's ears or head. In cases of perceptual illusion, however, one's perceptual system continues to represent that one bears these spatial relations to distal objects and events even though these relations, the objects, and events do not exist (or do not exist as represented). In the case of the mindreading animal that sees the insect before it as a leaf, for example, its visual system represents it as having a direct line of gaze to a leaf—that is how things visually appear to it. Now, if the animal also knows that there is no leaf before it but an insect (e.g., as a result of its having just seen the insect land on the similarly colored/patterned background), then it has a reason not to believe what its visual system is telling it. However, perception, as noted above, is a very strong force in the animal mind. It is designed to fix quickly and immediately the animal's world-directed beliefs and actions. Thus, the animal's mind, in such an instance, is in a state of tension. Its visual percept is bent on making it believe one thing, and its reason is bent on making it believe (or not believe) another—so what is this animal to do?

One way that nature could have designed the minds of animals to resolve this tension is simply to allow perception in such cases to win by default, thus overriding the animal's reason. There is, though, a more adaptive and flexible (not to mention more judicious) way to resolve the tension—one that allows the animal's perceptual system to continue to fix a belief, as it is naturally disposed to do, but not the belief that the animal bears a spatial relation to an object that it knows is not there. This could be done rather easily if nature equipped the animal with the capacity to affix something like a qualifier to the subject–object spatial relation depicted in its perceptual belief, a qualifier that functions much in the way that 'seems' and 'appears' do in English. Thus, for example, instead of the animal's perceptual system causing the animal to believe 'I have a direct line of gaze to a leaf,' it causes it to believe 'I seem (or appear) to have a direct line of gaze to a leaf.' This qualified relational belief, by virtue of its distinct content, would be prohibited from functioning as its unqualified counterpart in determining the animal's world-directed actions. In particular, the qualified belief would not dispose the animal to act as if there were a leaf directly before it—any more so than the qualified sentence 'I appear to be standing before an oasis' typically disposes one to conclude that one must be standing before an oasis. In this way, perception is allowed to discharge its natural function of fixing a belief but without fixing a belief that the animal has reason not to accept. Having discharged its function, the animal's perceptual system can relax, as it were, allowing the animal time to decide whether, in the end, it should also believe (without qualification) what its perceptual system is telling it. In such a case, perception and reason are partially appeased. The animal's percept fixes a belief that is semantically and structurally similar to one that it would have naturally fixed (had the animal not known that there was no leaf before it), and the animal is not forced to believe something it has reasons not to.

As for the question of how probable it is that animals might have the ability to affix a qualifier to the spatial relations represented in their perceptual beliefs, it is relevant to note that nature appears to have designed many animals with the ability to affix other types of qualifiers—for example, temporal (*now*, *earlier*, and *future*), spatial (*here*, *there*, *near*, and *far*), quantitative (*more* and *less*), exclusory (*not*, *absent*, or *lack of*), and probable (*likely* and *unlikely*) qualifiers—to the relations and properties represented in their beliefs about states of affairs in the world.[13] And so I

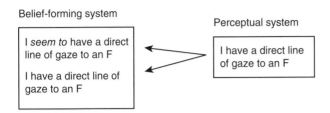

Figure 3.1
Nonillusory setting in which the animal has no reason to doubt that it has a direct line of gaze to an F.

see no serious problem with speculating that nature might have also equipped some animals with the ability to affix a qualifier to the subject–object relations represented in their perceptual beliefs that function much in the way that the qualifiers 'seems' and 'appears' do in English.

It is likely, furthermore, that once nature rigged up an animal's mind to affix such a qualifier to the subject–object spatial relation depicted in its perceptual beliefs when the animal knows (or has reason to believe) that there is no distal object or event as depicted in its percept, the mechanism would quickly generalize to those cases when the animal knows (or has no reason to doubt) that there is such a distal object or event. It would be far less costly in terms of cognitive processing if the animal's belief-forming system always attached such a qualifier to its perceptual inputs than if it did so only when the animal knew (had reason to believe) that it was under an illusion and that there was no such distal object or event in its direct line of gaze. In nonillusory settings, then, the animal's perceptual system would immediately fix two kinds of beliefs: an unqualified belief that matches the content of the inputted percept and a qualified belief that affixes 'seems' or 'appears' to the relational component of the content of the percept (see figure 3.1).

In contrast, when the animal is in illusory settings in which it has reasons to doubt what its perceptual system is telling it, the animal's perceptual system would be allowed to fix only a qualified belief (initially), allowing the animal's reasoning systems time to determine whether it should also fix an unqualified perceptual belief, as well (see figure 3.2).

Once this general mechanism is in place, the animal would be capable of understanding how the world appears to it in any environmental setting—illusory or otherwise.

It is important to note that this model of introspection is not a version of an inner-sense model of introspection, which I take to be a good thing,

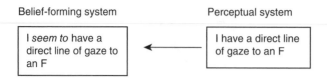

Figure 3.2
Illusory setting in which the animal has reason to doubt that it has a direct line of gaze to an F.

since there are a number of well-known, and apparently intractable, problems with inner-sense models of introspection (see Shoemaker 1996). On inner-sense models, introspection is understood to be a type of inner scanning of a subject's internal states, where the states are classified into mental categories by virtue of their detected (scanned) intrinsic, qualitative properties or (on some inner-scanning models) their detected functional properties (see Lycan 1996; Goldman 1993). The growing consensus in philosophy is that there really are no intrinsic qualitative properties (qualia) of mental states (Tye 1995), and that introspection does not classify an agent's current mental states into types by virtue of their detected functional properties (Goldman 1993). Thankfully, the above model of introspection avoids these problems by being a version of the displaced-perception model of introspection (Dretske 1997). On the displaced-perception model, an agent's introspective awareness of the type of mental state that he or she is in is fixed not by the agent's awareness of any intrinsic or functional properties of the state itself but by virtue of a reliable process involving only the representational content of the state. Thus, on the version of the model outlined above, an animal's introspective awareness of its own state of perception is understood as resulting from a reliable process that takes the content of the animal's percept (e.g., *I have a direct line of gaze to an F*) as input and yields an introspective belief regarding how things perceptually appear to the animal (e.g., *I appear to have a direct line of gaze to an F*) as an output. No inner awareness of the perceptual state's intrinsic or functional properties is involved, just a reliable process from the percept's representational content to the introspective belief about how things perceptually appear to the animal.

What is more, the process of displaced perception, unlike that of inner scanning, is likely to be a process that animals use in domains outside their own minds. A dog, for example, may be said to know (hear) that its master is home by hearing the sound of the key in the front door. In such a case, the dog has a displaced perception that its master is home by virtue of being directly aware of something else, the sound of the key in the door. The process is thus similar to that of an animal's coming to be introspectively aware that it appears to bear a direct line of gaze to an F, for example, by virtue of its being directly aware of something else— namely, its having a direct line of gaze to an F (which is not an internal mental state of the animal but a relation that the animal's percept depicts the animal as bearing to an external object). In this way, the above displaced-perception model of introspection is not forced to credit animals with having a unique cognitive ability, such as that of scanning their own internal states, that they are unlikely to possess in advance of being able to introspect their own mental states. If evolution is the tinkerer it is known to be (Jacob 1977), then it is more likely that it would use an already existing cognitive ability in animals, such as displaced perception used in the external domain, to endow them with the ability to introspect their own perceptual states than to invest them with a radically new cognitive ability. For this reason, I believe, displaced-perception models of animal introspection are, all things being equal, preferable to inner-sense models.

After coming to assess how the world perceptually appears to them, the next stage in evolutionary development would be animals coming to make the same type of assessment of *others*. On the face of it, the cognitive process most likely to allow this to occur would be some type of analogical- or similarity-based process. The process itself need not be any more sophisticated than the disposition to classify a novel object as belonging to a certain class as a result of a perceived similarity known to be possessed by an exemplar of the class. Taking a particular lion as an exemplar of a predator, for example, an animal will be naturally disposed to classify other animals it encounters as predators the closer they resemble this lion. Analogical-like processes of this sort are nothing more than inductive generalizations from a single case (compared to enumerative generalizations from many cases) and seem to be rather common within the animal kingdom. Numerous studies with birds and monkeys, for example, strongly indicate that these animals readily classify novel stimuli as belonging to a given class as a result of how similar they are to what the animals take to be an exemplar or prototypical member of this class (Astley & Wasserman 1992; Aydin & Pearce 1994; Jitsumori 1996; Vogels 1999; Werner & Rehkämper 2001; Smith et al. 2008). On the basis of these findings, it is surely not implausible to suppose that a mindreading animal might take itself as an exemplar of minded subjects and classify others as like-minded by means of the very same exemplar-based categorization process that animals appear to use generally. We can call such a view the self-exemplar model of mental state attribution.[14]

On such a model, for example, we can make sense of how an animal which introspectively knows that, to it, it appears to have a direct line of gaze to an F (e.g., a leaf) while gazing at what it knows to be a G (e.g., an insect) would be inclined to classify a conspecific that it observes having a direct line of gaze to the same (or a similar) G as an animal that, to it, appears to have a direct line of gaze to an F. From the animal's perspective, the process might look something like the following:

1. *Perception/belief*: I have a direct line of gaze to a G.
2. *Introspection*: I appear to have a direct line of gaze to an F.[15]
3. *Exemplar formation process*: By conjoining the representations in 1 and 2, the animal forms a self-representation, R, of itself as having a direct line of gaze to a G and as itself appearing to have a direct line of gaze to an F. R is used as the animal's exemplar of an animal that, to it, appears to have a direct line of gaze to an F.
4. *Perception/belief*: The conspecific over there has a direct line of gaze to a (or the very same) G.
5. *Classification process*: Since the animal's representation of the conspecific in 4 and its self-exemplar R both depict the subjects involved as having a direct line of gaze to a (or the very same) G, the animal classifies the conspecific as being an animal that, to it, appears to bear a direct line of gaze to an F.

I am assuming here that subject–object spatial relations depicted in perceptual beliefs, such as the relation of having a direct line of gaze to an object, are an important point of similarity in the self-exemplar model of mental state attribution. There may be others, of course. The points of similarity used by the mindreading animal to classify others as like-minded subjects, as well as how these points of similarity are weighed against each other, is an open empirical question. Nevertheless, the mindreading animal can certainly tell in its own case that some of these features are relevant. It can determine in its own case, for example, that when it alters its own line of gaze to objects in its environment (e.g., turning its head away from the camouflaged insect), it alters the line of gaze that it appears to bear to things (e.g., it no longer appears to bear a direct line of gaze to a leaf). Thus, it can come to view having a direct line of gaze to an object as an important point of similarity in classifying another animal as being like-minded.

Once the mindreading animal is capable of understanding how the world appears to others in various environmental settings—illusory or not—it can begin to keep track of how others (as well as itself) behave in these types of settings in terms of how things appear. The animal can notice, for example, that conspecifics (as well as itself) tend to eat objects that, to them, look like food; that they tend to flee from objects that, to them, look like lions; that they tend to respond to noises of a certain volume that, to them, sound like the cries of their offspring; and so on.[16] These empirical generalizations, it is important to note, are about observed correlations between types of behaviors and types of subjective states of mind; they are not simply about observed correlations between types of behaviors and types of objective, observable environmental facts. A mind-reading animal can appeal to such generalizations as a way to correctly predict a naive agent's behavior in an illusory environmental setting. For in such settings, the way things appear to the naive agent is what will determine its behavior.[17]

This, then, completes my attempt to sketch a prima facie plausible account of the psychological processes involved in attributions of states of perceptual appearing by animals that is consistent with the ARM theory. It is important to note, in light of our discussion of the shortcomings with the reinterpretation hypothesis's account of mental state attribution in animals, that on the ARM theory, attributions of states of perceptual appearing by animals are attributions of relations—specifically, the relation of *appearing to have a direct line of gaze to*—holding between an agent and a possible object or event in the environment; they are not attributions of hidden inner causal states. The attributed relation, moreover, is an intentional relation since the possible object or event in the relation need not be thought by the attributing animal to be actual. Furthermore, it is a relation that the attributing animal can know holds in its own case via introspection. Thus, by the traditional marks of the mental—intentionality and introspectibility—attributions of perceptual appearing, on the ARM theory, count as clear cases of mental state attributions—yet, as noted, they do not require the attributing animal to understand anything about inner causes of overt behavior or to encode perceptually disparate patterns of behavior into superordinate causal classes, as required by the reinterpretation hypothesis. For this reason, the ARM theory's account of mental state attribution in animals is to be preferred to the reinterpretation hypothesis's account.

The question that is before us now is how to test the ARM theory empirically and do it in such a way as to overcome the logical problem. To this, we now turn.

3.5 Experimental Protocols That Can Solve the Logical Problem

The ARM theory and the experimental framework described in section 3.2 provide a recipe for designing experience-projection (EP) protocols that can overcome the logical problem. The recipe in general is this. First, allow an animal to learn that while in a particular illusory setting, s, objects appear to it to be one way (as F) but are in fact another (e.g., are G—where being G excludes being F). Second, make sure that neither the animal nor any other agent that it may have observed have ever engaged in r-like behaviors when confronted by objects that are G (or confronted by objects that are G in s-type settings) but have done so when confronted with objects that are (as well as appear to be) F. Third, test to see if the animal anticipates that an agent will engage in r-like behavior in the illusory setting s where the agent is confronted with an object that is G. A mind-reading animal, on the ARM theory, would be expected to make such a prediction by understanding how the object appears to the agent (it appears to it to be F) on the basis of the objective facts in the situation (that the agent has a direct line of gaze to a G-type object in environmental setting s). A complementary behavior-reading animal, on the other hand, would not be expected to make such a prediction since the objective facts it has access to—that the agent has a direct line of gaze to a G-type object in environmental setting s—do not provide it with any reason to expect such behavior. Three different kinds of experimental designs that follow this recipe are described below.

3.6 Visual Perspective Taking with Chimpanzees using Transparent Colored Barriers

Using Hare et al.'s (2000) experiment as a model, I describe here a visual perspective-taking experimental protocol that overcomes the logical problem. As in Hare et al.'s (2000) experiment, a subordinate and a dominant chimpanzee are housed in separate rooms that are on either side of a middle area where they compete for food. The chimpanzees' rooms are equipped with guillotine doors that can be raised enough to allow the animals to see the middle area and each other without allowing them to enter the room. The chimpanzees will compete for two types of food placed in the middle room. The first type is a highly desirable yellow banana; the second type is not even real food but a plastic banana that is colored orange (or dark orange). From a distance, the only discernible difference between the real and fake bananas is their respective colors.

In the preliminary phase of the experiment, the doors of the chimpanzees' rooms are opened fully, and while the dominant chimpanzee is in the center of his own room and the subordinate is in the center of his own room (or inside the dominant chimpanzee's room), a single piece of food (a yellow real banana or an orange [or dark orange] fake banana) is placed either inside the subordinate's room or inside the dominant's room. The chimpanzees are then allowed to compete for the food. In this stage of the experiment, it is plausible to suppose that the subordinate will learn that he can retrieve those yellow bananas that are visibly and physically inaccessible to the dominant chimpanzee (e.g., those that are placed inside his own room while he but not the dominant chimpanzee is there), and that the dominant chimpanzee will retrieve those yellow bananas that are visibly and physically accessible to him (e.g., those placed in the middle area or in its own room) but not the orange bananas that are similarly placed (after the dominant's discovering that they are fake.)

In the pretraining phase of the experiment, the subordinate is exposed to two different types of transparent barriers: a clear transparent barrier that does not change the apparent color of objects behind it and a red transparent barrier that causes yellow objects behind it to look orange and orange objects to look slightly darker orange. (Different colored transparent barriers can be used.) Through the placement of various yellow and orange objects behind the barriers, the subordinate is shown or allowed to discover (if a mindreader) that he can see (and, hence, has direct line of sight to) objects placed behind either type of barrier, but that he sees yellow and orange objects behind the red barrier as orange and dark orange, respectively, and yellow and orange objects behind the clear barrier as yellow and orange, respectively. Moreover, the subordinate is allowed (or trained if necessary) to retrieve the objects he sees placed behind the barriers. This can be achieved by making the objects interesting for the chimpanzee and encouraging him to retrieve them.[18]

After the training phase, the chimpanzees are returned to their respective rooms and run through the following test.[19]

Alternative barrier test   A red barrier and a clear barrier are placed in the center of the middle area about 2 meters apart. A yellow banana is placed on the subordinate's side of the red barrier and an orange banana is placed on the subordinate's side of the clear barrier (see figure 3.3). The doors are then raised enough to allow each chimpanzee to see the barriers, the food, and each other; the doors are then raised further to allow the chimpanzees to enter the room; the subordinate is given a slight head start.

Now for the relevant predictions. If the subordinate chimpanzee is a mind-reader, as represented by the ARM theory, then we would expect him to use his understanding of how the respective bananas look to the dominant chimpanzee as a way to predict the dominant chimpanzee's behavior in the critical tests. Thus, if the subordinate chimpanzee is such a mindreader, then one would expect that, from his experiences in the preliminary stage of the experiment, he would learn something like the following:

(a) If it appears to the dominant chimpanzee that he has a direct line of gaze to an orange banana in a particular location, then he will not attempt to retrieve the banana from that location. However, if it appears to the dominant chimpanzee that he has a direct line of gaze to a yellow banana in a particular location, then he will try to retrieve the banana from that location.

And from his experiences in the pretraining phase of the experiment, the mindreading subordinate is expected to learn something like the following:

(b) When I have a direct line of gaze to a yellow (or orange) object behind the red barrier, it appears to me as if I have a direct line of gaze to an orange (or dark orange) object behind the barrier.

Armed with this knowledge, the mindreading subordinate chimpanzee, on the ARM theory, is expected in the test situation to understand that the dominant chimpanzee, by virtue of his having a direct line of gaze to a yellow banana behind the red barrier, *sees* the banana *as* orange. Under-standing this subjective fact about the dominant chimpanzee, together with his knowledge of (a) above, the mindreading subordinate chimpanzee could then predict and choose in the critical tests as follows:

(c) The yellow banana behind the red barrier appears to the dominant chimpanzee *as* being orange, and so he will not attempt to retrieve it—so take the yellow banana! (See figure 3.3.)

Now let us consider this mindreading chimpanzee's complementary behavior-reading counterpart. To reach the complementary behavior-reading counterpart, we need to replace the mindreading chimpanzee's judgments of perceptual appearing in (a) with their objective, observa-tional grounds, which in this case are judgments about what the dominant had a direct line of gaze to. In the preliminary phase of the experiment, for example, it was on the objective, observable fact that the dominant had a direct line of gaze to an orange banana that the mindreading chim-

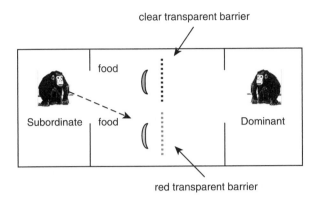

clear transparent barrier

food

food

Subordinate   food

Dominant

red transparent barrier

Figure 3.3
Expected performance of mindreading chimpanzee in the alternative barrier test.

panzee based his judgment that it appeared to the dominant that he had a direct line of gaze to an orange banana. Thus, from his experience in the preliminary phase of the experiment, the complementary behavior-reading chimpanzee would, at most, be capable of making certain judgments concerning the dominant's line of gaze, such as the following:

(a′) If the dominant chimpanzee has a direct line of gaze to an orange banana in a particular location, then he will not attempt to retrieve the banana from that location. However, if he has a direct line of gaze to a yellow banana in a particular location, then he will attempt to retrieve the banana from that location.

Since the complementary behavior-reading chimpanzee does not have the mental state concept of visual appearing, he cannot appreciate how yellow or orange objects behind the red barrier in the pretraining phase *visually appear* to him. Thus, the most that the complementary behavior-reading chimpanzee could learn from this phase of the experiment would be the following:

(b′) Neither the red nor the clear barriers block my line of gaze to objects behind them.

At most, knowing (b′) would enable the subordinate to understand in the test condition that the dominant chimpanzee has a direct line of gaze to the yellow banana behind the red barrier. However, from his knowledge of this, plus his knowledge of (a′) above, the complementary behavior-reading chimpanzee would be expected to predict and choose quite differently in the critical test from his mindreading counterpart. The

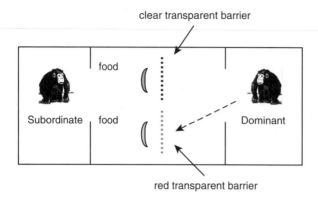

Figure 3.4
Expected performance of complementary behavior-reading chimpanzee in the alternative barrier test.

complementary behavior-reading chimpanzee would be expected to predict and choose as follows:

(c′) The dominant chimpanzee has a direct line of gaze to the yellow banana behind the red barrier and will, thus, attempt to retrieve it—so *don't* take the yellow banana! (See figure 3.4.)

The complementary behavior-reading hypothesis, therefore, predicts that the subordinate will behave quite differently in this test from what the mindreading hypothesis predicts. Thus, this experimental protocol has the capacity to distinguish a mindreading chimpanzee from its complementary behavior-reading counterpart.

What the protocol cannot do, of course, is distinguish the above mindreading chimpanzee from *all* conceivable behavior-reading counterparts. However, no experimental protocol can do that, and so this is not a mark against the present protocol as a solution to the logical problem. There are (minimal) behavior-reading hypotheses that may yield the same prediction of the subordinate's behavior in the critical tests as the above mindreading hypothesis, but what is important to note about these minimal behavior-reading hypotheses is that they are, by definition, not the above complementary behavior-reading hypothesis and, hence, do not constitute the logical problem for the above mindreading hypothesis. There is, moreover, no general argument to suppose that these alternative hypotheses cannot in principle be distinguished from the mindreading hypothesis by running further control tests or experiments (see Lurz 2009a for further support of this claim). As noted in the previous chapter, solving the logical problem does not require demonstrating how one can experimentally distinguish a mindreading hypothesis from *any* behavior-reading hypothesis—for no experimental approach can do that. It requires rather showing how to distinguish experimentally a mindreading hypothesis from its complementary behavior-reading hypothesis—and the above experimental protocol does just that.

3.7 Visual Perspective Taking with Chimpanzees using Size-Distorting Barriers

The visual perspective-taking protocol presented above can be realized in different ways, and it may be that some of these ways are easier or more practicable to run, or are less cognitively demanding for the animals involved. Thus, it is useful to show how the experimental protocol could be implemented with different stimuli and apparatuses. In this section, I show how the experimental protocol can be run using clear transparent barriers that distort the size of objects placed behind them, such as magnifying and minimizing lenses. However, before doing this, it is important to look at a recent appearance–reality study with chimpanzees using such lenses.

Carla Krachun and colleagues (2009) recently ran an appearance–reality (AR) discrimination test with chimpanzees using magnifying and minimizing lenses. Before testing, the researchers confirmed that their chimpanzees possessed an untrained disposition to choose (by pointing to) the larger of two grapes presented to them. In the demo trial of the experiment, the chimpanzees were presented with a clear magnifying lens which had a small grape already placed behind it (making it look like a large grape) and a minimizing lens which had a large grape already placed behind it (making it look like a small grape). The chimpanzees consistently pointed to the magnifying lens over the minimizing lens when requesting a grape, demonstrating that they were fooled by the distorted size of the grapes behind the lenses. In the test trial, the chimpanzees watched while a small grape was placed behind the magnifying lens and a large grape was placed behind the minimizing lens. In this situation, the animals were allowed to see the distortion in the size of the grapes when placed behind the lenses. It was discovered that more than half of the animals in these test trials selected the minimizing lens over the magnifying lens when requesting a grape.

The results certainly seem to suggest, as the researchers maintain, that chimpanzees can distinguish between the apparent size of an object (a grape) and its real size. On what might be called a 'strict' interpretation of their results, the chimpanzees can be interpreted as understanding that the grape behind the lens looks small (large) but is in fact large (small). There is, however, a less strict interpretation of Krachun and colleagues' results. According to the image-tracking hypothesis, the chimpanzees do not actually understand that the grape behind the lens which looks to them to be a small (large) grape really is a large (small) grape; rather, they understand that *the image* projected on the distorting lens (not the grape causing the image), which looks like a small (large) grape behind the lens, is correlated with (and thus can be used to keep track of) the real large (small) grape behind the lens. The hypothesis does have some intuitive backing. After all, projecting images on their surfaces is what lenses do, and chimpanzees (as well as other animals) are known to use other kinds of images on surfaces, such as those on mirrors, videos, and photographs, to track and locate hidden objects (for apes, see Gallup 1982; Menzel et al. 1985; Boysen & Kuhlmeier 2002; Poss & Rochat 2003; for pigs, see Broom et al. 2009; and for capuchin monkeys, see Poti & Saporiti 2010). Thus, it would seem that the data from Krachun et al. (2009) are consistent with both of these interpretations.[20] Moreover, since an image on a lens and the object behind it that produces the image are necessarily confounding variables, it would be impossible to tease apart these two interpretations by running further test with distorting lenses.[21]

Be this as it may, both interpretations do imply that the chimpanzees are at least capable of understanding that something (be it an image on a lens or an actual grape behind the lens) looks to them a certain way (e.g., *as* a small grape behind the lens) even though nothing in the environment is that way. And that is all the appearance–reality distinction needed for a mindreading chimpanzee to pass the following visual perspective-taking test.[22]

In the preliminary stage of the experiment, a subordinate and a dominant chimpanzee compete for two different size bananas (or grapes) in a middle area like the one described in the previous experimental protocol. By the placement of different size bananas, the subordinate learns that he can retrieve the food only when the dominant chimpanzee does not have a direct line of gaze to it (e.g., such as when the food is placed inside the subordinate's room). The subordinate also learns that the dominant chimpanzee will retrieve the larger of two bananas to which he has a direct line of gaze or a small banana if this is the only food item to which the dominant chimpanzee has such access.

In the pretraining phase of the experiment, the subordinate is intro-duced to three different kinds of clear transparent barriers that are distinguished by different colored trim: a black-trimmed, nondistorting barrier which does not change the apparent size of objects behind it; a red-trimmed, minimizing barrier which makes objects behind it look smaller than they are; and a blue-trimmed, magnifying barrier which makes objects behind it look larger than they are. Through the placement of various objects behind the barriers, the subordinate comes to learn, if he is a mindreader, that he can see (and, thus, has a direct line of gaze to) objects behind all three barriers (or images on the distorting barriers) but that the objects behind (or the images on) the distorting barriers *look* to be different in size from what they really are (or different from what is really behind the barriers).[23]

In the testing phase of the experiment, the subordinate and dominant chimpanzees compete for food placed behind the different barriers described above. Here are two (of many) tests that could be run using the barriers. In the magnifying/minimizing barrier test, a small banana is placed on the subordinate's side of a blue-trimmed, magnifying barrier, and a large banana is placed on the subordinate's side of a red-trimmed, minimizing barrier. And in the magnifying/nondistorting barrier test, a small banana is placed on the subordinate's side of a blue-trimmed, mag-nifying barrier, and another small banana is placed on the subordinate's side of a black-trimmed, nondistorting clear barrier. The tests are then run much in the same way as those in the previous section, with the subordi-nate chimpanzee being given a small head start, and so on.

The mindreading hypothesis, according to the ARM theory, assumes that the subordinate chimpanzee is capable of making an appearance–reality distinction of some degree (strict or otherwise) with the distorting lenses in the pretraining phase. It then predicts that the subordinate chim-panzee will optimize his choice of bananas by using his knowledge of the size-distorting effects of the barriers to anticipate the dominant chimpan-zee's behavior in the presence of such barriers. In the magnifying/minimiz-ing barrier test, for example, the hypothesis predicts that the mindreading subordinate will try to take the large banana in front of the red-trimmed, minimizing barrier since he understands that this banana (or the image it projects on the barrier) looks to the dominant chimpanzee to be a small banana behind the barrier and, thus, the dominant chimpanzee will *not* try to retrieve the banana from that location, whereas the small banana in front of the blue-trimmed, magnifying barrier (or the image it projects

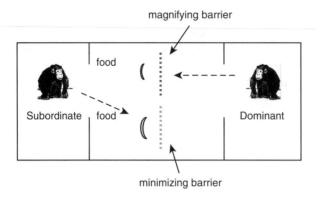

Figure 3.5
Expected performance of mindreading subordinate in the magnifying/minimizing test.

on the barrier) looks to the dominant chimpanzee to be a large banana behind the barrier and, thus, the dominant chimpanzee *will* try to retrieve the banana from that location (see figure 3.5).

And in the magnifying/nondistorting barrier test, the hypothesis predicts that the subordinate will try to take the small banana in front of the black-trimmed, nondistorting barrier since he understands this banana looks to the dominant chimpanzee to be a small banana behind the barrier, whereas the banana in front of the blue-trimmed, magnifying barrier (or the image it projects on the barrier) looks to the dominant chimpanzee to be a large banana behind the barrier and, thus, the dominant chimpanzee will attempt to retrieve the banana from that location (see figure 3.6).

The complementary behavior-reading hypothesis, however, would predict neither of these things. On this hypothesis, the subordinate chimpanzee is incapable of making an appearance–reality distinction of any kind since such a distinction would require him to have mental state concepts of perceptual appearing. All that the behavior-reading chimpanzee could possibly comprehend as a result of his exposure to the barriers in the pretraining phase is either (i) that none of barriers block his line of gaze to objects behind them, or (ii) that blue- and red-trimmed (but not black-trimmed) barriers block his line of gaze to objects behind them as a result of the intervening images on the barriers' surface. (In this respect, these barriers would be understood by the behavior reader as opaque.)

Thus, we have two possible complementary behavior readers to consider. To simplify matters, let us just examine how the first of these

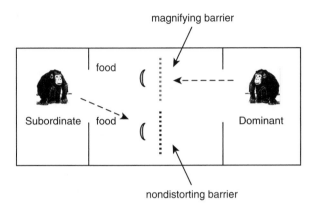

Figure 3.6
Expected performance of mindreading subordinate in the magnifying/nondistorting test.

behavior-reading subordinates would be expected to perform in the first test, and how the second behavior-reading subordinate would be expected to perform in the second test. In the magnifying/minimizing test, a behavior-reading subordinate of the first type would be expected to understand that the dominant chimpanzee has a direct line of gaze to an actual large banana behind the red-trimmed, minimizing barrier—the subordinate chimpanzee would not understand that the banana looks small to the dominant chimpanzee. Thus, given his past experiences with the dominant chimpanzee's having a direct line of gaze to large bananas, this behavior-reading subordinate would be expected *not* to try to take the banana in front of the red-trimmed, minimizing barrier (as the mindreading chimpanzee is expected to), for the dominant chimpanzee in the past has always attempted to take the larger of two bananas to which he has a direct line of gaze.

Now, in the magnifying/nondistorting barrier test, a behavior-reading subordinate of the second type would be expected to understand that the dominant chimpanzee has a direct line of gaze to the banana behind the black-trimmed, nondistorting barrier (for there is no image on the barrier to interfere with the dominant chimpanzee's line of gaze) but that the dominant chimpanzee's line of gaze to the other small banana behind the blue-trimmed, magnifying barrier is blocked by the image that the banana projects on the barrier. In effect, the subordinate would treat the black-trimmed barrier as transparent and the blue-trimmed barrier as opaque. Thus, given his past experience with the dominant chimpanzee's retrieving small bananas when they were the only food to which he had a direct line of gaze, this behavior-reading subordinate would be expected *not* to try to take the banana in front of the black-trimmed barrier (as the mindreading chimpanzee is expected to). In either case, neither type of complementary behavior-reading chimpanzee would be expected to perform in the same way as its mindreading counterpart on these tests. Thus, this experimental protocol, as with the colored-barrier one above, is capable of solving the logical problem. (See Lurz and Krachun [under review] for an alternative perspective-taking protocol with chimpanzees that also uses size-distorting lenses and that also solves the logical problem.)

Again, there may be possible behavior-reading hypotheses that yield the same prediction as the mindreading hypothesis for both of these tests. However, these minimal behavior-reading hypotheses are either not complementary behavior-reading hypotheses and, therefore, do not constitute a logical problem for the mindreading hypothesis under consideration or can be distinguished from the mindreading hypothesis under consideration by running further controls (see Lurz 2009a for further support of this claim).

3.8   Visual Perspective Taking with Ravens using Deceptive Amodal Completion Stimuli

Transparent colored screens and size-distorting lenses are not the only kinds of illusion-inducing apparatuses that can be used to test for perceptual appearing attribution in animals—nor are they even the most ecologically plausible apparatuses to use. Animals, after all, do not normally encounter transparent colored screens or magnifying/minimizing lenses in their natural environments. However, they do encounter other kinds of illusion-inducing objects. In all natural environments, for instance, partially occluded objects and sounds (particularly, species-specific calls) can appear whole or continuous to animals even when they really are not. The perception of partially occluded objects and sounds as whole and continuous typically goes by the (unusual) title of amodal completion in cognitive science and has been studied quite extensively in animals and humans for many years.[24] My concern here is with the animal data, of course. Animals from various taxa—bees, fish, mice, birds, monkeys, and apes—have been shown to perceive certain types of partially occluded objects and sounds as whole and continuous (see Kanizsa et al. 1993; Sato et al. 1997; Sugita 1997; Braaten & Leary 1999; Miller et al. 2001; Nieder 2002; Petkov et al. 2003, 2007; Fagot & Barbet 2006; Nagasaka et al. 2007; Sovrano & Bisazza

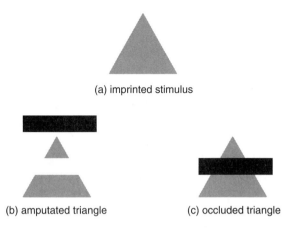

(a) imprinted stimulus

(b) amputated triangle   (c) occluded triangle

Figure 3.7
Stimuli used in Regolin and Vallortigara (1995).

2008; Seeba & Klump 2009). In Regolin and Vallortigara (1995), for example, newly hatched chicks were imprinted on a complete triangle (see figure 3.7a). When they were given two new stimuli—a partially occluded triangle (figure 3.7c) and an amputated triangle (figure 3.7b)—they responded to the former (figure 3.7c) exactly as if they were seeing the imprinted stimulus (figure 3.7a).

What is more, the researchers discovered that chicks imprinted on a partially occluded triangle (figure 3.7c) responded in the same way to the novel stimulus of a whole triangle (figure 3.7a) but not to the amputated triangle (figure 3.7b, minus the black bar overhead), despite the fact that the amputated triangle was physically more similar to the partially occluded triangle which acted as the imprinted stimulus. Thus, the chicks seem to see figure 3.7c as a partially occluded *whole* triangle.

What researchers have not investigated thus far is whether some animals can make an appearance–reality distinction involving amodal completion stimuli, and whether they can use this knowledge to predict another agent's behavior in an illusory setting by understanding that the occluded stimulus in the setting (which the animals know is actually amputated or discontinuous) appears to the naive agent to be whole and continuous. The type of experimental protocol that I have been advocating in this chapter can be easily extended to test this hypothesis. Three experimental designs are described below, one for ravens, one for chimpanzees, and one for dogs.

Through an ingenious series of experiments, Bugnyar and Heinrich (2005) discovered that ravens, when pilfering caches along with other competing pilferers, take into consideration the relative dominance status of their opponent as well as whether their opponent had a direct line of gaze to the original caching event. As a rule, dominant ravens typically eat first at feeding sites and will attack any subordinate raven (other than their own partners) that attempts to feed while or before they do (Heinrich 1999).[25] As a result, subordinate ravens generally refrain from taking food from sites while a dominant raven is currently eating there or is standing close by or on top of the food. The question Bugnyar and Heinrich investigated in their study was whether subordinate ravens ever changed their pilfering tactics when in the presence of a dominant raven that was *ignorant* of the location of hidden food at a site. In their experiment, a subordinate raven (focal subject) and a dominant raven (co-observer) watched from adjacent cages while a human experimenter hid a piece of meat in an open area of the aviary. Along with observing the caching event, the focal subject was able to observe that the dominant co-observer in the adjacent cage had a direct line of gaze to the caching event, too. In a cage next to the focal subject and co-observer, another dominant raven (the nonobserver) was housed. An opaque barrier prevented this raven from seeing the caching of the meat. From the calls and noises the nonobserver made from inside its cage, the focal subject was made aware of its presence and could see that the nonobserver's line of gaze to the caching event was blocked by the opaque barrier in its cage. A few minutes after the caching of the meat, the focal subject was released into the aviary along with either the dominant co-observer or the dominant nonobserver.

The researchers discovered that focal subjects were 10 times quicker to pilfer the cache of meat in the presence of the dominant co-observer than in the presence of the dominant nonobserver and were more likely to consume the cached meat with the nonobserver dominant than with the co-observer dominant. "Speeding up pilfering with knowledgeable dominants," the researchers suggested, "appears to be a best-of-a-bad-job tactic for subordinates, whereas delaying pilfering with ignorant dominants pays off" (Bugnyar & Heinrich 2005, p. 1645). Learning over repeated trials was ruled out as an explanation of the subordinates' performance since focal subjects' behavior was unchanged from first to last trials, and behavioral cueing by dominant co-observer ravens was ruled out as well since focal subjects often approached the cache site *before* their dominant co-observer showed any signs of approaching the site. Rather, it is more likely, as the researchers argue, that the subordinate ravens' performance was based upon their memory of whether the dominant raven competing for the cache site had or lacked a direct line of gaze to the initial caching event.

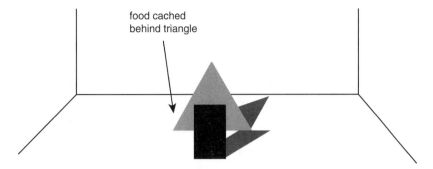

food cached
behind triangle

Figure 3.8
Partially occluded amputated triangle placed in the aviary as seen from the perspective of the ravens. The experimenter hides meat behind the triangle.

Bugnyar and Heinrich's experimental design does not solve the logical problem, but a version of it using deceptive amodal completion stimuli, I believe, can. In the pretesting phase of this experimental protocol, a subordinate raven observes while an experimenter places an amputated triangle (or some other variety of amputated figure) in the middle of the aviary. Once the figure is in place, the raven watches while the experimenter places an occluder in front of the amputated portion of the triangle (see figure 3.8).

Once the occluder is in place, the screen that was blocking the dominant raven's cage during the process is removed. At this point, the dominant raven has full visual access to the aviary and its contents, and the subordinate in the adjacent cage can see this.

Next the ravens watch while a human experimenter hides a piece of meat behind the occluded amputated triangle. The ravens can see the caching event as well as the fact that each has a direct line of gaze to the event. The experimenter hides the meat at one of the corners of the triangle's base. For this particular example, the experimenter hides the meat behind the far left-hand corner of the triangle's base. It is important that in hiding the meat, the experimenter takes care not to indicate to the ravens behind which side of the triangle the meat has been placed. From the birds' perspective, it should seem as if the experimenter could have hidden the meat anywhere along the triangle's base.

After the placement of the meat behind the left corner of the occluded amputated triangle, an opaque screen is raised in the dominant raven's cage, blocking its view of the aviary. The subordinate raven can see that the dominant raven no longer has a direct line of gaze to the aviary.

Following this, the subordinate raven watches while the experimenter removes the occluding structure (in this case, the black square) from in front of the amputated triangle. The shape behind the occluder is revealed again to be an amputated triangle—quite different from the way the object *looked* to the birds while it was behind the occluder. (I assume, though this will need to be tested, that ravens, like many other animals, will see occluded objects, such as the one depicted in figure 3.8, as being whole behind the occluder. It may turn out, of course, that ravens are more apt to see certain familiar types of occluded objects or shapes as whole or continuous, and that these objects and shapes should be used for the experiment. However, this can be easily determined by applying the experimental methods that scientist have used for years to test for amodal completion in other animals with ravens.)

Once the occluder is removed, the amputated triangle is moved a few feet to the left. At this point, a whole triangle (which looks exactly like the amputated triangle save the missing section) is placed a few feet away from the amputated triangle. The placement of the whole triangle has to be such that had the meat been hidden behind the right corner of the occluded triangle, it would now be behind the left corner of the whole triangle (see figure 3.9). The distance between the amputated and whole triangles can be lengthened by increasing the length of the triangles' bases.

Next, the opaque screen from dominant raven's cage is removed, allowing the dominant raven to see both shapes in the aviary. Both ravens are then released into the aviary to pilfer.

Predictions are as follows. If the subordinate raven is capable of attributing seeing-as, as understood on the ARM theory, then it is expected to make an appearance–reality distinction regarding the shape behind which

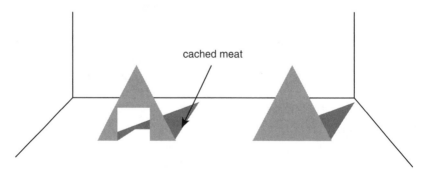

Figure 3.9
Removal of occluder and placement of the two shapes.

it observed the meat being cached and to use this knowledge to make sense of how the dominant raven likely saw the occluded shape as being, as well as how the dominant raven is likely to act in the test trial on the basis of this past visual appearance. In particular, as a result of observing the amputated triangle before the placement of the occluder, as well as observing it after the removal of the occluder, the subordinate raven is expected to understand that this shape is in fact an amputated triangle though it looked like a whole occluded triangle at the time of the caching when the occluder was placed in front of it. Armed with this knowledge of the difference between the apparent and the real shape of the occluded figure, the subordinate raven is expect to understand that to the dominant raven (who did not see the placement or removal of the occluder) it visually appeared as if the food was cached behind a whole occluded triangle. Thus, the subordinate raven should anticipate that the dominant raven will try to pilfer from behind the whole triangle in the test trial since that is the shape the occluded object looked to the dominant raven to have during the caching event of the meat. The mindreading subordinate, thus, should treat the dominant raven as if it were misinformed of the meat's location. Hence, it is expected to behave much in the way that the subordinate ravens did in Bugnyar and Heinrich's study that were paired with a non-observer (ignorant) dominant conspecific—that is, it should pilfer the meat behind the amputated triangle 10 times slower than the subordinate ravens pilfered the hidden meat in Bugnyar and Heinrich's study that were paired with a co-observer (knowledgeable) dominant raven.

This is not to be expected from the subordinate raven according to the complementary behavior-reading hypothesis, however. The objective, mind-independent observable fact on which the subordinate mindreading raven is hypothesized to judge that the dominant raven saw the shape behind which the meat was cached *as* an occluded whole triangle is that the dominant raven had a direct line of gaze to (what was in fact) an occluded amputated triangle. This observed, objective fact will be what the complementary behavior-reading raven is expected to use to predict the direction of the dominant raven's pilfering behavior. However, it is unclear how this fact would help the subordinate raven predict that the dominant raven will likely try to pilfer from behind the whole triangle in the test trial rather than from behind the amputated triangle. If anything, it would appear that if the behavior-reading subordinate had any expectation of the dominant raven's future pilfering behavior based upon the objective, observable facts, it would be that the dominant raven will try to pilfer from behind the amputated triangle since that *is* the shape behind which the meat was cached while the dominant raven had a direct line of gaze to the caching. The complementary behavior-reading subordinate raven, then, would be expected to treat the dominant raven as if it were knowledgeable of the food's location. Thus, given the results from Bugnyar and Heinrich's study, the subordinate raven here is expected to behave much in the way that the subordinate ravens in Bugnyar and Heinrich's study did when paired with a co-observer (knowledgeable) conspecific—that is, it is expected to pilfer the meat behind the amputated triangle 10 times faster than the subordinates in Bugnyar and Heinrich's study that were paired with a nonobserver (ignorant) dominant raven.

Thus, this protocol appears to be capable of discriminating between a subordinate raven that can attribute seeing-as and its complementary behavior-reading counterpart that cannot. However, in reply, it could be suggested that the complementary behavior-reading subordinate might actually believe that the dominant raven had a direct line of gaze to a whole occluded triangle at the time of the caching. Perhaps, the subordinate raven thinks that the amputated triangle temporarily becomes a whole triangle when it is behind the occluder (after all, that is how the figure looks to the raven while it is behind the occluder), and that it changes back to an amputated triangle when it is removed from behind the occluder. If the subordinate raven had such an understanding of the protean capacity of the amputated triangle, then it might conceivably believe that the dominant raven (like itself) actually had a direct line of gaze to a real whole occluded triangle at the time of the caching. And if the subordinate raven continued to believe this of the dominant raven at the time of the test trial, then it is not implausible to suppose that it might well expect the dominant raven to try to pilfer the meat from behind the whole triangle in the test trial—since that is the occluded shape the dominant raven had a direct line of gaze to during the caching—even though the subordinate knows the meat to be cached behind the currently reformed amputated triangle. Thus, on this complementary behavior-reading hypothesis, the subordinate raven would be expected to behave just in the way its mindreading counterpart is expected to.

There are at least three different ways to control for this possibility, however. The first two involve administering a kind of appearance-reality (AR) discrimination test to determine whether ravens do indeed take occluded objects to change their shapes in the way suggested above. In the next chapter, I will discuss in more depth the importance of running AR tests with animals and will outline a novel AR task using a violation of expectancy methodology. Here I offer a simple match-to-sample task and a simple discrimination task instead, both of which it is reasonable to think ravens would be capable of undertaking.

In the match-to-sample AR test, the ravens are initially trained to match a sample shape (e.g., a whole triangle) to one of two simultaneously presented target shapes (e.g., a whole triangle [correct match] and an amputated triangle [incorrect match]). Once the ravens reach criterion on this task, they are administered a test trial in which they observe the sample shape placed behind an occluder. The critical test is one in which the ravens observe an amputated shape, such as the amputated triangle depicted in figure 3.7b, placed behind an occluder and resulting in a display that looks like an occluded whole triangle, such as that depicted in figure 3.7c. The target shapes in such a test would then be a whole triangle and an amputated triangle. If the ravens take the amputated triangle to have changed into a whole triangle when it is behind the occluder, as the above hypothesis suggests they would, then they should select the whole triangle from the target pair. However, if the ravens take the occluder figure to be an amputated triangle behind the occluder, then they should select the amputated triangle from the target pair.

There is no guarantee how ravens will perform on this test, of course. The point here is merely that the test, in combination with the above experimental protocol, can be used to determine whether the subordinate raven in the original protocol treats the dominant raven as if it were misinformed of the location of the meat because it understands that (a) the dominant raven saw the amputated triangle behind which the experimenter cached the meat *as* a whole occluded triangle or because it understands that (b) the dominant raven had a direct line of gaze to the experimenter caching meat behind (what the subordinate took to *be*) a whole occluded triangle.

In the simple AR discrimination test, a raven watches from its cage while the experimenter places the amputated triangle in the middle of the aviary, then places the occluder in front of it, and finally caches the meat behind the amputated triangle, as depicted in figure 3.8. After the raven has observed all of this, its cage is then blocked by a screen, preventing it from seeing anything in the aviary. At this point, the experimenter removes the occluder, moves the amputated triangle a few feet to the left, and then places the whole triangle a few feet to the right, as depicted in figure 3.9. The screen from the raven's cage is removed and the bird is allowed into the aviary. Now if the raven truly believes that it had a direct line of gaze to the experimenter caching food behind a whole occluded triangle, as the above behavior-reading hypothesis implies that it should, then, by mere association alone, the raven should believe that the meat is behind the whole triangle and should search there when released into the aviary. However, if the subordinate raven believes instead that the experimenter cached the food behind an occluded amputated triangle, then, by mere association alone, this subordinate raven should believe the meat is cached behind the amputated triangle and should search there when released into the aviary. Thus, this simple discrimination test can be used, as the match-to-sample task above, to determine whether the subordinate raven in the original experimental protocol treats the dominant raven as if it were misinformed of the location of the meat because it understands that (a) the dominant raven saw the amputated triangle behind which the experimenter cached the meat *as* a whole occluded triangle or because it understands that (b) the dominant raven had a direct line of gaze to the experimenter caching meat behind (what the subordinate took to *be*) a whole occluded triangle.

Finally, the third way to control for the above complementary behavior-reading hypothesis is to change the location of the subordinate raven in the pretesting phase of the original perspective-taking protocol. Thus, in this version of the perspective-taking protocol, the subordinate and dominant ravens are at opposite ends of the aviary, instead of in adjacent cages. The front of the dominant raven's cage is covered with a screen, which the subordinate raven can clearly see from its present location. As in the original protocol, the subordinate raven watches while the experimenter places the amputated triangle in the middle of the aviary. In this version of the protocol, however, the experimenter places the occluder on the far side of the amputated triangle (as depicted in figure 3.10), not in front of the amputated triangle, as in the original protocol. Thus, from the subordinate's perspective, the amputated triangle does not appear to be a whole occluded triangle.

After the experimenter has set up the amputated triangle and occluder, the screen in front of the dominant raven's cage is removed, and both birds watch while the experimenter hides the meat on the subordinate's side of the amputated triangle. The subordinate, of course, can see that the dominant raven now has a direct line of gaze to the occluder and the amputated triangle but does not have a direct line of gaze to the location where the meat is hidden. After the meat has been hidden, the dominant raven's cage is again covered with a screen, and the subordinate is transported in its own cage to the dominant raven's side of the aviary. The subordinate's cage is now placed next to the dominant raven's cage. From its new vantage point, the subordinate can now see that the amputated triangle *looks* like

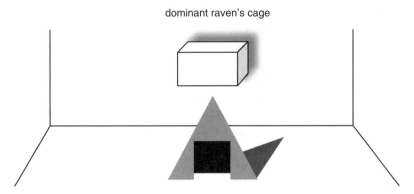

Figure 3.10
View of occluded amputated triangle from subordinate raven's perspective during the pretesting phase of the experiment. Note that the occluder is placed on the far side of the amputated triangle rather than in front.

a whole occluded triangle (or if it is the type of behavior reader suggested above, that the amputated triangle is now a whole occluded triangle). The experimenter proceeds as in the original protocol and, with the subordinate raven watching, removes the occluder in front of the amputated triangle, moves the amputated triangle a few feet to the left, and places a whole triangle a few feet to the right of the amputated one, resulting in the original configuration shown in figure 3.9. The screen in front of the dominant raven's cage is removed, and both ravens are allowed into the aviary.

On this version of the protocol, the complementary behavior-reading raven would have no reason to think that the dominant raven had a direct line of gaze to a whole occluded triangle at the time of the caching. For at the time of the caching, the occluded triangle did not look like a whole occluded triangle from the subordinate's perspective. Hence, such a behavior-reading raven would have no reason to think that the dominant raven in the test trial would try to pilfer from behind the whole triangle rather than from behind the amputated triangle. Nevertheless, the subordinate raven, if capable of attributing seeing-as, would have exactly the same general grounds for thinking that the dominant raven saw the occluded amputated triangle as a whole occluded triangle as it did in the original protocol. Hence, the seeing-as attributing subordinate raven is expected to behave just as it did in the original protocol—that is, to delay pilfering from behind the amputated triangle.

Thus, with the proper controls in place, the above experimental protocol has the power to discriminate between subordinate ravens that are
capable of attributing seeing-as from their complementary behavior-
reading counterparts that cannot. There is no guarantee, of course, that
subordinate ravens will behave as the mindreading hypothesis here predicts. However, there is no guarantee that they will not, either. The point
behind the protocol is to demonstrate in concrete terms how the logical
problem can be overcome for tests of cognitive state attribution in animals.

3.9 Visual Perspective Taking with Chimpanzees using Deceptive Amodal Completion Stimuli

The following experimental protocol is modeled on the anticipatory
looking/violation of expectancy protocols used by Southgate, Baillargeon,
and others to test for mental state attribution in infants (see Southgate
et al. 2007; Song & Baillargeon 2008). The objective here is to test whether
chimpanzees are capable of anticipating the actions of a human by understanding how an illusory amodal completion stimulus previously looked
to the human.

Before the chimpanzee arrives in the testing area, an experimenter
(Experimenter 1) places a table in front of the testing cage that separates
the chimpanzee and the experimenter. In the middle of the table, the
experimenter places a lidded box with an amputated triangle painted on
its side (see figure 3.11).

The box is placed behind an occluding rectangle or post (e.g., a black
PVC pipe), giving the appearance of an occluded whole triangle on the
box. The experimenter then places an interesting object on the table. The
object has to be something that will capture the chimp's attention long
enough for it to watch the events in the habituation phase of the experiment. The object could be, as shown here, an apple or a new toy that
makes noise when squeezed.

The habituation phase proceeds as follows. After the table has been set
up, the chimpanzee is allowed into the testing area to view the table and
its contents straight on. After the chimpanzee has viewed the table, another
experimenter, Experimenter 2, enters the testing area where the table and
Experimenter 1 are located. Experimenter 2 sits down in front of the table
and views the table's contents straight on (see figure 3.12). Experimenter
2, at this point, has her back to the chimpanzee and has the same view of
the table and its contents as the chimp.

After Experimenter 2 is seated in front of the table, Experimenter 1 gives
a signal (e.g., rings a bell or says "Go") to indicate to Experimenter 2 (as

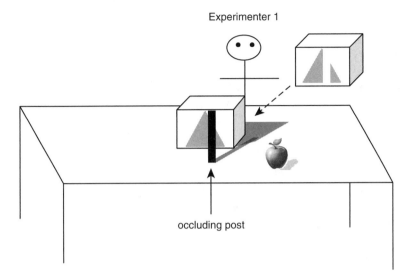

Figure 3.11
Initial setup of table.

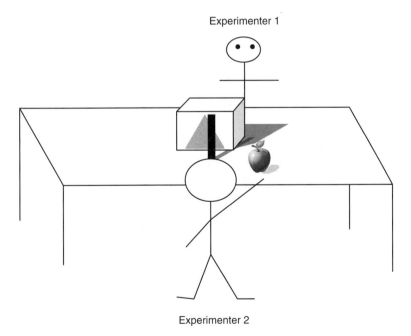

Figure 3.12
Habituation phase.

well as the observing chimpanzee) that he or she is allowed to manipulate the apple (or toy). The chimpanzee than watches while Experimenter 2 picks up the apple, examines it, and perhaps even takes a bite out of it, after which Experimenter 2 hands the apple to Experimenter 1, who then places it inside the box and closes its lid. This ends the habituation phase.

Test trials are conducted as follows at this point. Experimenter 2 turns around and faces away from the table or perhaps walks out of the testing area so that he or she can no longer see the table and its contents. While Experimenter 2 is no longer able to see the table and its contents, Experimenter 1 moves the box on the table about a foot to the left or to the right of center. In moving the box from behind the occluder, the chimpanzee can now see that the shape on the box is not as it appeared to be, a whole triangle, but an amputated triangle. After moving the box, the experimenter then places another box (which the chimpanzee could not see until now) on the table. This box has a whole-triangle painted on its side and is placed at the opposite end of the table and equidistant from the occluder as the amputated-triangle box (see figure 3.13).

After the experimenter has put the two boxes in place, she opens the amputated-triangle box and removes the apple. (This is done for the purpose of reducing a potential reality bias in the chimpanzee, which

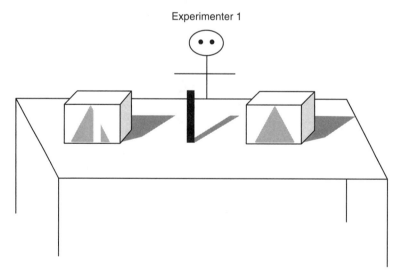

Figure 3.13
Experimenter 1 reveals the deceptive amputated-triangle box and places the whole-triangle box on the table.

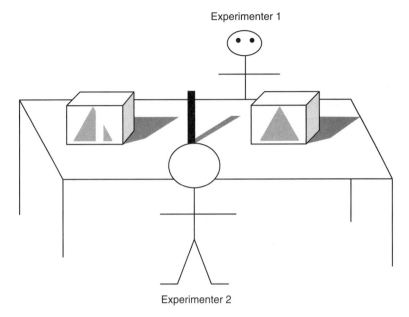

Figure 3.14
Test trial, in which Experimenter 2 returns and reaches for one of the two boxes.

might cause the animal during the test trials to simply look at the box with the apple in it.) Experimenter 2 then turns around or returns to the testing area and faces the table (see figure 3.14).

Once Experimenter 2 is seated and facing the boxes on the table, Experimenter 1 rings the bell (or says "Go"). After a brief pause (during which time the chimpanzee's looking responses to the boxes are measured), Experimenter 2 reaches for one of the two boxes. In the whole-triangle test, Experimenter 2 reaches for the whole-triangle box. In the amputated-triangle test, Experimenter 2 reaches for the amputated-triangle box.

Predictions are as follows. If the chimpanzee can take up the visual perspective of Experimenter 2, as understood on the ARM theory, then it is expected to understand that the experimenter during the habituation stage likely saw the triangular figure on the box as it appeared, that is as a whole occluded triangle. On the basis of its perceptual appearing attribution, the chimpanzee should expect Experimenter 2 to reach for the whole-triangle box in the test phase since that is the box that visually appears to the experimenter to be the one in which the apple was placed earlier. Thus, the chimpanzee should be surprised (look longer) at Experimenter 2's action (or the box toward which the action is directed) in the

amputated-triangle test compared to the whole-triangle test. Also, immediately after Experimenter 1 rings the bell (or says "Go") and right before
Experimenter 2 reaches for a box, the chimpanzee should anticipate
Experimenter 2 reaching for the whole-triangle box, and so it should look
to this box first rather than the amputated-triangle box after the bell rings
(or the experimenter says "Go"). Thus, the box to which the chimpanzee
looks to first prior to Experimenter 2's reaching, as well as how long it
looks after the experimenter has reached, can be used to determined
whether the chimpanzee anticipates the experimenter reaching for the
whole-triangle box.

A complementary-behavior reading chimp, on the other hand, in its
anticipation of Experimenter 2's future reaching, is expected to rely upon
only the objective, mind-independent facts presented to it in the habituation phase. The relevant objective, mind-independent facts in this case
are that the apple was placed inside the box with the amputated triangle
on it, and that Experimenter 2 had a direct line of gaze to this event save
the portion of the box blocked by the occluder. However, on the basis of
these facts it is difficult to understand why the chimpanzee would expect
Experimenter 2 reaching for the whole-triangle box. On the contrary, it
would seem that if the complementary behavior-reading chimpanzee had
any expectation at all, it would be that Experimenter 2 will reach for the
box with the amputated triangle on it. After all, this is the box that Experimenter 2 had a direct line of gaze to while Experimenter 1 placed the apple
inside it. Thus, the complementary behavior-reading chimpanzee should
be surprised (look longer) at Experimenter 2's action (or at the box to which
it is directed) in the whole-triangle test rather then in the amputated-
triangle test. Also, immediately after Experimenter 1 rings the bell and
right before Experimenter 2 reaches for a box, the chimpanzee should
anticipate Experimenter 2 reaching for the amputated-triangle box, and,
hence, it should look at this box first rather than the whole-triangle box
after the bell rings and before Experimenter 2 reaches.

Thus, this experimental protocol too can discriminate between an
animal that is capable of attributing states of perceptual appearing to other
agents and its complementary behavior-reading counterpart that cannot.
Obviously, further controls will have to be run in order to rule out possible
minimal mindreading hypotheses that might yield the same prediction as
the perceptual-appearing attributing hypothesis being tested. For example,
it is possible that the chimpanzee merely expects agents to reach for novel
items, the whole-triangle box being the novel item in the test trials.
However, this possibility can be easily controlled by running a habituation

trial in which a whole-triangle box is used instead of an amputated-triangle box. In the test trial, then, the amputated-triangle box is novel, and so the chimpanzee, on this hypothesis, is expected to anticipate Experimenter 2 reaching for it. However, the chimpanzee that is capable of attributing states of perceptual appearing to agents would still be expected to anticipate Experimenter 2 reaching for the whole-triangle box since that is the box that visually appeared to Experimenter 2 to be the one in which the apple was placed earlier.

It is also possible that the chimpanzee believes that the amputated triangle actually changes into a whole triangle when it is behind the occluder and, thus, believes that Experimenter 2 had a direct line of gaze to the apple being placed inside a box with a whole triangle on its front. On the basis of this, the chimpanzee might well expect Experimenter 2 to reach for the whole-triangle box in the test trial. This hypothesis, of course, is analogous to the alternative complementary behavior-reading hypothesis that we considered above for the raven protocol, and similar controls can be used to eliminate it, as well. The chimpanzees, for example, can be tested on a simple AR match-to-sample or discrimination task, much like the one described above for the ravens, to determine whether they indeed take amputated figures behind occluders to change their shape. Thus, I do not see that this possibility, any more so than in the raven protocol, undermines the present protocol's capacity to discriminate between chimpanzees that can attribute seeing-as from their complementary behavior-reading counterparts that cannot.

3.10   Visual Perspective Taking with Dogs using Deceptive Amodal Completion Stimuli

For the last experimental design described in this chapter, I wish to show how the above type of experimental approach with deceptive amodal completion stimuli can be extended to resolve an issue concerning emergent matching in animals. Emergent matching (sometimes called 'fast mapping') is the ability to match, without additional training, an unfamiliar name with a novel item within a set of familiar objects (Wilkinson et al. 1998). In humans, emergent matching comes online relatively early. Children as young as three are able to select the novel item from among a set of familiar items when a speaker requests an item from the set using an unfamiliar word (Carey & Bartlett 1978). It has been argued that emergent matching is partly responsible for young children's remarkable ability to learn roughly 10 new words each day.

Emergent matching is not exclusive to humans, however. It has been demonstrated in chimpanzees (Beran 2010), dolphins (Herman et al. 1984), sea lions (Schusterman et al. 2002), African gray parrots (Pepperberg & Wilcox 2000), and different breeds of domestic dog (Aust et al. 2008). Perhaps its best-known demonstration has been in a border collie named Rico (Kaminski, Call, & Fischer 2004). Rico was trained by his owners to retrieve some 200 different objects by their distinct names.[26] To test Rico's emergent matching abilities, Kaminski and colleagues placed an unfamiliar item in an adjacent room among seven familiar items of which Rich knew their names. When Rico's owner requested a familiar item by its familiar name, Rico ran into the adjacent room and retrieved the correct item 37 out of 40 times. When Rico was asked to retrieve an item using an unfamiliar word, he quickly went to the adjacent room and retrieved the novel item. What is more, he retrieved the novel item in these tests from the very first session of the experiment and was overall correct in matching the novel item with the novel word in 7 out of the 10 sessions.[27] (For each session, the researchers used a different novel item.)

To understand emergent matching in dogs, it is helpful to see it as a kind of semantic disambiguation effect, as it is sometimes called in psycholinguistics. When Rico's owner asks for an item using an unfamiliar name, the dog is presented with a request to fetch an item using an unfamiliar word. What is being requested is thereby rendered indeterminate to the dog. By some process or other, Rico is capable of disambiguating the request in such cases by mapping the new word onto the novel item. From an evolutionary perspective, this should not be too surprising, I should think. Dogs, after all, have coevolved with humans, and so it is quite plausible, as some researchers have argued, that they have been artificially selected over thousands of years for their ability to respond adaptively to demonstrative (i.e., pointing) or verbal requests made by humans (see Hare et al. 2002; Call et al. 2003; Miklósi et al. 2003; Reid 2009). Of course, such requests can quite easily be rendered semantically indeterminate by the requester's use of an unfamiliar word or, in some cases, by the environment itself. Thus, it is plausible to suppose that some breeds of dogs (especially working dogs like border collies) may have been selected for their talent in disambiguating such indeterminate requests when they occur.

A central issue within animal emergent matching research, however, is whether animals disambiguate such indeterminate requests by understanding the communicative *intention* of their requester or by some nonmindreading process such as exclusion learning.[28] On a social-pragmatic account of animal emergent matching, animals are hypothesized to know to match a new word or request to a novel item by way of figuring out, from the context of utterance of the new word or request, what their requester's communication intentions are. In such cases, the animals are thought to reason according to something like the principle of contrast—roughly, had the requester intended to refer to (to command me to fetch) the familiar object x, he or she would have used the familiar word/request 'x,' but since he or she used the unfamiliar word/request 'y,' he or she must be referring to (commanding me to fetch) the novel object y. According to the exclusion learning account of animal emergent matching, however, the animal is understood to select the novel item requested by an unfamiliar word not by figuring out what the requester intended or meant by the word or request but by a process of elimination applied directly to the items in the set. On this account, the animal is hypothesized to reason on the assumption that objects have only one name, and so when given an ambiguous request with a new word, the animal simply 'eliminates' (i.e., refrains from selecting) the objects whose names it knows until it encounters an object that it does not know the name of, at which point it selects the novel object. By such means, the animal matches the new word to the novel item without having any appreciation of what the requester might have intended to mean in using the new word.

Within the context of the debate of this chapter, the exclusion learning account can be understood as providing a kind of behavior-reading account of emergent matching in animals that is complementary to the mindreading explanation advocated by the social-pragmatic account. To date, no one has figured out how to distinguish these two hypotheses experimentally (Markman & Abelev 2004). The protocol illustrated above with ravens and chimpanzees, I believe, can be modified to do this. Although this modified protocol can be run with any type of animal shown to be capable of emergent matching, I illustrate it here with border collies.[29]

In the training phase of the experiment, a group of border collies is individually trained to retrieve an item (e.g., a sock toy) from a box that is in front of a familiar but partially occluded object (e.g., an occluded fire hydrant) when its owner says "bring me the blee"—or some such unfamiliar word (see figure 3.15).[30]

The details of the training are as follows. In a testing room, an experimenter places two boxes a few yards apart. In each, an identical looking sock toy is placed. Directly behind one of the boxes (called the target box), the experimenter places an amputated fire hydrant or some other object that is familiar to the dog and has been similarly amputated (see figure 3.16a).[31] After the testing area has been set up, the door to the room is

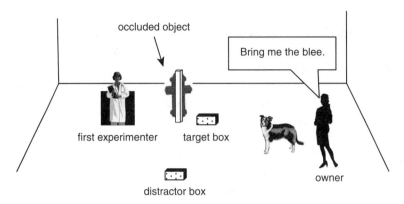

occluded object

Bring me the blee.

first experimenter   target box

distractor box   owner

Figure 3.15
General setup for experiment with border collies.

opened, and the dog is brought in by a second experimenter (not its owner). The experimenter has the dog sit or heel a few yards in front of and equidistant between the two boxes. The first experimenter gets the dog's attention (if need be) by calling its name or by some other attention-getting means. With the dog watching, the first experimenter places an occluder (e.g., a $2 \times 6 \times 36$ inch board) in front of the hydrant (see figures 3.15 and 3.16b). With the occluder in place, the hydrant now deceptively appears to be a whole and continuous hydrant behind an occluder. How the dogs will see such occluded objects, of course, will need to be tested. However, given the rather robust findings from the many amodal completion studies with a wide range of animal species, it is intuitively plausible that the dogs will see the occluded hydrant (or some other familiar object) as whole and continuous, despite their having seen that the object is really amputated.

After the placement of the occluder, the first experimenter stands a few feet behind the occluded hydrant and between the two boxes. At this point, the dog's owner opens the door to the testing room, enters, and takes over from the second experimenter. The owner greets his or her dog, looks at each box, and finally stares directly between them. The owner then requests the dog to fetch the "blee." Upon fetching the item from the target box (the one before the occluded hydrant) and bringing it to its owner, the dog is rewarded with food or praise. If the dog retrieves the item from the distractor box, it is not rewarded and is asked again to fetch the "blee" from the target box.

After the dog has brought its owner the item from the target box and been rewarded, the second experimenter returns and takes over from the owner, who now leaves the testing room, closing the door behind him or her. While the owner is out of the room, the first experimenter gets the dog's attention again. While the dog is watching, the experimenter removes the occluder before the hydrant, revealing again the true form of the amputated hydrant. At this point the trial ends.

Additional training trials are run in the same manner except that on some of the trials, the location of the hydrant and (hence) the target box is changed on a pseudorandom basis. On some trials, for example, the occluded hydrant and target box are located in front of and to the right of the dog, as shown in figure 3.15; on other trials, they are located in front of and to the left of the dog (not shown). Given the extraordinary ability of border collies to learn new words for new items, it is reasonable to think that the dogs in this experiment will come to learn to fetch the sock toy from the target box when its owner says "Bring me the blee." Figure 3.16 shows the sequence of events in the training trials involving the placement and removal of the occluder before the amputated hydrant.

After reaching criterion on training trials, the dogs are individually administered two types of tests. In both tests, the dog is presented with two nonoccluded hydrants—one of the hydrants is a whole and continuous hydrant (see figure 3.17a) and the other is the (now familiar) amputated hydrant (see figure 3.17b). Directly in front of each hydrant is a box with a sock toy inside. After the placement of the hydrants, the owner enters the testing room and takes over from the second experimenter.

As in the training trials, the owner greets his or her dog, looks at each box, and then stares straight between them. At this point, one of two tests is run. On the old name test, the owner asks the dog to fetch the "blee." On the new name test, the owner asks the dog to fetch an item using an unfamiliar word (e.g., "dax"). In both tests, the dog must decide from which of the two boxes it is to fetch. The problem, of course, is that neither box is in front of an occluded amputated hydrant, which was the exact stimulus used to identify the "blee" toy in the training trial. The mindreading and complementary behavior-reading hypotheses under consideration give different predictions regarding the dogs' retrieval choices for these two tests.

Predictions are as follows. If border collies are capable of seeing-as attributions, as this is understood on the ARM theory, then they would be expected to understand that their owners in the training phase see the occluded hydrant before them *as* being whole and continuous. And if the

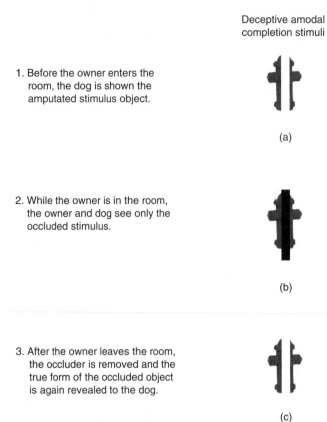

Deceptive amodal
completion stimuli

1. Before the owner enters the
   room, the dog is shown the
   amputated stimulus object.

(a)

2. While the owner is in the room,
   the owner and dog see only the
   occluded stimulus.

(b)

3. After the owner leaves the room,
   the occluder is removed and the
   true form of the occluded object
   is again revealed to the dog.

(c)

Figure 3.16
Placement and removal of the occluder before the amputated hydrant during training trials.

(a)   (b)

Figure 3.17
Placement of the (a) nondeceptive hydrant and (b) deceptive hydrant in the test
trials.

dogs also learn unfamiliar word–novel object pairings by figuring out the communicative intention of the requester during the context of utterance, as this is understood on the social-pragmatic theory, then the dogs would be expected to take their owner's mistaken perception within the context of utterance as determining what he or she likely *meant* to request with the word "blee." In effect, the dogs ask themselves: In the context in which my owner uses "blee," which sock toy is he or she intending for me to fetch by it? Given their understanding of the illusory context in which the owner introduces "blee," these mindreading dogs are expected to understand that it is likely the toy from the box before the object that *looks* to be an occluded whole hydrant. Hence, according to this mindreading-cum-social-pragmatic hypothesis, the dogs in the old word test would be expected to retrieve the toy from the box before the whole hydrant (see figure 3.17a). That is the box, after all, that is sitting in front of the object which *to the owner* looks to be the object that marked the location of the "blee" item in the training trials. In the new word test trial, on the other hand, these mindreading dogs are expected to retrieve the toy from the box in front of the amputated hydrant (see figure 3.17b). For on the social-pragmatic account, the dogs are expected to follow something like the principle of contrast and think, "Had my owner wanted me to retrieve the item from the box before the object that looks like a whole hydrant, he would have said 'blee'; since he said 'dax,' he must mean the other box."

On the complementary behavior-reading hypothesis, the dogs are expected to retrieve in just the opposite manner. Being complementary to the mindreading dogs under consideration, these behavior-reading dogs would base their retrieval choices on the objective, observable facts that their mindreading counterparts are hypothesized to use in assessing their owners' communicative intentions. In the training phase, these facts were that the owners had a direct line of gaze to an occluded amputated hydrant when requesting a "blee," and that the dogs were rewarded for retrieving the toy from the box before the occluded amputated hydrant. On the basis of these facts, the behavior-reading dogs are expected to understand that their owners' request for a "blee" is a request for the toy before an amputated hydrant or (perhaps) an amputated hydrant that is occluded. Since there is no occluded hydrant in the test trial, the behavior-reading dogs are expected on the old name test trials to retrieve from the box before the next closest thing—the amputated hydrant (see figure 3.17b). That is the box, after all, that is sitting in front of the hydrant which is most similar (in terms of its objective, observable features) to the hydrant that marked the location of the "blee" item in the training trials. And by exclusion learning, these dogs are expected on the new word test trials to fetch from the box before the whole hydrant (see figure 3.17a). On the assumption that objects have only one name, and that the "blee" toy is the one in the box before the amputated hydrant, the dogs are expected to infer that the "dax" is the toy in the box before the whole hydrant. Thus, the complementary behavior-reading dogs are expected to perform very differently on these two tests from their mindreading counterparts.

As with the previous experimental designs in this chapter, it is quite possible that a minimal behavior-reading hypothesis can be fashioned to yield the same predictions as the mindreading hypothesis under consideration. But again, it is important to stress that minimal behavior-reading hypotheses do not cause the logical problem. There is no general argument, as there is for complementary behavior-reading hypotheses, for thinking that minimal behavior-reading hypothesis cannot be addressed by conventional measures of running further controls.

It is, of course, possible that border collies are behavior readers and yet when presented with amputated objects that they have seen being occluded, such as the hydrant in the training trials, they take the objects, once occluded, to be whole and continuous (just as they appear). (We considered a similar possibility in the raven and chimpanzee protocols above.) It is possible, then, that these behavior-reading collies in the above experiment might actually believe that the amputated hydrant when placed behind the occluder becomes a whole hydrant. As a result, it can be hypothesized that these dogs come to understand "blee" as a request for the toy in the box before the whole hydrant (or the whole occluded hydrant) and are thereby predicted to retrieve from the very same boxes that the mindreading dogs are predicted to retrieve from on the two test trials.

Again, this possibility can be eliminated by running controls similar to those described in the raven and chimpanzee protocols above. What is more, by using a violation-of-expectancy procedure, this alternative behavior-reading hypothesis can be experimentally distinguished from the mindreading hypothesis under consideration, for if, as this hypothesis supposes, border collies believe of the amputated occluded hydrant that it is really a whole occluded hydrant, then they should not be surprised to find the hydrant whole were they allowed to walk behind the occluder and view the hydrant from the backside. (This trick can be easily done by having the first experimenter surreptitiously slide the missing sections of the hydrant into place, much like a revolving door used by magicians or found on some children's toys.) In fact the dogs, on this hypothesis, should be more surprised to find the hydrant still amputated when seen from behind. On the other hand, the mindreading hypothesis being tested, which assumes that the dogs draw an appearance–reality distinction regarding the occluded amputated hydrant, predicts that the dogs will expect an amputated hydrant behind the occluder. The mindreading hypothesis, then, predicts that the dogs would be more surprised to see that the hydrant has become whole when viewed from behind the occluder. Since dogs generally look longer at unexpected events (see, e.g., West & Young 2002; Pattison et al. 2010), these behaviors can be used as a way to measure the animals' expectations and level of surprise regarding the occluded amputated hydrant. The mindreading hypothesis predicts longer looking (and perhaps, smelling and/or barking) time from the dogs when they are shown that the hydrant behind the occluder is whole and continuous, whereas the behavior-reading hypothesis predicts longer looking (smelling, and/or barking) time from the dogs when they are shown that the hydrant behind the occluder is amputated. These two hypotheses, therefore, can be experimentally distinguished by rather conventional means.

In the end, of course, it is quite possible that border collies are simply unable to perform as the mindreading hypothesis here predicts. It is also quite possible that they can. After all, before Kaminski, Call, and Fischer's (2004) study, who would have thought that border collies were able to learn by emergent matching? Only by running the experiments will we know. And even if border collies are unable to perform as the mindreading hypothesis here predicts, it is possible that other animals capable of emergent matching (e.g., chimpanzees, African gray parrots, sea lions, and dolphins) can. Again, there is only one way to find out.[32]

3.11   Conclusion

Povinelli and colleagues' argument against mindreading of any kind in animals is shown to be unconvincing. This, in turn, motivated the optimists' position to solve the logical problem for cognitive state attributions in animals. In the remainder of the chapter, I showed how the logical problem can be solved both in theory and in practice. On the theory side, a new evolutionary account of perceptual appearing attribution in the animal kingdom—the ARM theory—was proposed. On the practice side, a series of experimental protocols, in line with the ARM theory, were described and shown to be capable of solving the logical problem for attributions of seeing-as. These experimental protocols are realistic enough to think that some animals may be capable of passing them. The issue is now in the hands of the experimentalists—and, of course, the animals.

4 Solving the Logical Problem for Belief Attribution

The reasoning of the previous chapter is extended here to show how the logical problem can be overcome for tests of belief attribution in animals. The current debate in the field is initially examined. The main philosophical and empirical arguments against belief attribution in animals are discussed and shown to be inconclusive, and the few empirical studies that have been interpreted as indicating the existence of belief attribution in animals are shown to be incapable of solving the logical problem. What is needed to move the debate and the field forward, it is argued, is a fundamentally new experimental approach for testing belief attribution in animals, one that is capable of distinguishing genuine belief-attributing subjects from their complementary behavior-reading and perceptual-appearing-attributing counterparts. In the last few sections of the chapter, I present three different kinds of experimental protocols that can deliver the required evidence.

4.1 Davidson's Argument against Belief Attribution in Animals

One of the best-known arguments against belief attribution in animals is by Donald Davidson (1980, 2001).[1] The argument itself is notoriously obscure in parts, but its general outline can be stated fairly clearly. Roughly, the idea is that "[m]uch of the point of the concept of belief is that it is the concept of a state of an organism which can be true or false, correct or incorrect," and thus any creature that possesses the concept of belief must possess the corresponding concepts of truth and falsity (2001, p. 104). The concepts of truth and falsity that apply to beliefs, however, have an important objectively normative dimension to them, making it difficult to see how animals might come to possess them. In holding false beliefs, for instance, one is said to be 'mistaken' or 'wrong' about things, while in holding true beliefs, one is said to be 'correct' or 'right.' And getting things right with true beliefs and wrong with false ones is not simply a subjective, personal matter; it is, Davidson maintains, objective in the sense that it is determined (in most cases) quite independently of oneself, or the fact that one holds the belief, or any subjective satisfaction or frustration that might ensue from one's holding or acting on it. As we all know, merely believing a proposition does not generally make it true, no matter how personally satisfying believing it may be.

Not implausibly, Davidson intuits that the only way for a creature to come to grasp "the concept of objective truth" is through understanding and participating in a public language in which there are shared standards of ascribing truth and falsity to assertions and sentences (2001, p. 104). Without the intersubjective standards of a linguistic community to appeal to, so the argument goes, there would be no way for a creature to make any sense of how it or others might get things right or wrong, or in what way its or others' beliefs might be true or false, on objective (i.e., nonsubjective or nonpersonal) grounds.[2] Since animals clearly do not understand or participate in such a language, Davidson concludes, they cannot come to possess the concept of belief with its attendant concepts of objective truth and falsity.[3] It is but a short step from here to the conclusion that animals cannot attribute beliefs, for possessing the concept of belief is surely a requirement.

The question is whether this last step here is valid. Must a creature possess the concept of belief as something that can be objectively true or false in order to be said to attribute beliefs? The answer, I submit, is no. To see this, we first need to note that in Davidson's argument two different concepts of belief are run together which need to be distinguished. The term 'belief' admits of a distinction, sometimes called an act–object distinction.[4] In speaking of someone's beliefs, for example, we may be speaking about his or her act of believing something, such as when we say things of the form 'S believes that *p*.' Yet in other cases, we may be speaking about the propositions the subject believes, such as when one says things of the form 'S's belief *is* that *p*' or 'S's belief (that *p*) logically entails this or that proposition.' In the object sense of belief, beliefs are thought of as bearers of truth and falsity, as propositions construed of as believed. And it is clearly this sense of belief that is appealed to at the beginning of Davidson's argument. However, in the act sense of belief, beliefs are not propositions but relations between a subject and something else. A subject's act of believing something is not something that is true or false—although, of course, what the subject believes may be, depending on what one takes the objects of believing to be (more on this below).[5]

At a minimum, then, to attribute beliefs to others requires the deployment of an act concept of belief. To think (or represent) that someone believes that *p*, one must deploy the concept *believes*. However, for reasons that Davidson has given, it is intuitively unlikely that animals understand the object notion of belief with its attendant concepts of objective truth and falsity. Does this mean, then, that animals cannot possess an act concept of belief sufficient to allow them to attribute beliefs to others? The answer depends upon whether animals' act concept of belief must be thought to be the concept of a *propositional* attitude. For implicit in Davidson's claim that the concept of belief is the concept of a state of an organism that can be true or false is the idea that belief attributions are attributions of propositional attitudes. It assumes that were animals capable of thinking (representing) the following state of affairs

(1)   S believes that *p*

they would need to represent it as S/believes/that *p*, where the subject S is represented as bearing the relation *believes* to the proposition picked out by the nominal clause 'that *p*.'

Fortunately this is not the only way that a state of affairs such as (1) can be represented. It is quite possible, as Arthur Prior (1971) once argued some years ago, that sentences like (1) can be parsed as S/believes that/*p*, where the subject S is understood as bearing a relation *believes-that* to the state of affairs denoted by the sentence '*p*.'[6] In parsing (1) in this fashion, all reference to the proposition *that p* and, hence, all need to understand objective truth and falsity as a consequence, are eliminated. There is nothing in such a parsing of (1) that refers to or denotes an entity that is objectively true or false. Neither S, nor the relation believes-that, nor the state of affairs denoted by the sentence '*p*' is something that can be said to be objectively true or false.

It is quite possible and, I shall argue below, not implausible to suppose that animals, were they capable of attributing beliefs, would represent a situation as depicted in (1) in a similar way.[7] On this Prior-inspired model, animals would be understood to attribute beliefs without attributing propositional attitudes.[8] They need only represent other agents as bearing a type of relation—the relation believes-that—to states of affairs.[9]

Of course, states of affairs and propositions are similar. They are both abstract entities that contain individuals, properties, and relations, for example.[10] And like a proposition's capacity to be true or false, a state of affairs can either obtain or fail to obtain. The state of affairs of Obama being president, for example, is an actual state of affairs; the state of affairs of McCain being president is not. Thus, a state of affairs, such as McCain's being president, can be thought of or represented by a subject without the subject's believing in it. As a result, there is no difficultly on the Prior-inspired model of explaining how an animal might attribute incongruent beliefs to others—that is, beliefs in states of affairs that the animal itself does not believe in. In doing so, the animal would simply represent an agent as bearing the relation believes-that to a state of affairs in which the animal itself does not believe.

There are, however, differences between states of affairs and propositions. States of affairs, for one, are generally taken to individuate more coarsely than propositions. This is so, on some accounts, because propositions, unlike states of affairs, are thought to contain finely individuated modes of presentations of the individuals, properties, and relations that they contain. As a result of this difference, it is to be expected that, on the Prior-inspired model, belief-attributing animals would be unable to anticipate those types of behaviors in other agents that can only be predicted by way of attributing beliefs understood as relations to fine-grained propositions. I do not see, however, that this is a problem for the Prior-inspired account. Although states of affairs may individuate more coarsely than propositions (at least in some cases), it does not follow that they cannot be used to make reliable predictions of other agents' behaviors on the assumption that the agents bear the relation believes-that to them. After all, a crudely sketched treasure map, to use an analogy, may not make all the subtle distinctions in terrain that a professional cartographer's map does, and yet for all that, the map may well be sufficient to predict where one needs to go to get the treasure and (more to the point) where someone else who is following the map is likely to go to find the treasure.

Another point of contrast, and the one that is most important for our critique of Davidson's argument, is that states of affairs, unlike propositions, are not bearers of objective truth and falsity. In fact, on a rather standard view of states of affairs, they actually provide a reductive account of what makes propositions objectively true or false.[11] In addition, the notion of obtaining in the case of states of affairs is not normative in the way that the concepts of truth and falsity are. States of affairs do not aim to obtain as propositions and beliefs (in the object sense) aim to be true. This is because states of affairs, unlike propositions, are not by their nature representational entities. There is nothing wrong or deficient with a state of affairs by virtue of its not obtaining, as there is with a false proposition or belief (in the objective sense). As a result, one cannot run the same sort of argument that Davidson does for the dependency of the concepts of objective truth and falsity (and thus belief in the object sense) on language with the concepts of obtaining and states of affairs. If belief attribution in animals involves representing others as standing in the believes-that relation to states of affairs, then there is simply no reason to think that animals must possess any understanding of objective truth and falsity, or any understanding of the object sense of belief, as Davidson's argument demands.[12]

One might object that the ability to attribute congruent and incongruent beliefs to others amounts to understanding the difference between true and false beliefs, and that even on the Prior-inspired model, belief attribution in animals (if it exists) would require animals to have at least an implicit grasp of the notions of truth and falsity. Not so. To see this, imagine an animal attributing a congruent or an incongruent belief to a subject, S, on the propositional-attitude model. In the congruent case, the animal would be taken to think (represent) something of the form:

(2) p & S/believes/that p

And in the incongruent case, the animal would be taken to think (represent) something of the form:

(3) not-p & S/believes/that p

In (2) and (3), the far left-hand 'p' and 'not-p' denote, respectively, the state of affairs that the attributing animal itself believes in.[13] The nominal clause 'that p' in (2) and (3), however, denotes the proposition *that p* to which the attributing animal represents S as bearing the believes relation. In case (2), the state of affairs denoted by the far left-hand 'p,' of course, makes the proposition denoted by 'that p' true—the relation between the former and the latter is that of truth-making. Following Davidson, it is not implausible to suppose that any animal capable of thinking (2) is expected to have some grasp of this truth-making relation between the state of affairs it believes in and the proposition that it represents S as believing. Similarly in (3), the state of affairs denoted by 'not-p' makes the proposition denoted by 'that p' false, and, not implausibly, any animal capable of thinking (3) is expected to have some grasp of this false-making relation between these two entities. Thus, the propositional-attitude model of congruent and incongruent belief attribution is simply another way of running Davidson's argument that animals, if they are thought to attribute beliefs, must possess some understanding of the notions of truth and falsity that are applicable to propositions.

However, the above line of reasoning does not apply to the Prior-inspired model. In attributing a congruent belief, according to this model, the animal is understood as thinking (representing) something of the form:

(4) p & S/believes that/p

And in attributing an incongruent belief, the animal is understood to think (represent) something of the form:

(5)   not-p & S/believes that/p

In case (4), the state of affairs denoted by the far-right hand 'p,' which is what S is represented as bearing the believes-that relation to, is the very same state of affairs denoted by the far-left hand 'p,' which is the state of affairs that the attributing animal believes in. However, the relation of identity is not the truth-making relation between a proposition and the state of affairs that makes the proposition true. Hence, in thinking (4), the animal needn't have even an implicit grasp of the concept of truth. In case (5), on the other hand, the state of affairs denoted by the far-right hand 'p' excludes the state of affairs denoted by the far left-hand 'not-p.' But the relation of exclusion between states of affairs is not the false-making relation between a proposition and a state of affairs that makes the proposition false. And so in thinking (5), the animal needn't have even an implicit grasp of the concept of falsity. Hence, the attribution of congruent and incongruent beliefs on the Prior-inspired model does not require an implicit grasp of the ideas of truth and falsity.

The Prior-inspired model is not simply a way of making sense of how animals might attribute beliefs without attributing propositional attitudes. There are independent grounds to prefer the model to a propositional-attitude model of animal belief attribution. First, there is no evidence that animals understand or are able to represent propositions, or that they have any grasp of the concepts of objective truth and falsity applicable to propositions. By contrast, there is rather strong evidence that some animals are capable of representing actual states of affairs in their environment as well as representing other agents as standing in relations to such states of affairs (i.e., states of affairs that the animals themselves believe in). In chapters 2 and 3, for example, we reviewed evidence that showed that scrub jays, ravens, and chimpanzees all appear to know whether competing rivals have or lack a direct line of gaze, or a direct line of hearing, to actual states of affairs in the world.

Furthermore, there is evidence that these very same animals are capable of entertaining representations of nonactual states of affairs in their creative practical reasoning strategies. In cases of insight learning and tool manufacturing, for example, chimpanzees and corvids have shown signs of being able to solve problems by 'trying out' possible solutions (i.e., by considering nonactual states of affairs) before acting on a solution that in their mind seems to work the best (see Köhler 1927; Heinrich & Bugnyar 2005; Dufour & Sterck 2008; Osvath & Osvath 2008; Bania et al. 2009; Bird and Emory 2009). In Heinrich's (1995, 1999) now classic string-pulling test, ravens were presented with the novel problem of extracting a piece of meat that was tied to a string hanging from a perch. Given the length of the string and the strength of the knot fastening the meat (as well as the hardness of the meat), the birds could not extract the meat (or bits of it) simply by flying toward it, grabbing it in their beaks, and then flying off, for the meat would be pulled from their beaks by the taut string as they flew away. Rather, the only way for the birds to retrieve the meat was for them to stand on the perch above the string, pull the string up with their beaks, step on the slack in the string, and then repeat the process until the meat reached the perch—at which point the ravens could extract the meat by pulling it out of the knot with their beaks. Some of the ravens in Heinrich's study succeeded in solving the problem in precisely this way on the very first trial, without recourse to trial and error. It would appear, as Heinrich suggests, that these ravens 'mentally rehearsed' a solution to the problem in advance of executing it in action. Doing so, of course, would require the birds to represent a sequence of nonactual states of affairs in their minds—for example, entertaining the states of affairs of their standing on the perch, pulling the string up with their beak, and so on.[14]

More recently, Peter Carruthers (2006) has argued for a similar 'mental rehearsal' account of the tactical deception strategy observed by Menzel's chimpanzee, Belle. Recall that in chapter 1 I described Belle's innovative maneuver of fooling Rock (the alpha male in the group) by digging in a location where she knew the food was not hidden and then doubling back to retrieve the food from its hiding place while Rock busied himself searching in the location where Belle had initially dug. Carruthers writes as follows:

How, then, did [Belle] eventually hit upon her successful solution (going to dig in the wrong place)? I suggest that the best available explanation is that she used mental rehearsal creatively ... [H]aving abandoned her original plan [of retrieving the food from its known hiding place], Belle may have mentally rehearsed [the nonactual state of affairs of] going to dig in another, foodless, spot. (p. 144)

On the basis of this imagined nonactual state of affairs, Carruthers suggests, Belle was able to predict that Rock would likely follow her to this foodless location, push her aside, and take over the digging himself, at which point she could double back and retrieve the food from its hiding place. Carruthers' explanation of Belle's novel behavior is not at all implausible and is quite consistent with other accounts of prior planning and 'mental rehearsal' found in chimpanzees and other great apes (see, e.g., Biro & Matsuzawa 1999; Mulcahy & Call 2006; Osvath 2009).

And so at least two kinds of animal that are thought by some to be capable of attributing mental states—apes and corvids—have been shown to possess the individual capacities requisite for attributing beliefs on the Prior-inspired model: The capacity to represent others as bearing relations to actual states of affairs and the capacity to represent nonactual states of affairs. The question is whether these animals, as well as other types of animals that appear to possess these individual capacities (such as bottlenose dolphins; see Herman 2006), can bring them together to represent other agents as standing in relations to nonactual states of affairs. In chapter 3, it was shown how animals might conceivably come to do this for the relation of perceptual appearing. And later in this chapter, I shall attempt to show how animals can go from there to representing other agents as bearing the relation of believes-that to nonactual states of affairs. Thus, on the Prior-inspired model, I argue, we can offer a plausible bottom-up account of how animals might conceivably come to attribute beliefs. By contrast, we have no idea how animals, save through the acquisition of language, might come to represent propositions or other agents as bearing relations to propositions. As things stand, then, I believe we have some independent grounds to prefer the Prior-inspired model of belief attribution in animals to a propositional-attitude model.

4.2 Bermúdez's Argument against Belief Attribution in Animals

Although the Prior-inspired model addresses Davidson's argument against belief attribution in animals, it does not do so for a more recent argument against belief attribution in animals put forward by José Luis Bermúdez (2003, 2009). The reason for this, quite simply, is that Bermúdez's argument goes through whether one understands belief attribution in animals on the Prior-inspired model or on a propositional-attitude model (as Bermúdez himself does in presenting his argument). However, since it is the former model that is relevant for our purposes, I shall present Bermúdez's argument here as it applies to it.

Before presenting the argument, it is important to note up front that Bermúdez does not deny, as does Davidson, that animals can have beliefs.

On the contrary, he makes a rather strong case in Bermúdez (2003) that many animals have beliefs about worldly states of affairs (even rather sophisticated proto-causal conditional states of affairs), and that they can even engage in rudimentary forms of reasoning that employ such beliefs, which Bermúdez calls "proto-modus ponens" and "proto-modus tollens." He even grants the possibility that some animals—notably, chimpanzees—may be capable of attributing simple perceptual states, such as seeing objects and states of affairs, as well as simple goal-directed desires, to other agents. What Bermúdez denies, however, is that animal can attribute beliefs.

His argument for this thesis, as presented in Bermúdez (2009), consists of three main steps. The first concerns what he takes to be a fundamental difference between beliefs and perceptions vis-à-vis their effects on an agent's behavior. In many situations, an agent's having a particular perceptual state, unlike his having a particular belief, has rather direct and predictable impact on behavior:

In many contexts what a creature perceives has obvious and immediate implications for action—seeing a predator, or a food source, for example. The only elements of the background psychological profile that need to be brought into play are generic and universal. In these cases, therefore, there is correspondingly little or no need for the creature explicitly to represent the agent's psychological background profile. (p. 152)

Things are quite different for beliefs, according to Bermúdez. In most circumstances, an agent's having a particular belief does not feed directly into the agent's behavior: "Individual beliefs and desires feed into action only indirectly, as a result of an agent's specific psychological profile" (p. 151). Thus, as a result of this "holistic character" of belief in its relation to action, what an agent will do, given a particular belief he or she has, depends upon other things that the agent believes, as well as what he or she desires, and how he or she reasons from the contents of these beliefs and desires to the action to be performed. And so, Bermúdez argues, successful prediction of another agent's action by attributing a belief requires "tracking" the agent's own putative practical reasoning from the attributed belief to the predicted behavior, which in turn requires working through this reasoning in one's own mind.

The second step in Bermúdez's argument is the claim that working through the putative practical reasoning of another agent involves thinking and reasoning with sentences—in particular, conditional sentences. To illustrate, imagine on the Prior-inspired model attributing the following belief to the agent S:

(6)   S/believes that/the prey has gone behind the tree.

And, for the sake of illustration, suppose we can safely assume that S has the following desire, too:

(7)   S/desires that/it increase its chances of catching the prey.

Now, according to the first step of Bermúdez's argument, in order to predict what S will do in this situation, one must work out the practical reasoning that S is likely to go through in having the belief and desire represented in (6) and (7), respectively. For instance, one might know that the following conditional state of affairs obtains and is likely to be believed by S:

(8)   If the prey has gone behind the tree, then S's going around the tree will increase its chance of catching it.

And from (8) plus the content of S's belief in (6)—that is, the prey has gone behind the tree—one can go on to infer this:

(9)   Going around the tree will increase S's chance of catching the prey.

On the assumption that S is also rational and is likely to engage in the same logical inference that one has just performed in one's own mind, one can predict that S is also likely to have the following belief:

(10)   S/believes that/going around the tree will increase its chances of catching the prey.

Finally, given S's desire represented in (7), one can now go on to predict that S will likely go around the tree.

Bermúdez takes the above sort of imaginary scenario to be the paradigmatic method of predicting another agent's action on the basis of attributing a belief. However, note that a critical step in this process involves thinking about the conditional state of affairs denoted in (8). Thinking and reasoning about conditional states of affairs in the above manner, Bermúdez argues, can be done only by representing those states of affairs with conditional sentences. Analog modes of representations, such mental models, maps, or images, Bermúdez maintains, simply cannot capture the logically relevant 'if–then' structure of conditional states of affairs:

But it is clear that this canonical structure [of the conditional state of affairs in (8), e.g.)] cannot be captured in any sort of analog representation. We have no idea what a conditional map might look like, for example. (p. 162)

The final step in Bermúdez's argument is that the cognitive processes one employs in tracking the practical reasoning of an agent must inform one's own practical decision making (e.g., it must be available to inform you about what you should do if S rushes around to the other side of the tree) since, according to Bermúdez, all "practical decision-making takes place at the conscious level" (p. 159). From this, Bermúdez infers that the sentences employed in tracking the practical reasoning of an agent must be sentences to which one has conscious access, which means that they must be sentences in one's natural language since sentences in one's subpersonal language of thought (à la Fodor 1975) are, by definition, consciously inaccessible.

The upshot of these three steps is that since animals quite obviously cannot evaluate the logical inferences between conditional states of affairs by entertaining sentences (specifically, conditional sentences) in their natural languages, they cannot track the practical reasoning of other agents and, thus, cannot predict the behavior of other agents by attributing beliefs to them—which is tantamount to saying that animals simply cannot attribute beliefs.

There are various places in this argument to which one might object, but I shall concentrate on just two here (see Lurz 2007 for further comment). On empirical grounds alone, the truth of the conclusion of Bermúdez's argument appears highly suspect. There is fairly solid empirical evidence showing that children begin to attribute beliefs, and not just perceptual states, long before they are capable of consciously representing and evaluating the various logical and evidential relations among states of affairs or propositions. On a conservative estimate, children begin to attribute beliefs at around the age of 4 (see Wimmer & Perner 1983; Chandler et al. 1989; Wellman 1990; Clements & Perner 1994; Hala et al. 1991)—although there are now more than a few studies that appear to show that children as young as fifteen months can attribute beliefs (see, e.g., Onishi & Baillargeon 2005; Baillargeon et al. 2010). And there are a number of studies on children's reasoning abilities that show that children do not start to engage in explicit (conscious) assessment of the formal or logical properties of arguments or sets of propositions until early adolescence (Pillow 1999; Morris 2000; Moshman 2004). It is not until early adolescence, for example, that children start to make conscious judgments about the relative evidential strengths of arguments (Pillow 2002) or appeal to the logical form of arguments in distinguishing valid from invalid inferences (Moshman & Franks 1986), or identify logically inconsistent sets of propositions (Markmam 1979). Children do not even appear to be conscious of the inferences that they make until the ages of 4–6. In a well-known set of studies by Gopnik and Graf (1988) and O'Neill and Gopnik (1991), for example, children learned about the contents of a drawer by inferring it from a clue. Although the children demonstrated that they knew the contents of the drawer, three-year-olds showed no sign of being aware of their having inferred this knowledge from the clue, and four-year-olds showed very limited awareness (if at all) of their having acquired the knowledge through an inference. Children younger than four years appear to lack an explicit awareness of the inferences they make.[15] And if they are unaware of the inferences they make, they cannot consciously consider how the states of affairs/propositions represented in those inferences relate to each other logically and evidentially, as is required on Bermúdez's belief-attribution model. By Moshman's own estimate, conscious assessment of the logical/formal relation among states of affairs/propositions does not clearly emerge until ten or eleven years of age, long after children are quite capable of attributing beliefs.

This is not to say that children do not reason logically before this age, for they do. However, the reasoning of which they appear capable is quite often occuring independently of their conscious assessment of it (Gopnik 2009). What children appear to lack before early adolescence is not the ability to reason logically but the ability to assess at a conscious level the reasoning's logical and evidential properties. For these reasons, the received view in developmental psychology is that the inferential steps that young children go through in attributing beliefs (as well as other mental states) take place below the level of conscious accessibility (see Scott & Baillargeon 2009). And if this is true for belief attribution in children, then there is no reason to think it must be otherwise for belief attribution in animals—at least, no reason that is given in Bermúdez's argument.

The second objection to be raised is that the first step of Bermúdez's argument is contentious. There is no obvious dichotomy between perceptual state attribution and belief attribution along the line that is claimed. If it is true (as it surely is) that in many circumstances, a creature can reliably (enough) predict another agent's behavior by attributing a perceptual state to the agent without having to work out in its own mind the agent's putative practical reasoning—either because the type of perceptual state involved reliably produces a kind of behavior in such agents quite independently of any mode of practical reasoning or because the perceptual state leads to such behavior by way of a "generic and universal" mode of practical reasoning that the attributor can safely ignore for the purposes of making its prediction—then a creature can surely do the same by attributing similar kinds of beliefs. To use Bermúdez's own example, if a creature can predict the action of an agent (e.g., fleeing) by knowing that the agent sees (or seems to see) a predator directly in front of it without tracking the agent's practical reasoning in such a circumstance, then it can surely do the same if it attributes to the agent the belief that there is a predator directly before it. For the belief that a predator is directly in front of it, as much as the sight of a predator being directly in front of it, will, in most cases, lead the agent to flee quite independently of any practical reasoning it might do (in such circumstances, there may be no time to engage in such reasoning) or in terms of a practical reasoning schema that the attributor can simply take for granted (e.g., if there is a predator directly before you, run!) and, thus, need not attempt to track.

The point here is that some kinds of beliefs (e.g., beliefs regarding the location/presence of food, predators, or dominant/subordinate conspecifics) in certain populations of agents are just as reliably tied to specific kinds of behaviors (e.g., eating, fleeing, combating, mating) as are certain kinds of perceptual states. For this reason, it is quite reasonable to suppose that the kinds of beliefs that animals are most likely to attribute to agents will be those, like certain kinds of perceptual states, that are reliably tied to particular kinds of behavior in such agents, either because the practical reasoning in such cases is not a contributing factor to the agents' behavior (and, thus, needn't be tracked by the attributor) or because the practical reasoning that is a contributing factor is universal and generic (and, thus, needn't be tracked by the attributor).

Given their similarity to perceptual states, we can call such belief attributions *perceptual belief* attributions. Thus, it would seem that what Bermúdez's argument succeeds in showing is that animals are unlikely to be capable of attributing nonperceptual (or inferential) beliefs—that is, beliefs that the animal can anticipate producing a type of behavior in agents only by determining the unique (nonuniversal, nongeneric) practical reasoning schema that the agent is likely to employ in the situation. However, the argument says nothing against animals' attributing perceptual beliefs— that is, beliefs that the animal can anticipate producing a type of behavior in agents without the animal having to figure out the practical reasoning schema that the agent is likely to employ in the situation.

It might be wondered, however, what the difference is on the account that I am advocating here between an animal that attributes a perceptual state and one that attributes a perceptual belief. The answer, to be worked out in more detail in section 4.4 below, is that the latter attributions are (a) attributions of an intentional relation to other agents that is understood by the attributing animal to be *revisable* in light of countervailing evidence presented to the agents in a way that the relation of perceptual appearing (at its most basic level) is not, as well as (b) an intentional relation that can be directed at *abstract* (non-directly perceivable) states of affairs which the relation of perceptual appearing (again, at its most basic level) cannot. Put baldly, belief attributions in animals on the account that I am putting forward are attributions of epistemically revisable intentional relations that can take abstract (non-directly perceivable) states of affairs as intentional objects. Nothing on this model of distinguishing perceptual belief attributions from perceptual state attributions necessarily requires animals to be capable of tracking the practical reasoning of other agents in the way that Bermúdez's model of belief attribution requires.

Taking stock at this point, it appears that neither of the above philosophical arguments rules out the possibility that animals are capable of attributing beliefs. On the assumption that the above are the strongest a priori arguments that have been marshaled against belief attribution in animals, the issue would appear to be a thoroughly empirical one. And so, let us turn to the empirical data.

4.3   The Empirical Studies

There have been two general types of experimental protocols used to test for belief attribution in animals. The first, sometimes called the cooperative 'bait-and-switch' (or 'change-of-location') protocol, is designed to test an animal's ability to use an experimenter's helpful communicative gestures to choose between two containers, one of which contains hidden food. The second, called the competitive 'bait-and-switch' ('change-of-location') protocol, is designed to test an animal's ability to use a competitor's gestures or past selection behavior to choose among containers, one of which contains hidden food. Call and Tomasello (1999) ran one of the first cooperative 'bait-and-switch' experiments. In the training phase of their experiment, an ape (either a chimpanzee or an orangutan) watched while an experimenter hid a piece of food under one of two containers located behind an occluding screen. The screen prevented the ape from seeing which container the experimenter hid the food inside, but by the fact that the experimenter came up empty handed, the ape knew that the food was hidden somewhere behind the screen. During the baiting process, the ape also observed another experimenter (the communicator) standing behind the occluding screen and intently watching the baiting process. After the first experimenter baited a container, the occluding screen was removed, the containers were revealed to the ape, and the communicator stepped forward and placed a marker on top of the container that the first experimenter had baited. The ape was then allowed to choose one of the containers.

The apes (seven chimpanzees and two orangutans) eventually learned to choose the marked container and received the bait inside. In the false-belief test trials, the communicator was again shown to the ape to be watching the baiting process from behind the screen. After one of the containers was baited, the screen was removed. This time, however, the communicator turned his back to the containers before marking a container. The first experimenter then switched the location of the containers in full view of the ape but not the communicator. The communicator then turned back around and proceeded to mark the container at the location that he had seen baited earlier.

The researchers reasoned that if the apes were capable of attributing beliefs to the communicator, then they should understand that in the false-belief test condition, the communicator will mark the container (as he did in the training trials) where he last saw and (hence) currently believes the food to be hidden, even though the food is actually under the other container due to the switching of the containers by the first experimenter. Understanding the test situation in these terms, the apes would be expected to choose the container opposite to the one that the communicator actually marks.

However, the apes in Call and Tomasello's study consistently chose the marked (i.e., empty) container over the unmarked (baited) one on the false-belief tests trials—despite the fact that in the control trials, they were quite able to ignore the marked container for the unmarked one if they were shown the transference of the food from one container to the next.

Given the successes of chimpanzees on various competitive mindreading tests (e.g., Hare et al. 2000, 2001), it was thought that perhaps chimpanzees failed the 'bait-and-switch' test in Call and Tomasello's (1999) study because it involved cooperative communication about the location of food, which is not part of the natural communicative repertoire of chimpanzees. Therefore, more recently, Kaminski et al. (2008) ran a competitive 'bait-and-switch' experiment with chimpanzees. In their experiment, two chimpanzees (a subject and a competitor) participated in a competitive game over a highly desirable piece of food (e.g., a grape) hidden beneath one of three cups on a sliding table in a middle area (see figure 4.1).

At the start of the game, the chimpanzees watched while an experimenter baited one of three cups on the table. After the baiting, a screen was positioned (or lowered) in front of the competitor, blocking its view of the middle area. The screen also signaled to the subject chimpanzee that its competitor was blind to the events that were transpiring in the

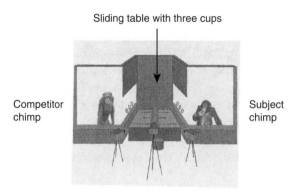

Figure 4.1
Experimental setup from Kaminski et al. (2008).

middle area. Once the screen was in place, the experimenter performed one of two types of manipulations on the cups and bait in front of the subject chimpanzee. In the unknown-lift trials, the experimenter removed the bait from underneath the cup and then replaced it back underneath the cup. In the unknown-shift trials, the experimenter removed the bait from underneath the cup and placed it underneath a different cup. After the experimenter manipulated the cups and the bait in one of these ways, a screen was positioned in front of the subject chimpanzee, blocking its view of the middle area. The screen before the competitor was then removed, and the table with the cups was slid over to the competitor's side. The competitor was then allowed to choose a cup by pointing at it. If the baited cup was chosen, the food underneath it was removed and given to the competitor; the cup was then returned to the table. If an unbaited cup was chosen, then the competitor was shown that the cup was empty and received no reward; the empty cup was then returned to the table. The subject chimpanzee, of course, could not see which cup the competitor had chosen; although from its prior training in the experiment, the subject chimpanzee presumably understood that the competitor had selected a cup at this point and had received the hidden bait if it chose correctly. After the competitor had made its choice and the cups had been returned to their original locations, the screen before the subject chimpanzee was removed. The table was then slid over to the subject chimpanzee's side. The subject chimpanzee was then allowed to make one of two choices: It was allowed to choose a cup on the table that (depending upon the competitor's choice) may or may not have the highly desirable piece of food underneath, or it was allowed to choose a cup that had been placed inside its booth which had a less preferable but guaranteed food reward inside (e.g., monkey chow).

Kaminski and colleagues reasoned that if the subject chimpanzees were capable of attributing beliefs, then they should understand that their competitor in the unknown-shift trials was likely to choose the empty cup on the table, given its mistaken belief regarding which cup was baited. The subject chimpanzees in such trials would be expected to choose the higher-quality baited cup on the table when it was allowed to choose. However, in the unknown-lift tests, the subject chimpanzees should understand that their competitor is likely to choose the baited cup on the table, given its correct belief regarding which cup was baited, and so the subject chimpanzees in these trials would be expected to choose the low-quality but guaranteed baited cup inside the booth.

Kaminski and colleagues found no such preferential choosing on the part of the subject chimpanzees. In fact, the subject chimpanzees were just as likely to choose the high-quality baited cup on the table in the unknown-shift tests as they were in the unknown-lift tests. The authors took these results, plus the findings from Call and Tomsello (1999), as positive support for the hypothesis that chimpanzees are unable to attribute beliefs.

As always, negative results are difficult to interpret. Although Kaminski and colleagues' interpretation is plausible, it is not the only plausible interpretation. There is another. Arguably, if animals are capable of attributing beliefs, then this is for the express purpose of producing reliable expectations of others' behavior, so it stands to reason that belief-attributing animals should be expected to excel at realistic (perhaps competitive) mindreading tasks that explicitly test their ability to anticipate others' behavior. However, the 'bait-and-switch' protocols, whether competitive or cooperative, are not designed to test an animal's ability to anticipate another's behavior; they are principally discrimination tasks, designed explicitly to test how animals will choose between different containers. What the experiment measures is success at choosing containers, not at anticipating others' behavior.[16] The subject chimpanzees in the test condition of Kaminski and colleagues' study, after all, do not even observe the competitor's choosing behavior. For all the subject chimpanzees knew, nothing was happening behind the screen in the critical test trials, or perhaps the subject chimpanzees (not unreasonably) assumed that the experimenter was extending to the competitor the same courtesy of lifting and/or shifting the bait around as he did for the subject. In either case, the subject chimpanzees may well have thought that when the screen before them was finally removed, they were actually choosing first, not after the competitor. This would explain why the subject chimpanzees in the unknown-lift and unknown-shift tests chose the higher-quality baited container on the table at the same rate—the chimpanzees assumed that in both cases, they were choosing first and that a container on the table remained baited.

Most recently, Krachun et al. (2010) received negative results from a 'bait-and-switch' protocol that was purposively designed to be neither a communicative–cooperative paradigm nor a competitive paradigm. In the training phase of the experiment, a chimpanzee observed while an experimenter (the baiter) placed a grape or a piece of banana inside a small yellow box with a lid. The baiter closed the lid on the box and placed it underneath one of two colored cups according to the following rule: If the food in the box was a grape, the baiter placed the box under the blue cup; if the food in the box was a piece of banana, the baiter placed the box under the white cup. After the baiter placed the box under the correct cup according to the above rule, the chimpanzee was then allowed to select one of the cups on the table. Five of the six chimpanzees tested on this phase of the experiment eventually learned to select the white cup if they had observed the baiter place a banana piece in the yellow box and the blue cup if they had observed the baiter place a grape in the yellow box.

Once the chimpanzees reached criterion on this phase of the experiment, they were then given a false-belief test and a true-belief test. In the former, the chimpanzee observed while the baiter placed a grape or a banana piece inside the yellow box (as in the training phase), closed the lid of the box, and then left the testing room. While the baiter was absent, the chimpanzee then observed another experimenter (the switcher) replace the contents of the box with the alternative food item (e.g., if the box contained a grape, the switcher removed the grape and replaced it with a banana piece). After the switcher switched the contents of the box and closed its lid, the baiter returned to the room. A screen was then raised in front of the chimpanzee, blocking its view while the baiter placed the yellow box under the appropriate cup according to what item the baiter (not the switcher) had placed inside it. The screen was then removed, and the chimpanzee was allowed to choose one of the cups. The design of the true-belief test was the same except that the baiter remained in the room and watched while the switcher switched the contents of the box.

The researchers reasoned that if the chimpanzees understood that the baiter in the false-belief trials had a mistaken belief regarding the contents of the yellow box, then they should choose the cup that corresponded to the yellow box's original contents and not to its actual contents. Likewise, if the chimpanzees understood that the baiter in the true-belief trials had a correct belief regarding the contents of the yellow box (having witnessed the switch by the switcher), then they would be expected to choose the cup that corresponded to the box's actual contents not its original contents.

What Krachun and colleagues discovered, however, was that, across the different test trials, their chimpanzees chose the cup according to the yellow box's *actual* contents. One rather plausible explanation of these results, the researchers suggest, is that the chimpanzees "might have unthinkingly carried the strategy they learned during the training trials over to the true and false belief test trials (e.g., choose based on the current contents of the yellow container)" (p. 162).[17] That is to say, the chimpanzees may have failed to comprehend the task presented to them in the training trials as one requiring the prediction of the baiter's future behavior in light of what the baiter currently believes about the contents of the box, but rather one requiring them to discriminate between colored cups according to a conditional rule which had nothing to do with the mental states of the baiter. Hence, it is not implausible to suppose that the failure of the chimpanzees on Krachun et al.'s (2010) test is due not to their inability to attribute beliefs but to their inability to understand the tasks at hand as requiring or involving mindreading as opposed to requiring or involving discrimination according to a non-mindreading-involving conditional rule.

Thus, it is not unreasonable to suppose that chimpanzees' failure on the above 'bait-and-switch' protocols are not indicative of their inability to attribute beliefs but of their difficulty with understanding the conditional rules, in some instances, of fairly complex and (from the animals' perspective) unnatural discrimination tasks, and in other instances, their failure to see the conditional discrimination tasks as involving the prediction of an agent's behavior in terms of what the agent believes. What the successes of the various competitive experimental paradigms in animal mindreading suggest, rather, is that the best way to test for mental state attribution in animals is with tasks that explicitly test for their ability to anticipate another agent's behavior.

As mentioned above, there have been a few animal studies using the 'bait-and-switch' paradigm that have yielded positive results. In Tschudin (2006), four dolphins were trained to use a tapping gesture by an experimenter (the communicator) to select a box (from among two) that contained a fish hidden inside. In the training phase of the experiment, a dolphin was presented with the communicator standing next to and observing another experimenter (the baiter) place a fish in one of two identical boxes behind an occluding screen. The screen prevented the dolphin from seeing which of the boxes was baited but allowed it to see (over the screen) that the communicator was intently watching the baiting process on the other side. After the box was baited, the baiter then removed the screen, and the communicator approached the baited box and tapped it. The dolphin was then allowed to select one of the two boxes by moving toward the box or by pointing its head/rostrum toward it. Selection of the baited box was rewarded by giving the dolphin the fish inside. Three of the four dolphins quickly learned to select the box that was tapped by the communicator.

After reaching criterion on the training phase, the dolphins were then immediately administered a series of false- and true-belief test trials in random alternating order. On the false-belief test trials, the dolphin watched the communicator on the far side of the screen observing the baiter placing a fish in one of the (behind the screen) boxes—just as in the training phase. The screen, again, prevented the dolphin from seeing which box was baited but allowed it to observe the communicator watching the baiting process on the other side. After the baiting, the screen was removed, and the communicator turned around and left the testing area, at which point the baiter switched the location of the boxes in full view of the dolphin. Once the boxes were switched, the communicator returned and tapped the empty box. The dolphin was then allowed to select one of the boxes. For the true-belief test trials, the procedure was the same except that the boxes were switched only after the communicator returned to the testing area. On these trials, the communicator (as well as the dolphin) witnessed the switching of the boxes. After the locations of the boxes were switched, the communicator tapped the baited box, and the dolphin was allowed to select a box.

Tschudin reasoned that if the dolphins were capable of attributing beliefs to the communicator and predicting her tapping behavior accordingly, then they should understand that the communicator, in the false-belief test condition, would have a mistaken belief regarding the location of the fish and, as a result, would tap the empty box; in which case the dolphins are expected to select the untapped box. And in the true-belief condition, the dolphins should understand that the communicator would have a correct belief regarding the location of the fish and, as a result, would tap the baited box; in which case the dolphins are expected to select the tapped box.

That is precisely how the dolphins behaved in the vast majority of the test trials. What is more, all three dolphins passed the false-belief test on the very first trial, and two passed the true-belief test on the first trial. This suggests that the dolphins were not selecting the baited box in the test trials by a quick (one-trial) learning process; rather, their successful first-trial performance apparently reflected their bringing prior knowledge to bear on the test conditions—knowledge gained either from their experiences in the earlier training trials or experiences gained outside the experiment altogether (or perhaps a combination of both).

Tschudin's study, unfortunately, did not control for possible confounds, such as the possibility of inadvertent cueing by the communicator (who always knew the location of the baited box) or the detection by the dolphins of auditory differences between tapped-empty and tapped-baited boxes, or the possibility that the dolphins may have used their prior experience from an earlier false-belief pilot study to pass the tests trials in the current study.[18] There is, then, some concern about how strongly the results should be taken to support the hypothesis that dolphins attribute beliefs.

Nevertheless, even with the proper controls in place, I do not see that the design of the experiment can overcome the logical problem. To see this, let us examine Tschudin's belief-attributing hypothesis a bit more closely. According to the hypothesis, the dolphins use the correctness and incorrectness of the communicator's belief regarding the location of the fish, and not the tapping of the box, as their basis for selecting the baited box in the test trials. And so, on this hypothesis, the dolphins are understood to follow something like the following rule during the test trials:

Belief-Attributing Rule   When the communicator has an incorrect belief about the location of the fish, choose the box opposite to the one she taps; when the communicator has a correct belief about the location of the fish, choose the box that she taps.

Of course, the dolphins cannot follow this rule directly since they lack direct access to the communicator's beliefs. Therefore, they must follow it by appealing to the observable cues that they take as evidence of the respective belief states in the communicator. What are these observable cues? Well, in the false-belief trials, the grounds for thinking that the communicator mistakenly believes the fish is at a location that it is not are surely the fact that the communicator was absent during and (thus) did not have a direct line of gaze to the moving of the baited box to its new location; in the true-belief trials, the grounds for thinking that the communicator correctly believes the fish is at its new location are the fact that the communicator was present during and (thus) had a direct line of gaze to the moving of the baited box to its new location.

However, if these are the grounds that the dolphins use to follow the Belief-Attributing Rule above, then the question arises why they could not have performed as they did simply by following the Complementary Behavior-Reading Rule, as Tschudin himself expresses it:

[W]hen the communicator lacks visual access [to a change in the location of the baited box], choose the opposite box; when the communicator has visual access [to a change in the location of the baited box], choose the box indicated. (p. 425)

Tschudin considers and quickly rejects the Complementary Behavior-Reading Rule explanation of the dolphins' performance on the grounds that such a rule would have to have been learned by the dolphins during the testing trials since, prior to the test trials, the dolphins had no experience with selecting a baited box under such conditions.[19] And yet, as the data from the study show, there was no indication of learning during the test trials.

Of course, the Belief-Attribution Rule is subject to the same concern since the dolphins never had any experience of selecting the baited boxes under such conditions before the test trials, either. Thus, if the criticism is decisive for the complementary behavior-reading explanation, it is decisive for the belief-attributing explanation. Clearly, then, for the belief-attributing hypothesis to overcome this objection, it must be argued that the Belief-Attributing Rule somehow falls out of a more general belief-attributing rule or ability that the dolphins learned or knew prior to the testing phase of the experiment. For example, it may be argued that since foraging tactics in dolphins are often learned through observing conspecifics, specifically calves observing their mothers (Mann & Sargeant 2003; Sargeant & Mann 2009), it is possible that dolphins know from observing conspecifics (or even from observing their own foraging behavior) that dolphins tend to believe food to be at the location that they originally saw it in (as evidenced by their focusing their echolocation on or orienting their bodies toward that location) unless they saw the food move (either on its own or inside a vessel, such as inside their own or another dolphin's mouth) to a new location, in which case they tend to believe the food to be in the new location (again, as evidenced by their focusing their echolocation on or orienting their bodies toward the new area).

It is possible, then, that Tschudin's dolphins may have applied this background knowledge of dolphin behavior and beliefs during acts of foraging to the communicator as a way to predict the correctness and incorrectness of the communicators' belief regarding the location of the fish in the test trials. Thus, on such a model, we can at least begin to make sense of how the dolphins might have been able to predict that the communicator would believe (mistakenly), in the false-belief trial, that the fish is in its original location (since that is where she last saw it) and signal that location by tapping the box, despite the dolphins knowing the fish to have been moved to a new location; and how the communicator would believe (correctly), in the true-belief trial, that the fish is in its new location and signal that location by tapping the baited box (since the communicator saw the fish-containing box moved to this new location).

Although such a model can conceivably explain how the dolphins came to follow the Belief-Attribution Rule without learning it simply from their experiences in the test trials, an analogous model can be given to explain how the dolphins came to follow the Complementary Behavior-Reading Rule without their learning it simply from their experiences in the test trials, too. It is just as plausible that dolphins learned from their experience of observing conspecific foraging (or even from observing their own foraging behavior) that dolphins tend to focus their echolocation beam on or orient their bodies toward those locations where they originally had a direct line of gaze to food unless they have had a direct line of gaze to the food's being moved (either on its own or inside their own or another dolphin's mouth) to a new location, in which case they tend to focus their echolocation beam on or orient their bodies toward this new location.

Thus, it is possible that Tschudin's dolphins applied this sort of background knowledge to the communicator as a way to determine the location of the fish in the test trials. The dolphins, then, can be understood to predict that the communicator, in the false-belief trial, will tap[20] the box (similar to the way a dolphin might focus its echolocation beam) at the location that the communicator *originally* had a direct line of gaze to while the fish was placed there, despite the dolphins' knowing that the fish has since been moved to a new location; and that the communicator, in the true-belief trial, will tap the box (again, similar to a dolphin focusing its echolocation beam) at the location where the fish has been moved while the communicator had a direct line of gaze to its change of location. Thus, on a very similar model, it appears that we can also make sense of how the dolphins might have come to follow the Complementary Behavior-Reading Rule without their having to learn the rule during the test trials.

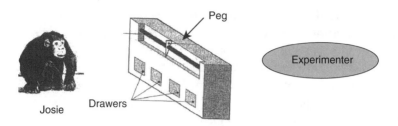

Figure 4.2
Experimental setup from O'Connell and Dunbar (2003).

For these reasons, I do not see that Tschudin's study, even with the proper controls in place, can adequately discriminate between belief-attributing and complementary behavior-reading dolphins.

O'Connell and Dunbar (2003) received positive results from one of their chimpanzees (Josie) in a cooperative 'bait-and-switch' study which used a mechanical-like apparatus instead of the standard boxes or containers. In the training phase of the experiment, Josie was trained to use the location of a peg on a box-like apparatus to locate the baited drawer from among a row of four drawers that were set within the apparatus. The peg itself was fastened to a fan belt, and its location (relative to drawers below it) could be changed by turning a crank behind the apparatus that moved the belt (see figure 4.2).

During the training, Josie watched while the experimenter, with food in hand, positioned the peg over one of the drawers. The experimenter then moved behind the apparatus and placed the food inside the drawer marked by the peg. The apparatus itself prevented Josie from seeing which drawer the experimenter had baited; however, since the experimenter always returned from behind the apparatus empty handed, Josie had reason to believe that the bait was hidden inside one of the four drawers. After the experimenter baited the appropriate drawer and returned from behind the apparatus, the apparatus was then pushed toward Josie, and she was allowed to select one of the drawers by pointing to it.

Once Josie successfully learned to select the drawer under the peg and was rewarded for doing so by receiving the food within it, she was administered a series of randomly alternating false- and true-belief test trials. In the former trials, Josie watched while the experimenter positioned the peg over a drawer and then moved behind the apparatus to bait the drawer as in the training trials. However, unlike the training trials, once the experimenter was behind the apparatus and occupied with baiting the drawer,

Josie saw the peg move to a new position directly over a different drawer (in fact, the experimenter secretly turned the crank behind the apparatus, moving the peg on the belt to its new location). The experimenter did not return to the front of the apparatus at this point to observe the peg's new location but simply proceeded with the baiting process. Thus, on the false-belief test trials, the experimenter did not see that latest peg position before baiting. The conditions were much the same for the true-belief test trials except that, after the peg was moved to its new location, the experimenter returned from behind the apparatus, with food still in hand, and looked at the peg's new location. After viewing the new location of the peg, the experimenter moved behind the apparatus and baited the box that was currently marked by the peg.

O'Connell and Dunbar reasoned that if Josie understood that, in the false-belief test trials, the experimenter had a mistaken belief regarding the current location of the peg (since the experimenter only last saw the peg at its old position, not at its new one), then she should expect the experimenter to bait the drawer that the peg was originally hanging over (i.e., where the experimenter last saw it hanging), not the drawer that the peg was currently hanging over, and thus, Josie on these trials should select the drawer that the peg was previously hanging over when she is allowed to choose a drawer. On the true-belief trials, however, the researchers reasoned that if Josie understood that the experimenter had a correct belief regarding the current location of the peg (having seen its new location), then she should expect the experimenter to bait the drawer that the peg is currently hanging over (the last place the experimenter saw it in), not the drawer that it was hanging over earlier, and, thus, Josie on these trials should select the drawer that is currently indicated by the peg when she is allowed to choose.

The researchers discovered that, as predicted, Josie selected the previously marked drawer on the false-belief test trials and the currently marked drawer on the true-belief test trials significantly more often than would be expected by chance. They concluded from these results that Josie was capable of attributing beliefs at the level of a four-year-old child.

Unfortunately, O'Connell and Dunbar's study does not overcome the logical problem, and so it does not determine whether Josie is a belief-attributor or a complementary behavior reader. Josie's performance can just as well be explained in terms of her learning from the training trials to choose the drawer which the experimenter last had a direct line of gaze to the peg being over, as opposed to her learning to choose the drawer that the experimenter last saw and (hence) currently believes the peg to be over.

Finally, Krachun et al. (2008) ran a competitive 'bait-and-switch' experiment with chimpanzees that used looking time as a measure and received positive results. In the experiment, a chimpanzee competed with a human competitor for food hidden in one of two containers. In the false-belief test, the chimpanzee observed while one of the two containers was baited behind a screen while the competitor watched. While the competitor left the room or turned around, the chimpanzee witnessed the experimenter switch the locations of containers. The competitor returned to the table and "unsuccessfully" reached for the empty container. The chimpanzee was then allowed to choose. Krachun and colleagues discovered that although chimpanzees failed to choose the baited container on false-belief trials, they did look more at the baited container on these trials than on the true-belief trials (i.e., trials where the competitor had witnessed the switch in the location of the containers). The researchers guardedly interpreted these results as indicating a possible "implicit" understanding of false belief in chimpanzees.

A chief problem with Krachun and colleagues' study, however, is that since it is (like the other 'bait-and-switch' studies) a discrimination task, the animals' differential looking times on the test trials were not indications of the animals' anticipation of where the competitor would reach, but rather, as the researchers acknowledge, the animals' level of uncertainty over which container had the bait in it. The fact that the chimpanzees looked more often at the baited container in the false-belief trials than in the true-belief trials indicated that the chimpanzees were less certain of their choices in the former than the latter trials. However, their being less certain of their choice in the false-belief test may have had little to do with their understanding the competitor's false belief. As the researchers point out, there were reasons for the animals to be uncertain in the false-belief test trials that had nothing to do with the competitor's false belief. In the false-belief trials, but not in the true-belief trials, the experimenter performed the switching of the containers in a decidedly deceptive manner— smiling mischievously and glancing occasionally at the door or the competitor's back. This may have suggested to the animals that something was underhanded, perhaps making them wonder whether the competitor's indicated choice of containers (by his "unsuccessful" reaching) was a reliable indicator of the hidden food, as it had been in the past trials. Also, in the warm-up and pretest trials, the competitor always had a direct line of gaze to the containers while the experimenter manipulated them. It was only on the false-belief test trials that the competitor's line of gaze to the containers was first blocked or absent while the experimenter switched them. This difference between these preceding trials and the false-belief test may have made the animal feel uncertain, or confused, about whether the container indicated by the competitor was the baited container. From their previous experience, the chimpanzees may have thought that the competitor's indicative gestures were reliable because the competitor had a direct line of gaze to the manipulation of the containers. When this condition was absent in the false-belief test, the chimpanzees may have become less certain of the reliability of the competitor's indicative gesture.

These shortcomings of Karchun and colleagues' experiment strongly suggest that what the looking-time response needs to indicate in a false-belief task is not uncertainty about the location of the baited container but knowledge—specifically knowledge of another agent's future behavior. Hence, the false-belief test should be one in which the test animal is required to anticipate another agent's behavior, and a violation-of-expectation or anticipatory-looking methodology can be used to measure the animal's level of expectation of the other agent's future behavior. In the remaining sections, I describe three experimental designs that employ one or the other of these methodologies and, I argue, can successfully distinguish belief-attributing animals from their complementary behavior-reading (as well as their simple perceptual-appearing-attributing) counterparts.

4.4   From Perceptual Appearing Attribution to Belief Attribution

The experimental approach outlined herein is generated by the ARM theory discussed in the previous chapter. According to ARM, the capacity to attribute states of perceptual appearing in animals evolved (insofar as it did) for the purpose of enabling animals to anticipate other agents' behaviors in settings in which the animals' competing behavior-reading counterparts could not. In many situations, the way things perceptually look or sound to an agent is a better predictor of its behavior than the way things objectively are for the agent and its environment. Behavior-reading animals—animals that are unable to attribute mental states at all—can appeal only to the latter sorts of objective, mind-independent facts to anticipate other agents' future behaviors (e.g., facts about an agent's past behaviors, or facts about an agent's line of eye gaze to an object or event in the environment). Animals that are capable of attributing states of perceptual appearing, on the other hand, are able to appeal to the subjective way objects and events perceptually appear to other agents and, as a result, are in a better to position than their similarly placed behavior-reading counterparts to predict the behavior of other agents in illusory settings.

There are, however, two important ways in which animals capable of attributing states of perceptual appearing may be limited in their behavior-predicting practices in illusory settings. First, agents that are capable of distinguishing perceptual appearances from reality can sometimes see through illusory appearances when presented with countervailing evidence (i.e., a state of affairs that undermines the illusion) and can act on the way the world *really is* in the setting rather than on the way it perceptually appears to be. For example, an agent might see a straight stick placed in a glass of water as bent, but if the agent saw the stick while it was being submerged in the water (countervailing evidence), he or she may, if capable of distinguishing appearances from reality, believe that the stick is really straight and act on this fact (true belief) rather than on the way the stick currently looks to the agent to be (as bent). The agent's beliefs and subsequent behavior toward the stick's shape change (though the way the stick looks to the agent does not) as a function of whether the agent is presented with facts that undermine the perceptual illusion. This is a distinctive feature of beliefs as compared to perceptual experiences. Beliefs as a kind are revisable in light of countervailing evidence in the way that perceptual experiences (i.e., phenomenal appearings) as a kind are not (see Fodor 1983; Pylyshyn 1999).

However, a simple, inflexible perceptual-appearing-attributing animal, one that predicts other agents' behaviors *solely* on the basis of how it represents the world as perceptually appearing to these agents, would be insensitive to such epistemic and behavioral variances across illusory settings by agents capable of making an appearance-reality distinction. A simple perceptual-appearing-attributing animal, for example, would be locked into predicting the agent's behavior described above in terms of how the stick in the water visually appears to the agent (as bent), irrespective of the fact that the agent was observed to have been presented with the event (i.e., the stick being straight while submerged in the water) which undermines the perceptual illusion. In which case, the simple perceptual-appearing-attributing animal would expect the wrong type of behavior from the agent: It would expect the agent to act toward the stick as if it were bent, while the agent (given its ability to distinguish appearance from reality in this case) will act toward the stick as it really is—straight. Given what was argued in section 3.3 in the preceding chapter, it seems likely that some of a perceptual-appearing-attributing animal's conspecifics will themselves be capable of making distinctions between perceptual appearances and reality. Hence, a simple, inflexible perceptual-appearing-attributing animal is likely to expect the wrong kinds of behavior from such conspecifics in illusory settings where they have been presented with evidence that undermines the illusion.

However, I see no reason why an animal that is capable of attributing states of perceptual appearing could not come to learn to predict such agents' behaviors in illusory settings in a more flexible way, in a way that reliably tracks the changes in the beliefs and subsequent behaviors of such agents. And, as noted, there will certainly be a selective pressure for perceptual-appearing-attributing animals to come to do this if many of their conspecifics (or other frequently encountered agents) are capable of distinguishing appearances from reality in illusory settings where they are presented with countervailing evidence to the illusion. Thus, for example, a perceptual-appearing-attributing animal could come to learn from its encounters with such conspecifics and other such agents to discriminate between the following two kinds of illusory settings:

Illusory setting (A) In this sort of setting, the following facts obtain. (i) The other agent has a direct line of gaze to a state of affairs Fx (e.g., the stick in the water being straight); yet (ii) it *appears* to the agent as if it has a direct line of gaze to a different state of affairs Gx (e.g., the stick in the water being bent); and (iii) the agent has been presented with an event (e.g., the straight stick being submerged in the water) which the perceptual-appearing-attributing animal itself takes to be evidence of the x being F and not G (e.g., the stick in the water being straight and not bent).

Thus, the perceptual-appearing-attributing animal could learn to predict other agents' behaviors in illusory settings of type (A) in terms of their having a direct line of gaze to the state of affairs Fx (the stick in the water being straight) and not in terms of their appearing to have a direct line of gaze to the state of affairs Gx (the stick in the water being bent).

Illusory setting of type (B) is similar to type (A) except that the other agent involved has not been observed by the perceptual-appearing-attributing animal to be presented with countervailing evidence:

Illusory setting (B) In this type of setting, (i) the other agent has a direct line of gaze to a state of affairs Fx (e.g., the stick in the water being straight); yet (ii) it *appears* to the agent as if it has a direct line of gaze to a different state of affairs Gx (e.g., the stick in the water being bent); and (iii) the agent has *not* been observed to have been presented with an event (e.g., the straight stick being submerged in the water) which the perceptual-appearing-attributing animal takes as evidence of the x being F and not G (e.g., the sick in the water being straight and not bent).

In illusory settings of type (B), the perceptual-appearing-attributing animal could learn to predict other agents' behaviors in terms of their appearing to have a direct line of gaze to the state of affairs Gx (the stick in the water being bent) and not in terms of their having a direct line of gaze to the state of affairs Fx (the stick in the water being straight).

I see no reason why an animal capable of attributing states of perceptual appearing could not come to learn to use its perceptual appearing attributions in this flexible way, and if it did, its perceptual appearing attributions would be more like attributions of belief states (intentional states that as a kind are revisable in light of countervailing evidence) than attributions of simple perceptual states (intentional state that as a kind are generally not revisable in light of countervailing evidence). For this reason, I believe, we would be entitled to say of such a perceptual-appearing-attributing animal that it is capable of attributing perceptual *beliefs* (or, if one demands, belief-like states) to other agents.

The other way that an animal capable of attributing states of perceptual appearing may be limited in its ability to predict other agents' behaviors in illusory settings is that some agents in such settings may act on how a state of affairs appears to them at an abstract level of description and not merely in terms of how the state of affairs perceptually appears to them to be at a (more-or-less) concrete, phenomenological level of description. For instance, even in those cases where agents fail to see through the deceptive appearances of a perceptual illusion (perhaps, as a result of their not being presented with countervailing evidence) and are subsequently deceived by the illusion, the illusory state of affairs on which the agents act and are deceived may not be the determinate, directly perceivable state of affairs which they phenomenally seem to see or hear but a more abstract, determinable state of affairs which, due to the aid of cognition, they mistakenly cognize or believe to obtain. A straight stick in a glass of water and a bent stick in an empty glass, for example, may each visually appear to an agent to have a specific, determinate shape—they both look bent—and yet the sticks may also cognitively appear to the agent to have the more abstract, determinable property of being same-shaped or congruent (a property possessed by any pair of objects having the same determinate shape). Thus, the agent, if in possession of the abstract concept of congruency, may be said to see the sticks as congruent (in addition to seeing them as bent).

Arguably, this sense of 'seeing-as'—sometimes called the 'epistemic' sense of 'seeing-as'—requires the agent to possess and deploy an abstract concept and, thus, deserves to be considered a type of perceptual belief.[21] If the agent here is (let us imagine) looking for any congruently shaped objects (and not necessarily just objects that share a particular bent shape) and is subsequently fooled by the apparent congruency of the sticks, we can say that the agent acted on a mistaken perceptual belief (or cognitive appearing).

However, if an animal that is capable of attributing states of perceptual appearing is not capable of representing such abstract states of affairs, then it will be unable to predict the behavior of those agents that are fooled by and act on the apparent existence of such abstract states of affairs in illusory settings. If such an animal is, say, incapable of understanding that the agent described above sees the sticks as congruent, and understands only that the agent sees the sticks as being bent, then it will be unable to predict what the agent is likely to do next (especially if this is the first time that the agent has been observed seeing objects as having that determinate bent shape and, thus, has never before been observed reacting to the presence of objects as having that shape). However, a perceptual-appearing-attributing animal that *is* capable of representing the agent as seeing the sticks as congruent (and not simply as bent) would be capable of predicting what such an agent is likely to do next (even if this is the first time that the agent has been observed seeing objects as having that particular bent shape). Thus, if a perceptual-appearing-attributing animal can represent agents as seeing or hearing states of affairs or objects as being Φ, where 'Φ' is an abstract concept such as congruency, then given what was said above regarding the epistemic sense of 'seeing-as,' we would be entitled, I believe, to say that such a perceptual-appearing-attributing animal is capable of attributing perceptual *beliefs* (or, if one prefers, states of cognitive appearing) to other agents.

Of course, not all perceptual-appearing-attributing animals may be capable of representing such abstract states of affairs. Some may be limited to representing other agents as simply seeing or hearing states of affairs or objects as being Ψ, where 'Ψ' is a (more-or-less) determinate, directly perceivable property (or set of properties) such as a particular color, shape, spatial relation, or sound. Of such perceptual-appearing-attributing animals (unless capable of using their perceptual-appearing-attributing skills in the flexible manner discussed above), we can say that they are capable of attributing only simple or determinate states of perceptual appearing to other agents, in contrast to their more sophisticated perceptual-appearing-attributing counterparts whose perceptual appearing attributions can be understood as attributions of perceptual beliefs (or states of cognitive appearing).[22]

And so on the ARM theory, perceptual appearing attribution in animals should reflect at least two general levels of development. The first involves what can be called simple or determinate perceptual appearing attribution. At this level, perceptual-appearing-attributing animals predict other agents' behaviors in terms of how they think first-order, determinate states of affairs perceptually appear to these agents. These perceptual-appearing attributors, however, are inflexible in their use of their perceptual appearing attributions, deploying them in all settings to predict other agents' behaviors, even in those settings (such as illusory settings of type [A]) where agents may not act according to the way first-order, determinate states of affairs perceptually appear to them to be. The second level of development is perceptual belief attribution. I have just argued that there are two varieties of perceptual belief attribution in perceptual-appearing-attributing animals that are of interest. The first involves perceptual-appearing-attributing animals using their perceptual appearing attributions in a flexible way that tracks the changes in beliefs and behaviors of agents in illusory settings of type (A) and (B). In using their perceptual appearing attributions in this flexible manner, I claim, these animals' perceptual appearing attributions take on the status of perceptual belief attributions. The second variety of perceptual belief attribution involves perceptual-appearing-attributing animals that are capable of representing other agents as bearing the perceptual appearing relation to abstract states of affairs. In doing so, I claim, these animals' perceptual appearing attributions can be understood as attributions of perceptual beliefs (or states of cognitive appearing).

To test the ARM theory empirically, we would need an experimental method capable of distinguishing (a) those animals capable of attributing simple states of perceptual appearing from (b) those capable of attributing such perceptual beliefs as defined above. All of the belief-attribution studies surveyed above, unfortunately, rest upon a particular view of the difference between belief attribution and perceptual state attribution that prevent them from being able to experimentally distinguish (a) and (b). The view itself, quite correctly, is based upon an undeniable fact about beliefs and perceptions—namely, that past veridical perceptions (e.g., having seen food placed in location x) can sometimes lead a subject to later act on a mistaken belief at a time when the veridical perception no longer exists (e.g., the competitor/communicator now incorrectly believes that the food is still in location x even though it has been moved to location y). The studies, therefore, assume that if chimpanzees and dolphins are capable of attributing beliefs, and not just occurrent perceptual states, then they should be able to predict an agent's behavior on the basis of the agent's currently held false belief in the absence of the veridical perception that caused it. The chief problem with this approach is that an agent's currently held false belief will always be confounded with the agent's having had a past veridical perception (as well as the agent's having had a direct line of gaze to the perceived object or event), and, as a result, the animal's successful prediction of the agent's action can just as well be explained in terms of its attributing a past veridical perception (or a past direct line of gaze to an object or event) to the agent.

Luckily, there are two other ways of understanding the difference between belief attribution and perceptual state attribution in animals that escape this problem. Both of these approaches reflect a distinctive feature of belief in relation to perception—namely, revisability and abstractness. As mentioned above, a distinctive feature of beliefs (at least, as a kind of mental state) is that they are revisable in light of countervailing evidence in the way perceptual states (as a kind) generally are not.[23] As a result of measuring the lines in a Muller–Lyer diagram (see figure 4.3), for example, one's belief about the lines' unequal length changes, despite the lines' continuing to look unequal, and this change in one's belief naturally leads to a change in one's behavior.

Thus, an animal capable of attributing perceptual beliefs (or belief-like states), and not just perceptual states, is expected to be sensitive to the behavioral difference between (1) an agent that perceives (sees or hears) an object as F but has countervailing evidence that the object is F and (2) an agent that perceives (see or hears) an object as F but has no such countervailing evidence. In section 4.6–4.7 below, I describe two experimental protocols for testing chimpanzees' and monkeys' sensitivity to this epistemic difference; for obvious reasons, I call these tests revisability tests.

Figure 4.3
Muller–Lyer diagram.

The other distinctive feature of belief (and thought and cognition in general) is its ability to allow subjects to represent states of affairs in the world that cannot be represented by means of perception alone. Such states of affairs are routinely called 'abstract.' Of course, abstractness comes in degree, and so it is unlikely that there will be any sharp distinction between perception and belief on this measure. Be this as it may, the point here is merely that the more abstract a state of affairs a mental state represents the more the state belongs to cognition than to perception. Intuitively, on any metric of abstractness, representing an object as having a second-order or determinable property is more abstract than representing an object's first-order, determinate properties. Consider, for example, the determinable property of having shape in general. Intuitively, representing an object as having shape in general is more abstract than representing it as having a determinate shape, such as square or circular. And for similar reasons, representing a pair of objects as being congruent or incongruent in shape is more abstract than representing each of the determinate shapes of the objects, and even more abstract than representing both objects as having the same/different determinate shape(s).

Following David Premack (1983), cognitive scientists have come to call relations of same/difference in second-order or determinable properties *second-order relations* and relations of same/difference in first-order or determinate properties *first-order relations*, taking mental representations of the former (abstract) relations as a mark of genuine cognition. It would be ideal, then, in developing a test for belief attribution in animals to run an experiment that tested for the capacity to attribute an intentional relation (such as cognitively appearing) to abstract states of affairs involving second-order or determinable relations. Just such a protocol can be developed, I believe, and I attempt to do this in section 4.9 below. To distinguish this type of belief-attribution test from the revisability tests, I call it the abstract belief-attribution test.

4.5   A Simple Appearance–Reality Screening Test

In sections 4.6 and 4.7, I describe two revisability tests. Both require testing animals on their ability to distinguish appearances from reality (AR) involving deceptive amodal completion stimuli. In this section, I describe a simple AR test using visual amodal completion stimuli; in section 4.7, I do the same for auditory amodal completion stimuli.

As noted in chapter 3, many types of animals are susceptible to amodal completion illusions. Here I want to describe the results from one such study with chimpanzees that is relevant to the AR test I am proposing.

Figure 4.4
In (a), the top and bottom black bars attach to the gray occluding rectangle and move in a congruent manner, giving the appearance of a straight black bar moving behind the rectangle. In (b), the top and bottom black bars attach to the gray occluding rectangle and move in opposite directions, giving the appearance of separate (broken) black bars moving in opposite directions on top of the rectangle.

Using a two-choice delayed match-to-sample task, Sato et al. (1997) showed that an adult chimpanzee reliably matched a unified straight bar when presented with an occluded figure (see figure 4.4a) whose top and bottom portions were aligned and moving in a congruent manner but matched a broken bar when presented with an occluded figure (see figure 4.4b) whose top and bottom portions were misaligned and moving in an incongruent manner.

This and other amodal completion experiments have been taken as evidence that chimpanzees see occluded figures as having certain features (e.g., being straight or unified) even though the figures may not in fact have such features. Thus, chimpanzees appear to be susceptible to a type of visual illusion. What researchers have not yet investigated is whether chimpanzees (or any other animal) can distinguish the apparent from the real shape of an occluded object in those cases where they are given clear countervailing evidence that appearances are deceptive.[24] The AR task described below asks whether chimpanzees, when given evidence that an occluded figure is actually bent or disjointed despite its looking straight or whole to them, take the figure to be as it really is (i.e., as bent or disjointed) or as it visually appears to be (i.e., as straight or whole). If chimpanzees are capable of distinguishing appearance from reality in such cases, then they should take the occluded figure to be bent or disjointed, appearances to the contrary. If, on the other hand, they are incapable of making such a distinction, then they should take the occluded figure to be as it appears (i.e., as a straight or whole object behind an occluder).

Although different methods can be used to try to answer these questions (e.g., match-to-sample tasks such as those used in Sato et al. 1997), I present here a habituation/dishabituation procedure using computer

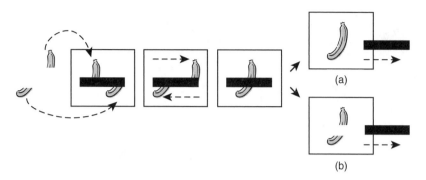

Figure 4.5
Simple appearance–reality test using computer animation.

animated stimuli. Figure 4.5 provides an illustration of a series of still frames from a video that could be used in such an experimental protocol. In the habituation phase of the experiment, the animal is shown a video (such as depicted in figure 4.5) of two pieces of a disjointed object (e.g., two pieces of banana [as shown] or two pieces of a rod) being placed on top of an occluder. (Note that the width of the rectangular occluder is the same size as the missing section between the two banana pieces. Thus, when the banana pieces align themselves on top of the occluder in the third frame, there will still be a missing portion between them that is the width of the occluder.) The object's continued disjointedness can be further demonstrated to the animal by having the pieces move in opposite directions, as Sato et al. (1997) did with the misaligned bars. The pieces are then brought into alignment, giving the illusion of a whole occluded object, as illustrated by the third frame in figure 4.5. The stimulus in the third frame is shown to the animal long enough to induce amodal completion (say, half a second or more).[25] This ends the habituation phase of the experiment.

Given the results from Sato et al. (1997), we have reason to believe that chimpanzees will see the figure in the third frame in figure 4.5 as an occluded *whole* banana. The question is whether the chimpanzees will believe the figure to be as it appears (a whole banana behind an occluder) or as it really is (aligned banana pieces on top of a rectangle). If the former, then chimpanzees should expect to find a whole banana behind the occluder when it is suddenly removed, but if they believe the latter, then they should expect to find banana pieces once the occluder is removed. These expectations can be determined by violating them and measuring the animals' looking times. Chimpanzees, like many animals, are known to look longer at unexpected events than at expected ones (see, e.g., Cacchione & Krist 2004; Slocombe et al. 2010).

The testing phase occurs immediately after the habituation phase. In the testing phase, the occluding bar is suddenly removed (or the occluded object is brought out from behind the occluder) to reveal the object as whole (figure 4.5a) or as disjointed (figure 4.5b).[26] If chimpanzees are able to make an appearance–reality distinction in the case of occluded objects, then they should be able to comprehend that, from the countervailing evidence given in the habituation phase, there really is not a whole banana behind the occluder, despite its coming to look that way once the pieces are aligned. Such chimpanzees, then, should be surprised (look longer) at the presence of a whole banana (figure 4.5a) and be unsurprised (look less) at the presence of banana pieces (figure 4.5b) once the occluder is removed. On the other hand, if chimpanzees are unable to make an appearance–reality distinction and simply think "If it looks like a whole banana, then it is a whole object banana," then they should be surprised (look longer) at the presence of banana pieces (figure 4.5b) and be unsurprised (look less) at the presence of a whole banana (figure 4.5a) once the occluder is removed.[27]

However, it is possible that a chimpanzee could pass this simple AR test without discriminating between the way the stimulus in the third frame of figure 4.5 looks to it (as a whole occluded banana) and the way it knows the stimulus to really be (aligned banana pieces attached to the top of the occluding bar), for the chimpanzee might simply fail to attended to the third (critical) frame in the video and simply attended to the first and second frames of the habituation phase (where it was shown banana pieces) and the concluding frame of the testing phase (where it was shown either banana pieces or a whole banana on the screen). In this case, the chimpanzee might well be surprised to see a whole banana on the screen in the last frame of the testing phase but unsurprised to see banana pieces, given that it saw banana pieces and not a whole banana in the first and second frames of the habituation phase. Thus, such a chimpanzee would not have made any discrimination between the way the stimulus in the third (critical) frame looks to it and the way it knows the stimulus to really be, yet it would give the same differential looking in the testing phase of the experiment as a chimpanzee that made such a discrimination.

It is important, then, to makes sure that the chimpanzee attends to the (critical) stimulus presented in the third frame above and does so long enough to induce amodal completion. An eye tracker or a video camera embedded in the computer monitor can be used to determine whether the

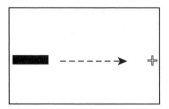

Figure 4.6
Training phase, in which the chimpanzee learns to use the joystick to move the
rectangle on the computer screen over to the cross.

chimpanzee did in fact attend to the critical stimulus for the required
length of time. However, it may be better to design the experiment so that
the chimpanzee is actually made to attend to the critical stimulus. One
way to do this is to complicate the simple AR test above in the following
way. In this version of the test, chimpanzees are first trained to use a joystick to move a rectangle on the computer screen to a designated location,
such as a cross located on the far side of the screen (see figure 4.6).[28]

To start the trial, the chimpanzee is taught to unlock the stationary
rectangle by touching it. Once unlocked, the rectangle can be moved by
means of the joystick. However, in its path toward the cross, the rectangle
will occasionally become locked again and remain stationary. The only way
for the chimpanzee to unlock the rectangle at this point is for it to touch
it again. Where or whether the rectangle will become stuck in its path
toward the cross will vary from trial to trial. Thus, as a result of not
knowing where or whether the rectangle will become stuck again, the
chimpanzee will need to monitor closely its movement across the screen.
Once the rectangle makes contact with the cross, the chimpanzee is
rewarded with food and the trial ends.

Once the chimpanzee has mastered the training phase, it is given a test
trial in which it is required to move the rectangle through a disjointed
banana (or some other amputated shape) on its way to the cross (see figure
4.7 below).

It seems plausible that the chimpanzee will notice the banana pieces on
the screen at the beginning of the test trial, given their unexpected presence. It also seem plausible that on test trials, the chimpanzee will, due to
its earlier training, proceed to unlock the rectangle by touching it and use
the joystick to move the rectangle toward the cross. On its way to the cross,
however, the rectangle unexpectedly becomes locked between the two
pieces of banana, as shown in the second frame in figure 4.7. To unlock

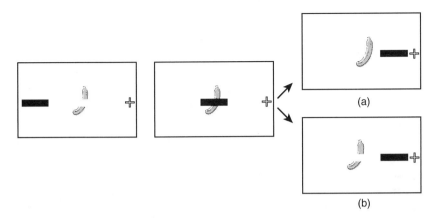

Figure 4.7
Testing phase, in which the chimpanzee is required to move the rectangle through the banana pieces to the cross. The rectangle unexpectedly becomes locked when it is between the banana pieces (second frame), and the chimpanzee must touch the rectangle to unlock it. This will require the chimpanzee to attend to the stimulus in the second frame. The chimpanzee is then shown one of two endings. In (a), the rectangle as it moves toward the cross reveals a whole banana underneath. In (b), the rectangle as it moves toward the cross reveals two banana pieces.

it, the chimpanzee must touch the rectangle again. This, of course, will require the chimpanzee to notice and attend to the stimulus in the second frame for a certain length of time. It is plausible to suppose that the length of time it takes the chimpanzee to notice that the rectangle is locked, to unlock it by touching it, and then to monitor whether the rectangle is responding to the joystick would be sufficient for the attended-to stimulus to induce amodal completion in the chimpanzee. Again, given the results from Sato et al. 1997, we have grounds to believe that such an occluded figure (when attended to for a sufficient length of time) will look to the chimpanzee to be an occluded whole banana.

Once it has unlocked the rectangle, the chimpanzee is then expected to continue moving the figure toward the cross and away from the banana pieces. At this point, two types of trials are run: (a) one in which the rectangle, once it is moved away from the banana pieces, reveals a whole banana behind it (figure 4.7a), and (b) one in which the rectangle reveals the original banana pieces (figure 4.7b).

The question is, given that the stimulus in the second frame looks to the chimpanzee to be an occluded whole banana (supported by Sato et al. 1997), does the chimpanzee take it to be an occluded whole banana or just two pieces of a banana aligned on top of the rectangle (as it has reason to believe the stimulus really is based upon its observation that the rectangle moved between the banana pieces earlier)? If the chimpanzee has the former view (if it is a phenomenalist, as it were), then it should not be surprised in test trial (a) to see a whole banana behind the rectangle once the rectangle is moved out of the way, but it should be surprised in test trial (b) to see two banana pieces instead. Such a chimpanzee, then, should look longer at the banana pieces in trial (b) than at the whole banana in trial (a); whereas, if the chimpanzee has the latter view—if it is capable of making an appearance–reality distinction, that is—then it should not be surprised in test trial (b) to see the banana pieces once the rectangle is removed, but it should be surprised in test trial (a) to see a whole banana instead. Such a chimpanzee, then, should look longer at the whole banana in trial (a) than at the banana pieces in trial (b). If, on the other hand, the chimpanzee simply ignores the stimulus presented in the second frame of figure 4.7 altogether, then it would not have noticed that the rectangle has become locked and, thus, would not have unlocked it, which would have prevented it from proceeding to either trial (a) or (b). Such a chimpanzee, then, would not (in fact, could not) give the same differential looking times for the two types of stimuli in the test trials that a chimpanzee capable of making an appearance–reality distinction is expected to.

4.6   Revisability Belief-Attribution Protocol No. 1

Those animals that test positive on this slightly more complex AR test can then be used as subjects on the following belief-attribution task using video animated stimuli. It should be mentioned at the start that the use of animated shapes and images on a computer and television screen is now a rather routine method in comparative and developmental psychology for testing mindreading abilities (specifically, goal attributions) in chimpanzees, young children, and adults, and it has generally yielded rather robust positive results (see Heider & Simmel 1944; Premack & Woodruff 1978; Gergely et al. 1995; Premack & Premack 1997; Uller 2004; Kuhlmeier et al. 2003; Surian et al. 2007; Csibra 2008; Campbell et al. 2009). Thus, although the belief-attribution experiment described below is quite novel, its methodology is generally taken by researchers to be a quite sound way of testing for mindreading capacities in nonlinguistic subjects, such as animals and young children—and so, on to the experimental design.

In the familiarization phase of the experiment, the test animal (e.g., a chimpanzee) is habituated to the movements of a conspecific in two sets

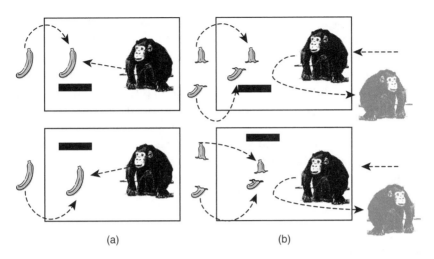

(a)   (b)

Figure 4.8
The test animal watches two sets of familiarization videos. In one set (a), the video chimpanzee is onscreen before the whole banana appears, at which point the video chimpanzee retrieves the banana. In the other set (b), the banana pieces come onscreen first, and then the video chimpanzee arrives, looks at the banana pieces, and departs.

of video scenes (see figure 4.8). In one set of scenes, figure 4.8a, the video chimpanzee is onscreen first, then the whole banana appears, at which point the video chimpanzee is shown to move toward the whole banana. In the contrasting sets of scenes, figure 4.8b, the banana pieces appear onscreen first, then the video chimpanzee arrives, sees the pieces and quickly departs. If the test animal is capable of attributing perceptual beliefs (see section 4.4 above), then the video chimpanzee's movements should suggest to the test animal that the video chimpanzee is attracted to stimuli that it has reason to believe are whole bananas and repulsed by stimuli that it has reason to believe are strange/unappealing banana parts. (To make it understandable to the test animals why the video chimpanzee might be repulsed by banana parts, the parts can be made to look strange or unappealing by giving their ends unusual shapes or colors as I have tried to do here. If this proves to be impracticable—perhaps, the viewing animal simply cannot comprehend why the video chimpanzee might be repulsed by banana parts no matter how unusual they may appear—then other stimuli can be used. For example, the stimuli may be, respectively, an attractive-looking ball [attractive stimulus] and a ball that has a jagged triangular wedge cut out of it [repulsive stimulus], making it look like an open mouth or a Pac-Man with intimidating-looking teeth.) If, on the other hand, the test animal is capable of attributing only simple states of perceptual appearing (see section 4.4 above), then the video chimpanzee's movements will be suggestive of its attraction to stimuli that visually look to it to be whole bananas and repulsed by stimuli that visually look to it to be strange/unappealing banana parts. And if the test animal is capable of behavior reading only, then the video chimpanzee's movements will be suggestive of its attraction to stimuli that are in fact whole bananas and repulsed by stimuli that are in fact strange/unappealing banana parts.

In the testing phase of the experiment, the test animal is shown the video chimpanzee presented with what looks to be a whole banana that is occluded by a bar (see figures 4.9 and 4.10). In test (I), the video chim-

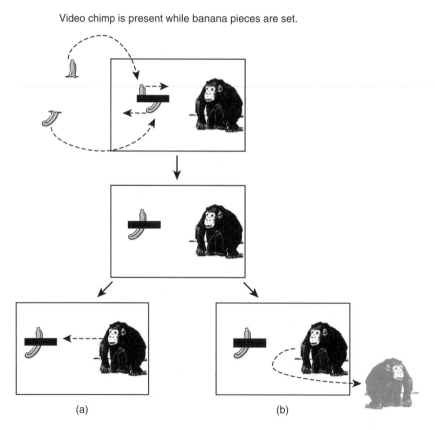

Video chimp is present while banana pieces are set.

(a)   (b)

Figure 4.9
Testing phase (I).

Banana pieces are set before video chimp arrives.

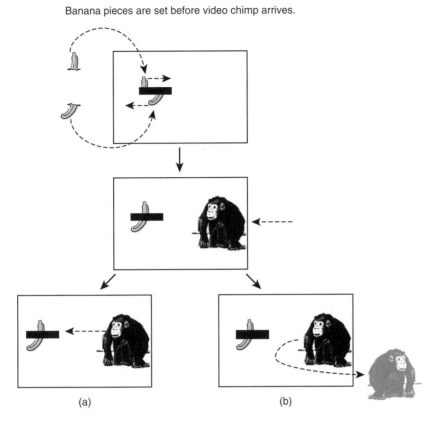

Figure 4.10
Testing phase (II).

panzee has 'reason to believe' that the apparent whole banana is not really a whole banana but banana pieces since the video chimpanzee was on the scene at the time that the banana pieces were fitted to the black bar and the pieces were moved in opposite directions, suggesting continued disjointedness (countervailing evidence). In test (II), however, the video chimpanzee has 'reason to believe' that the apparent whole banana *is* a whole banana since it looks that way and the video chimpanzee was not on the scene while the banana pieces were fitted to the bar and moved in opposed directions.[29] Each test video (I and II) has two different endings that are shown to the test animal. In (A) endings, the video chimpanzee is shown to be attracted to the apparent whole banana; in (B) endings, it is shown to be repulsed by the apparent whole banana. The question is which of these endings the test animal expects and which it find surprising.

Now for the predictions: If the test animal is a simple perceptual-appearing attributor (see section 4.4 above), then in both test cases (I and II), it should expect (A) the video chimpanzee to be attracted to the perceptually apparent whole banana behind the occluder since in both cases the stimuli presented to the video chimpanzee visually look to it to be an occluded whole banana, and in the habituation phase the video chimpanzee was always attracted to stimuli that visually looked to it to be whole bananas and repulsed by those that visually looked to it to be banana pieces. Thus, the simple perceptual-appearing-attributing animal ought to be surprised by the (B) endings in both test videos and, as a result, ought to look longer at these endings than at the (A) endings.

A belief-attributing animal, however, is predicted to have different expectations (see section 4.4 above). In test (I), for instance, it should expect (B) the video chimpanzee to be repulsed by the perceptually apparent whole banana behind the occluder since in witnessing the banana pieces being fitted to the bar and moved in opposite directions (countervailing evidence), the video chimpanzee has reason to believe that there is not a whole banana behind the bar (contrary to visual appearances), and in the past the video chimpanzee was always repulsed by stimuli it had reason to believe were not whole bananas. Thus, a test animal that understood the video chimpanzee's behavior in these terms should be surprised to see (A) the video chimpanzee being attracted to the aligned banana pieces in the test (I) and should, as a result, look longer at the (A) ending than at the (B) ending.

In test (II), however, the belief-attributing animal should expect (A) the video chimpanzee to be attracted to the perceptually apparent whole banana behind the occluder since it has reason to believe that there is a whole banana behind the bar, given that it looks that way to the video chimpanzee and, being absent during the placement and alignment of the banana pieces to the occluder, it has no reason to believe otherwise. What is more, in the past the video chimpanzee has always been attracted to stimuli that it had reason to believe (and no reason not to believe) were whole bananas. Thus the belief-attributing animal ought to be surprised by the (B) ending in test (II) and look longer at this ending than at the (A) ending.

The last prediction we need to consider is that of the complementary behavior-reading counterpart to our belief-attributing test animal. The complementary behavior reader, recall, is expected to uses the very same observable cues to anticipate the video chimpanzee's movements as our belief-attributing test animal is hypothesized to use to attribute its beliefs to the video chimpanzee. The question is whether the complementary behavior reader could use these cues to make the same predictions of the video chimpanzee's movements as our belief-attributing test animal. The answer is no, and here is why. In test (I), our belief-attributing test animal uses the observable cue of the banana pieces being fitted to the bar and moved in opposite directions *in the presence* of the video chimpanzee as its grounds for attributing the belief to the video chimpanzee that there is not a whole banana behind the bar. However, this observable cue was not present in the familiarization phase of the experiment, for the video chimpanzee in the familiarization phase was not present while the banana pieces were brought onto the scene and set in place. And so the behavior-reading test animal could not use this observable cue as its basis to anticipate the chimpanzee's behavior in the test condition.

It is possible, of course, that the behavior-reading test animal might rely upon some other observable cue in the familiarization trial to anticipate that the video chimpanzee in test (I) will be repulsed (B) by the banana pieces. For example, in the familiarization trials the video chimpanzee was always repulsed *once it came* to have a direct line of gaze with the stationary banana pieces. And so it might be suggested, using this cue, the behavior-reading chimpanzee would anticipate that the video chimpanzee in test (I) would be repulsed (B) once it came to have a direct line of gaze with the stationary banana pieces. Thus, on this hypothesis, the behavior-reading test animal should be surprised by the (A) ending in test (I) and look longer at that ending than at the (B) ending, just like the belief-attributing test animal is predicted to do.

There are two problems with this suggestion, however. First, the behavior-reading test animal in this suggested hypothesis is not a complementary behavior reader since it does not anticipate the video chimpanzee's behavior by means of the same observable cue that the belief-attributing test animal is hypothesized to use to attribute its belief. Thus, the suggestion is simply an admission that the experiment solves the logical problem since it accepts that a complementary behavior-reading test animal would not have the same expectation of the video chimpanzee's behavior in the test as its belief-attributing counterpart. The second problem with this suggestion is that if this were the observable cue that the behavior-reading test animal uses to anticipate that the video chimpanzee in test (I) would be repulsed (B), then this very same animal should expect the very same behavior from the video chimpanzee in test (II), for there too the video chimpanzee comes to have a direct line of gaze with stationary banana pieces.[30] However, this is precisely what the belief-attributing test animal does *not* expect the video chimpanzee to do in test (II). Hence, either way, the belief-attributing test animal is predicted to have different expectations of the video chimpanzee's behavior on the two tests (I and II) from either its complementary behavior-reading counterpart or the minimal behavior-reading counterpart that we are presently considering.

Finally it is worth mentioning that it is highly unlikely that a behavior-reading test animal could anticipate (B) in test (I) and (A) in test (II) by reflecting on how it would behave were it in the video chimpanzee's situation—for recall that the behavior-reading test animal (whether complementary or minimal) lacks mental state concepts, and so it is difficult to see how it would make sense of its being (B) repulsed by an object that looks to it to be an occluded whole banana in test (I) but (A) attracted to such an object in test (II) unless it could understand that in the former cases it would have *reason to believe* that things are not as they appear, and in the latter case that it would have *reason to believe* that things are as they appear. However, the behavior-reading test animal, lacking the requisite mental state concepts, would be unable to grasp this psychological difference. Thus, whether the behavior-reading test animal relies on associations of the video chimpanzee's movements from the familiarization phase of the experiment or whether it reasons from its own case, its expectations of (and thus its looking-time responses to) the video chimpanzee's movements in the test cases will be different from those of its belief-attributing counterpart.

Thus, this belief-attribution test has the power, unlike any currently being used, to distinguish genuine belief-attributing animals (e.g., chimpanzees) from their complementary behavior-reading counterparts, as well as from their simple perceptual-appearing-attributing compadres. (See Lurz 2010 for a demonstration of how the above protocol can also discriminate between genuine belief-attributing animals and those capable of attributing only states of knowledge and ignorance).

4.7 Revisability Belief-Attribution Protocol No. 2

Auditory amodal completion (sometimes called 'auditory induction' or 'auditory restoration') has been experimentally observed in monkeys (Miller et al. 2001), cats (Sugita 1997), and birds (Seeba & Klump 2009; Braaten & Leary 1999) and may well exist in other species (for review, see Petkov & Sutter forthcoming). In one of the first experiments of auditory amodal completion in monkeys, Miller et al. (2001) played recordings of three versions of a species-specific whistle to cotton-top tamarins. One version was a whole, complete whistle (whole whistle); another was a whistle with a block of silence placed in the middle (middle-silence whistle); and the third was a whistle similar to the second except that the block of silence was filled in with white noise (middle-noise whistle). The researchers discovered that the monkeys called back to the whole whistles (as is their normal response behavior) as well as to the middle-noise whistles. However, the monkeys did not respond when they heard the middle-silence whistles. The tamarins, it appears, took the middle-noise whistles to be whole whistles that were partially occluded by white noise.

More recently, Chris Petkov and colleagues (2003, 2007) received similar results with macaque monkeys. In their study, the monkeys were initially trained to detect with a lever release whether a foreground sound was discontinuous (i.e., had a middle-silence gap in it). In separate experiments, the authors used a macaque 'coo' call, a frequency-modulated tone, or a pure tone as the foreground sound to be detected. After the monkeys reached criterion in detecting the foreground sounds with middle-silence gaps, noise was faded into the gap and the researchers discovered that the monkeys treated the middle-noise sound as if it were the same as a whole sound (e.g., a whole 'coo' call). In other words, the macaques failed to detect the gap in the sound, and their psychophysical performance was very much like they were experiencing the illusion of a continuous foreground sound occluded by noise.

What the above research shows is that monkeys are able to treat two different auditory stimuli (a whole sound and a middle-noise sound) as belonging to the same auditory type (a whole foreground sound). What researchers have not yet investigated, however, is whether monkeys (or other animals) are able to treat two identical auditory stimuli as belonging to different auditory types. Can monkeys, for example, understand of two identical sounds (e.g., two identical middle-silence sounds) that one is as it phenomenally appears (a middle-silence sound) while the other is different from what it phenomenally appears (i.e., that it is really a whole foreground sound that is partially occluded)? If so, this would be evidence of a kind of appearance–reality distinction in monkeys for auditory stimuli. Such a discrimination would be analogous to that of understanding that a straight stick in water and the bent stick on land, though phenomenologically identical (they both look bent), are in fact different kinds of sticks (the one straight, the other bent). And if monkeys can make such an appearance–reality distinction with auditory stimuli, can they go on to use it to anticipate another agent's behavior in terms of whether they think the agent makes such a similar distinction as well? In this section, I describe an experimental protocol that can be used to test both of these possibilities. As with the experiment protocol described in sections 4.6 above, the one described here begins with a simple AR test.

Before describing the AR test, it is important to mention an underlying assumption of the experimental design. The assumption is that sounds can be partially occluded by physical barriers as well as by masking noises, and that in some instances, seeing that a physical barrier is what is responsible for the silent portion of a middle-silence sound will cause one to hear or interpret the middle-silence sound as a whole sound that is partially occluded. To illustrate, imagine watching a bee buzzing continuously as it weaves its way through a glade of trees. As it passes behind a large tree, the buzzing emitted by the bee will be (partially or wholly) occluded. As a result, you will not hear (or not hear as well) that portion of the buzzing that the bee is making while it is momentarily behind the tree. The sound that one phenomenally hears, however, is the sound of a middle-silence buzzing (that is the sound you would hear, e.g., were you to have closed your eyes and simply listened). Nevertheless, given what you saw, you will quite naturally amodally complete (restore) the missing part of the buzzing; you will interpret the middle-silence buzzing as a whole buzzing that is partly occluded by the tree. Your reason for doing so, of course, is that you witness the bee go behind the tree and, thus, take the tree, and not the bee, to be what caused the middle-silence gap in the buzzing. Although what you phenomenally hear (middle-silence buzzing) is one thing, what you take the noise to be (a whole buzzing) is another, and that is a type of auditory appearance–reality discrimination. The question is whether any animal might be capable of making a similar discrimination between two phenomenally identical middle-silence sounds, one of which the animal has reason to believe is different from how it phenomenally appears.

The AR test here aims to address this question. In the training phase of the experiment, the animals (e.g., macaque monkeys) are trained to judge whether a sample sound (e.g., a whole buzzing sound or a middle-silence buzzing sound) is the same as or different from a subsequent target sound produced by an onscreen object (e.g., a bee) moving across the computer screen.[31] If the target sound matches the sample (e.g., both are whole buzzing sounds), then the test animal viewing the video is rewarded for pressing the S shape on the touch-screen computer; if the sounds are different (e.g., the sample is a whole buzzing sound and the target is a middle-silence buzzing), then the animal is rewarded for pressing the D shape on the screen (see figure 4.11).

Offscreen sample sound (whole buzzing): Buzzzzzzzzzzzzzzzzzzzzzzzzzzzz

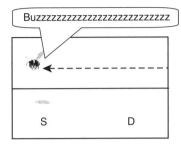 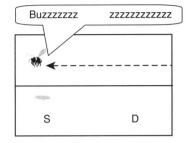

(a) Target sound: whole buzzing
    produced by bee on computer
    screen.

(b) Target sound: middle-silence
    buzzing produced by bee on
    computer screen.

Figure 4.11
While viewing the computer screen, the test animal is first presented with an off-screen sample sound: either a continuous, whole buzzing sound (as shown here) or a middle-silence buzzing sound (not shown here). After the sample sound is presented, the test animal watches while a bee flies across the scene on the computer while emitting either (a) a continuous, whole buzzing sound or (b) a middle-silence buzzing sound. After the bee exits the screen, the test animal is allowed to selected S or D on the computer. In the case illustrated here, since the sample is a whole buzzing sound, the animal is rewarded for selecting S if shown (a) and D if shown (b). If the sample had been a middle-silence buzzing, the animal would have been rewarded for selecting S if shown (b) and D if shown (a).

After the test animals reach criterion on this phase of the experiment, they are given a series of test trials (see figure 4.12). The tests are the same as the training trials except that the onscreen bee is shown to fly either behind an occluder—as in figure 4.12a—or in front of it—as in figure 4.12b. In both cases, what the animal hears is the same sound—a middle-silence buzzing.

Despite the target stimuli in test (a) and (b) being phenomenally the same sound, there is evidence presented visually in (a) that indicates that the sound is really an occluded whole buzzing sound, and evidence presented visually in (b) that indicates that it is just as it phenomenally appears: a middle-silence buzzing. For in (a), the silence is shown to be due to the bee going behind the occluder; whereas in (b), it is shown to be due to the bee itself. If the test animal can likewise make such an AR distinction, then we should expect it to take the auditory stimulus presented in (4.12a) as an occluded whole-buzzing sound and, thus, select S

Offscreen sample sound (whole buzzing): Buzzzzzzzzzzzzzzzzzzzzzzzzzzzzzz

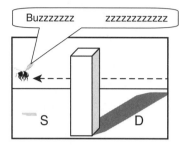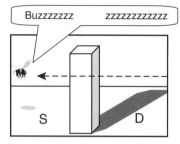

(a) Target sound: middle-silence
    buzzing while bee flies behind
    occluder.

(b) Target sound: middle-silence
    buzzing while bee flies in front
    of occluder.

Figure 4.12

While viewing the computer screen, the test animal is presented with the offscreen sample sound: either a continuous, whole buzzing sound (as shown here) or a middle-silence buzzing sound (not shown here). After the sample has been presented, the test animal then watches while the bee is shown flying behind the occluder (a) or in front of it (b). In both cases, the target sound presented to the animal is a middle-silence buzzing.

(if the sample was a whole buzzing) and to take the auditory stimulus presented in (4.12b) as a middle-silence buzzing and, thus, select D (if the sample was a whole buzzing).

Those animals that perform in this way are then allowed to participate in the following belief-attributing experiment. The experimental paradigm used here is that of anticipatory looking, as opposed to violation of expectancy used in the belief-attributing experiment described in section 4.6 above. (However, as noted below, one could easily run the experiment as a violation of expectancy.) In the experiment, the test animal is first habituated to a set of conditional behaviors of a human actor depicted in a video. In addition to the actor, the following props are used in the video: two different colored buttons on either side of the actor that light up, a wall behind the actor that blocks the actor's view of the events happening in the background, and an occluding rectangular post positioned behind the wall. The video itself is shown to the animal on a computer monitor mounted to a wall, and on the wall directly below the monitor are two covered trays in which food rewards are delivered. Each food tray is positioned directly under the colored buttons in the video (see figure 4.13).

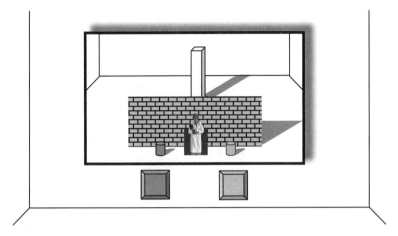

Figure 4.13
General setup for belief-attribution experiment from the perspective of the test animal. The squares on the wall below the computer monitor are the covered trays in which food rewards are delivered to the test animal.

The habituation trials begin with the human actor on the screen facing forward with his or her head cocked to one side as if prepared to hear a sound. At this point, one of two sounds is then played offscreen: either a continuous, whole buzzing sound or a middle-silence buzzing sound. After the sound is played, the buttons on either side of the actor illuminate. (The illumination of the buttons will serve as an indicator to the test animal that the actor is about to make a selection.) The actor waits for a few seconds and then proceeds to press one of the buttons according to the following conditional rule: If a whole buzzing sound was played, the actor presses the red button (and food is then immediately delivered into the covered food tray below that button); if a middle-silence buzzing sound was played, the actor presses the green button (and food is then immediately delivered into the covered food tray below that button). In either instance, after the actor has pressed a button, the test animal is allowed to raise the cover on the food tray and eat the food inside.

After a number of trials, it is hoped, the animal will eventually come to anticipate the actor's differential responses to the auditory stimuli. This can be measured by seeing which button or food tray the animal is prone to look to immediately after seeing the buttons in the video light up. The animal should look toward the button it expects the human to press (or toward the tray under the button to which it expects to find food). Once the animal demonstrates that it expects the actor in the video to behave in accordance with the above conditional rule, the following two sets of tests are run:

Ignorance test trials These trials are just like the habituation trials except that the auditory stimulus is produced by an onscreen bee that flies behind the wall and, hence, out of view of the (ignorant) human actor.[32] There are two types of ignorance trials that are run. In the behind-the-occluder ignorance trials, the onscreen bee flies behind the rectangular occluding post, similar to that shown in figure 4.12a above. The sound that the test animals hears in this case is a middle-silence buzzing—again, similar to that shown in figure 4.12a. After the bee exits from the screen, the two buttons beside the human actor light up. This ends the test trial. (Alternatively, one could also have the actor actually go on to select the red button on some of these trials and the green button on others, using a violation-of-expectancy paradigm to determine what the test animal expects the actor to do in each type of test trial.) In the in-front-of-the occluder ignorance trials, the bee is shown to fly in front of the rectangular occluder and to emit a middle-silence buzzing, similar to that shown in figure 4.12b. After the bee exits the screen, the trial continues just as in the behind-the-occluder ignorance trials.

Knowledgeable test trials In these test trials, the human actor is shown to be looking over the wall and at the bee as it comes onscreen. As with the ignorance trials, there are two types of knowledgeable trials. In the behind-the-occluder knowledgeable trials, the human actor observes while the bee is shown flying behind the rectangular occluder (similar to figure 4.12a). In the in-front-of-the-occluder knowledgeable trials, the actor observes while the bee is shown flying in front of the rectangular occluder (similar to figure 4.12b). In both cases, the auditory stimulus that is played is the same—a middle-silence buzzing.

Predictions are as follows. If the test animal can make the appearance–reality distinction presented in the auditory AR test above, and it can go on to use this discriminatory ability, according to the ARM theory of mindreading, as a way to understand what the human actor in the video is likely to believe regarding the true nature of the sound stimulus presented in the test trials, then the animal is expected to have the following expectations regarding the actor's beliefs and subsequent behavior. In both of the ignorance trials, as well as in the in-front-of-the-occluder knowledgeable trials, the belief-attributing animal should understand that the actor is likely to believe that the sound stimulus is as it phenomenally appears—as a middle-silence buzzing—and to act as he or she did in the habituation trials when he or she heard what he or she had reason to believe was a middle-silence buzzing—that is, to select the green button. In the behind-the-occluder knowledgeable trials, however, the belief-attributing animal should understand that the human actor is likely to believe, of the sound stimulus (i.e., middle-silence buzzing) presented, that it is really a whole buzzing sound that is partially occluded by the rectangular barrier and to act as he or she did in the habitation phase when he or she heard what he or she had reason to believe was a whole buzzing sound—that is, to select the red button. Thus, such an animal is expected to look first or more often at the green button (or the tray under it) after the buttons illuminate in the former set of test trials and at the red button (or the tray under it) after the buttons illuminate in the behind-the-occluder knowledgeable test trials.

This same differential looking is not expected from either a simple perceptual-appearing-attributing animal or a complementary behavior-reading animal. Regarding the former, since the sound that the actor phenomenally hears is the same in each test trial (middle-silence buzzing) and since the actor always selected the green button in the habituation phase when he or she heard what phenomenally sounded like a middle-silence buzzing, the simple perceptual-appearing-attributing animal should expect the actor to select the green button on all of the different test trials.

The complementary behavior reader, of course, is expected to use the very same observable grounds to anticipate the actor's behavior in the test trials that the belief-attributing test animal is hypothesized to use to attribute its beliefs to the actor. However, in the knowledgeable test trials, part of the observable grounds that the belief-attributing animal is hypothesized to use is the fact that the actor had a direct line of gaze to the bee while it flew in front of or behind the rectangular occluder. However, neither of these objective, observable features was presented in the habituation trials. Thus, either the complementary behavior-reading animal is expected to have no expectation of what the human actor is likely to do in the knowledgeable test trials, or it may simply expect the actor to behave as he or she did in the habituation phase when a middle-silence buzzing was presented—that is, select the green button.

It is quite possible, of course, that the complementary behavior-reading animal takes the middle-silence sound stimulus in the behind-the-occluder knowledgeable trials to be a whole buzzing sound and, thus, expects the actor to behave as he or she did in the habituation phase when a whole buzzing sound was presented—that is, select the red button. However, on this hypothesis, we would expect the complementary behavior-reading animal to predict the same behavior (select red button) on the behind-the-occluder ignorance trials, which is not what the belief-attributing animal is expecting the actor to do. Thus, it appears that no matter which way one tries to conceive of how the complementary behavior-reading animal might come to make determinate predictions of the human actor's behavior in the different test trials, these predictions will not be the same as those expected by the belief-attributing animal.

4.8   Representation of Abstract Relations by Primates

As argued in section 4.4., there are two ways of understanding the difference between belief attribution and perceptual state attribution in animals on the ARM theory. The first, which was examined in the last two sections, is in terms of revisability: Beliefs are revisable in light of countervailing evidence in the way that perceptual states are generally not, and animals capable of attributing beliefs should show signs of understanding this feature of beliefs. The other way to distinguish belief attribution from perceptual state attribution in animals, which is to be examined in this section, is in term of abstractness. Beliefs, unlike perceptual states, can be about increasingly more abstract states of affairs—states of affairs, for example, involving higher-order or determinable properties and relations. It takes little thought or cognition, for example, to recognize that the two objects before you are both square—one can simply see this; however, it does require some thought and cognition to recognize that the two objects are congruent (i.e., same shaped), distinct from what determinate shape they may appear to have. Their being congruent is not the same as their both being square since many object pairs are congruent even though their members are not both square. Thus, the state of affairs of the pair's being congruent is an abstract or higher-order state of affairs that is (we can say) determined by (but not reducible to) the more concrete (observable) state of affairs of each object in the pair being square. Thus, to recognize the pair as being congruent requires possessing and applying an abstract concept of congruency which represents a relational property that goes beyond what can be directly seen. And much the same can be said for states of affairs involving other types of higher-order or determinable relations (e.g., the relation same color or same function, etc.). To recognize such abstract states of affairs requires something more than just perception—it requires cognition, thought, and abstract concepts. Thus, to represent an agent as standing in an intentional relation, such as seeing-as, to such an abstract state of affairs—especially one on which the agent is known to be prepared to act—is tantamount to representing the agent as bearing a belief relation to the state of affairs (as argued in 4.4 above). The question to be examined in the next section is how researchers might go about testing whether animals (e.g., chimpanzees) can attribute such intentional relations to other agents.

Before proceeding to the experimental design, it is important to note that great apes (Oden et al. 2001), as well as some species of monkey (Burdyn & Thomas 1984; Bovet & Vauclair 2001), have been shown to solve analogical or conceptual match-to-sample tasks that ostensibly require them to represent second-order/determinable relations between pairs of objects. It was once thought (Premack 1988; Thompson & Oden 1993) that only linguistically trained apes were capable of solving such problems, but this has since been shown to be false by a number of studies with language-naive animal subjects (also with 29-week-old infant children; see Tyrrell et al. 1991). In one of the first of such animal studies (Oden et al. 1990), infant chimpanzees were allowed to manipulate a pair of objects attached to a board. The pair of objects were either the same in appearance (e.g., two bottle caps) or different (e.g., a strip of wood and a metal bracket). In the test trials, the chimpanzees were then given a pair of novel objects to manipulate, objects that they had never seen before. These pairs of novel objects were either the same in appearance (e.g., two plastic chains) or different (e.g., a length of garden hose and a plastic block). The infant chimpanzees, it was discovered, had a decided preference for handling the pair of objects in the test trials whose relation was different from that exemplified by the pair in the familiarization trial—quite irrespective of the objects' individual physical (determinate) characteristics. For example, if the chimpanzees had initially manipulated a pair of objects that were the same (or different) in appearance (no matter what particular characteristics of the objects determined their sameness/difference in appearance), the infant chimpanzees preferred to manipulate a pair of objects that were different (or same) in appearance in the test trial. The infant chimpanzees (much like infant children) appear to have an attraction to relational *novelty*. However, in order to be so attracted to relational novelty, the chimpanzees needed to go beyond simply representing in perception the determinate colors and shapes of the objects before them; they needed to represent (via cognition) the more abstract, higher-order relation of the objects being same-in-appearance or different-in-appearance, as well.

In a follow-up study, Thompson et al. (1997) went further to show that not only can language-naive chimpanzees represent such abstract, higher-order relations but adult language-naive chimpanzees can use these representations to solve conceptual match-to-sample tasks. (Infant chimpanzees, Oden et al. 1990 discovered, do not appear to be capable of using their representations of abstract, higher-order relations instrumentally for the purpose of solving such matching problems.) In their study, Thompson and colleagues presented language-naive, adult chimpanzees with a pair of objects (the sample pair) that were either identical (AA) in appearance or different (CD). The chimpanzees were then presented with two pairs of novel objects (the target pairs): One pair of target objects consisted of identical objects (BB); the other pair consisted of different objects (EF). The researchers discovered that their chimpanzees, without any differential reinforcement training, spontaneously and consistently selected the pair of target objects that exemplified the same higher-order relation exemplified in the sample pair. (Measures were taken to rule out successful performance by association.) What is more, the chimpanzees' performance remained at a consistently high level (80 percent) with novel problem sets. Success on these tests, Thompson and colleagues concluded, "strongly suggest[s] that [chimpanzees] judge the conceptual equivalence of relations between relations" (p. 35).[33] A more recent study by Jennifer Vonk (2003) has shown that even gorillas and orangutans are capable of making similar abstract same/different judgments about relations.[34]

Thus, the idea behind the experimental protocol that I describe below is to exploit this unique cognitive talent in chimpanzees (and other primates) to represent abstract, higher-order relational states of affairs and to see whether they can use it to represent that other agents bear intentional relations to such states of affairs.

4.9 Abstract Belief-Attribution Protocol

The following belief-attribution test employs a violation-of-expectancy paradigm with video animated stimuli similar to the one described in section 4.6 above. This experiment also requires the chimpanzees to take a prescreening AR test with visual amodal completion stimuli like the one described in section 4.5 above. Only those that pass the AR test are allowed to participate in the following experiment.

Figure 4.14
Habituation phase with congruent stimuli. While the computer-generated image (CGI) figure is onscreen and facing away from the trees (not shown here), (1) the congruent stimuli (red and blue rectangles) come from offscreen and place themselves behind the trees. (2) The CGI figure then turns around to face the occluded stimuli (as shown here). After looking toward each occluded shape, the CGI figure knuckle walks down the right path (white arrow).

In the familiarization phase of the experiment, the test animal is habituated to the movements of a computer-generated image (CGI) of a conspecific (perhaps one with which the test animal is familiar). Figures 4.14 and 4.15 show a still frame from the habituation videos. Note that the chimpanzee in the still frames is the CGI figure that the test animal is watching, not the test animal viewing the videos. The video sequence opens with the CGI figure standing in front of two trees. The CGI figure at this point is facing away from the trees and toward the test animal who is watching the video. While the CGI figure's head is turned away from the trees, two sample stimuli (e.g., a red and blue rectangle) from offscreen silently move onto the screen and place themselves behind the trees as shown in step (1) in figures 4.14 and 4.15. After the stimuli are in place, the CGI figure turns around to face the occluded stimuli, as shown in step (2) in figures 4.14 and 4.15. The CGI figure now has the same view of the occluded stimuli as the test animal. After the CGI figure has turned around and has looked at each of the occluded stimuli, it knuckle walks down one of the two paths. Thus, there will be two types of habituation videos shown to

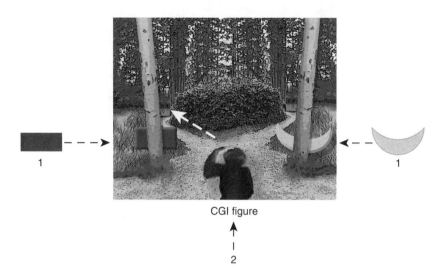

CGI figure
↑
|
2

Figure 4.15
Habituation phase with incongruent stimuli. While the computer-generated image (CGI) figure is onscreen and facing away from the trees (not shown here), (1) the incongruent stimuli (red rectangle and yellow crescent) come from offscreen and place themselves behind the trees. (2) The CGI figure then turns around to face the occluded stimuli (as shown here). After looking toward each occluded shape, the CGI figure knuckle walks down the left path (white arrow).

the test animal. In those videos where the sample stimuli are congruent shapes (as illustrated in figure 4.14), the CGI figure knuckle walks down the right path.

In those videos where the sample stimuli are incongruent shapes (as illustrated in figure 4.15), the CGI figure knuckle walks down the left path.[35]

The test animal is shown these two types of habituation videos a number of times to induce habituation (i.e., the expectation of the CGI figure's actions in the presence of congruent or incongruent stimuli). Various shapes (e.g., circles and triangles) of varying colors can be used as sample stimuli in the habituation videos.

In the testing phase of the experiment, the test animal watches two types of similar videos in which a novel set of occluding stimuli is used. In the 'look-same-but-are-different' video, two sample stimuli (e.g., an amputated orange oval and a whole blue oval) come on the scene. The pieces of the amputated orange oval align themselves to the sides of the left tree while the whole blue oval moves behind the right tree (see figure 4.16).

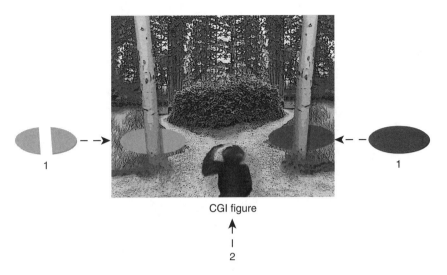

CGI figure

2

Figure 4.16
'Look-same-but-are-different' test video. While the computer-generated image (CGI) figure is onscreen and facing away from the trees (not shown here), (1) the incongurent stimuli come from offscreen and place themselves behind the trees. (2) The CGI figure then turns around to face the occluded stimuli (as shown here).

To reinforce to the test animal that the orange oval pieces attached to the left tree do not constitute a whole oval, the pieces themselves can be moved in opposite directions before they come to align themselves, much in the way that the banana pieces were moved in the AR task in section 4.5 above. Once the oval pieces are aligned, their final placement gives the appearance of a whole occluded oval. At this point, there appear to be two similarly shaped (congruent) objects behind the trees. After the placement of the sample stimuli, the CGI figure turns around to look at them, just as in the habituation videos. At this point, the test animal is shown one of two different endings to the video. In the 'surprise' ending, the CGI figure is shown knuckle walking down the left path.[36] In the 'expected' ending, the CGI figure is shown knuckle walking down the right path. For each ending, the test animal's looking time is measured.

The second test video is the 'look-different-but-are-same' video, in which two sample stimuli of the same shape (e.g., two PacMan shapes) come onto the screen and move behind the trees (see figure 4.17). The occluded stimuli, however, look to be of different shapes. The one on the left looks to be an occluded whole circle while the one on the right looks to be an occluded PacMan.

Figure 4.17

'Look-different-but-are-same' test video. While the computer-generated image (CGI) figure is onscreen and facing away from the trees (not shown here), (1) the same-shaped stimuli come from offscreen and place themselves behind the trees. (2) The CGI figure then turns around to face the occluded stimuli (as shown here).

After the placement of the stimuli, the CGI figure turns around and looks at each, as in the habituation videos. The test animal is then shown one of two endings. In the 'surprise' ending, the CGI figure is shown knuckle walking down the right path.[37] In the 'expected' ending, the CGI figure is shown knuckle walking down the left path. Again, for each of these endings, the test animal's looking time is measured.

It goes without saying that different types of 'deceptive' shapes can be used in the test videos (see figure 4.18), and that the quality of the images in the videos themselves will be more detailed than the schematic representations above.

The beauty behind the belief-attribution protocol presented here is that it is capable of discriminating between a belief-attributing test animal and its simple perceptual-state and behavior-reading counterparts. If those test animals that pass the AR task in section 4.5 are also capable of attributing beliefs involving second-order relations, then they should be able to understand that the CGI figure takes the right path when it believes the occluded objects are congruent, and it takes the left path when it believes the occluded objects are incongruent. Armed with this

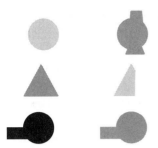

Figure 4.18
Various shapes that can be used in the experiment.

understanding of the CGI figure's behavior in the habituation videos, the test animal should be able to understand that in the 'look-same-but-are-different' video, the CGI figure likely believes that the occluded objects are congruent since they both perceptually look to have the same determinate shape and the CGI figure did not see the objects go behind or align themselves to the trees. Thus, on the basis of this belief attribution, the test animal should anticipate the CGI figure taking the right path and should look longer at the 'surprised' ending (in which the CGI figure takes the left path) than the 'expected' ending (in which the CGI figure takes the right path).

Likewise in the 'look-same-but-are-different' video, the test animal should understand that the CGI figure likely believes that the occluded objects are incongruent—again, since they look to have different determinate shapes and the CGI figure did not see the objects go behind the trees. Thus, the test animal should predict the CGI figure moving down the left path and anticipate the 'expected' ending and be surprised by the 'surprising' one, looking longer at the latter than at the former.

The test animal would not have such expectations of the CGI figure's actions, however, were it capable of attributing only simple perceptual states of first-order determinate states of affairs. Although such a perceptual-appearing-attributing animal would be capable of understanding that the CGI figure mistakenly sees the occluded objects as having the same determinate shape (both oval) in the first test video and different determinate shapes (circle and PacMan) in the second, it would not be able to predict the CGI figure's actions in the test trials on the basis of either of these kinds of first-order perceptual state attributions. Since the determinate shapes of the occluded objects on the test trials are novel, the CGI figure was never shown to have such first-order perceptual states in the habituation videos. Thus, such a perceptual-appearing-attributing animal would have no way of knowing how the CGI figure might behave on the basis of such novel first-order, determinate perceptual states. The point of introducing novel shapes (real and apparent) into the test videos is precisely to test the animals' ability to rise to the more abstract, second-order level of mental state attribution in their understanding of the CGI figure's actions.

The last prediction we need to consider is that of the complementary behavior-reading animal that passed the prescreening AR task described in section 4.5. This animal cannot attribute first-order or second-order perceptual states to agents (such as the CGI figure), but it can represent first-order and second-order relations in the world. Hence, this sort of test animal, through its viewing of the habituation videos, could come to understand that the CGI figure takes the right path when the occluded objects actually have the second-order relation of being congruent, taking the left path when the objects have the second-order relation of being incongruent. The question, then, is how such a behavior-reading animal would represent the second-order relation of the occluded objects in the test videos. Would it represent their relation as it actually is or as it appears to the test animal to be? If it represents the relation as it actually is, then the test animal would make the exact opposite predictions of the CGI figure's behavior in the test videos from its belief-attributing counterpart. This behavior-reading test animal, for example, would expect the CGI figure in the 'look-same-but-are-different' test video to knuckle walk down the left fork since the sample stimuli are in fact incongruent shapes, and this is how the CGI figure responded to incongruent figures in the habituation videos; and the animal would expect the CGI figure in the 'look-different-but-are-the same' test video to knuckle walk down the right fork since the sample stimuli are in fact congruent shapes, and this is how the CGI figure responded to congruent figures in the habituation videos.

On the other hand, if the complementary behavior-reading animal represents the sample stimuli in the test videos as having the second-order relations that they *appear* to have, then it would make the same predictions of the CGI figure's actions as its belief-attributing counterpart. However, it must be remembered that the point of the prescreening AR test was to screen out such subjects in the first place. If the test animal takes the occluded objects in the videos to have the second-order relation that they *appear* to have, despite the animal's being shown that the objects really do not instantiate this relations, then the animal is not able to make an appearance–reality distinction involving occluded objects, and so it would not be included as a subject in the above belief-attribution test. Thus, the only type of behavior-reading animal that could plausibly squeeze through the AR test is one that would be expected to represent the occluded objects in the test videos as having the second-order relation that the objects actually have, appearances to the contrary. And such a behavior-reading animal, as noted above, would be expected to react differently to the different endings in the test videos from its belief-attributing counterpart.

Thus, this type of experimental protocol, like those described in sections 4.6 and 4.7, appears to have the power to discriminate genuine belief-attributing subjects from their simple perceptual-appearing-attributing and complementary behavior-reading counterparts. It is important to note in closing that although the experimental protocols described in this chapter all involve the use of video animated stimuli, they can be run with live or real stimuli, as well. The visual perspective-taking protocols in chapter 3, which all use live/real stimuli, can, for example, be converted into revisability belief-attribution tests by introducing 'knowledgeable agent' trials in which the test animal is shown that the agent is also presented with the countervailing evidence of the perceptual illusion. And in Lurz (forthcoming), I describe a live version of an abstract belief-attribution test similar to the one described in this section. Thus, nothing in the nature of the experimental protocols described here prevents them from being run live.

4.10   Conclusion

Whether animals are capable of attributing beliefs, I have argued, is very much an open empirical question, the various philosophical and empirical arguments to the contrary notwithstanding. What are needed are better and more sensitive tests (in particular, tests that can discriminate genuine belief-attributing subjects from their simple perceptual-appearing-attributing and complementary behavior-reading counterparts) as well as an account of what belief attribution in animals might be if it is not the attribution of propositional attitudes. I have sketched three possible experimental protocols that can make the above discriminations and have defended a nonpropositional account of belief attribution that is applicable to animals. The rest is now in the hands of empirical researchers—and, of course, the animals.

Epilogue

So are animals mindreaders or complementary behavior readers? Do they, in particular, predict other agents' behaviors by attributing cognitive states to them, such as seeing, hearing, knowing, and believing? Or do they predict other agent's behaviors by simply representing the behavioral and environmental cues that serve as the observable grounds for attributing such states?

If the arguments in the past three chapters are sound, then the answer to these questions is that we simply do not know at present. This is disheartening news, I believe, only if there were no way forward to answering these questions. However, as I have argued, there *is* a way forward—though not one commonly recognized by researchers in the field. Although researchers may not presently know whether animals can attribute such mental states or just the observable grounds associated with them, they are now in possession of the sorts of experimental protocols that would provide the cleanest tests for whether animals can do so, for the protocols presented in the past two chapters—unlike those currently used in the field—are capable of discriminating between genuine cognitive state attributing animals and their complementary behavior-reading counterparts. The field of animal social cognition research, I believe, is in a position to answer its strongest methodological challenge—the logical problem.

The proposed experimental protocols have yet to be tested on animals. Of course, if they had been, there would have been little point in arguing for them. This does not diminish their significance, however. Their significance is in showing *how* empirical researchers might come to gain knowledge about animal mindreading, not *that* they already have it. Knowledge requires the elimination of relevant alternatives, and in the field of animal social cognition, the relevant alternative to animals being mindreaders, to their attributing cognitive states in particular, is the hypothesis that they are complementary behavior readers. To know that animals are capable of attributing such mental states requires eliminating the complementary behavior-reading alternative. The question that has bedeviled the field since its inception, as I have tried to show, has been how to eliminate this alternative hypothesis by experimental means. It is this question that I have tried to answer.

Notes

1. The term 'theory-of-mind,' or 'ToM,' is also frequently used in the field to mean the same as what is meant here by 'mindreading' or 'mental state attribution,' and unless otherwise indicated, that is how the term shall be used in this book.

2. This claim will be qualified a bit in chapter 2. My position, more precisely, is that the question of whether animals are capable of attributing cognitive states, such as seeing, hearing, knowing, and believing, is currently unsettled.

3. Of course, there is concern that if animals are discovered to be mindreaders, then given the arguments above that such animals deserve to be recognized as legal or natural persons, it may prove that mindreading animals should *not* be used in such invasive tests.

4. A screen is placed between the chimpanzee and the containers, blocking its view of the baiting process but allowing it to see that the knower (who is on the other side of the screen) has a clear view of the baiting process whereas the guesser (who is absent during the baiting process or is facing away from the process) does not.

5. Not too long after this, Povinelli et al. (1990) also found similar positive results with their chimpanzees using a similar knower–guesser test but received negative results with rhesus monkeys. However, see Heyes (1993, 1994) for criticisms of Povinelli et al.'s (1990) findings.

6. It now appears the children as young as three can attribute false beliefs—at least at an implicit level of representation (Clements & Perner 1994). Onishi and Baillargeon (2005) have recently argued that children as young as fifteen months can attribute false beliefs—although such claims are considered controversial by some researchers (see Perner & Ruffman 2005).

7. See also de Waal (1982) and Byrne (1995).

8. More recently, Bulloch et al. (2008) and Hostetter et al. (2001) used a similar seeing-vs.-unseeing experiment with two trainers and received, from the initial test

trials, positive results from their chimpanzees; Kaminski, Call, and Tomasello (2004) also received initial positive results with their chimpanzees using a seeing-vs.-unseeing protocol but with only one trainer. These studies will be discussed in further detail in chapter 2.

9. Kamar and Olson (1998) used a version of Heyes's experimental protocol on children from three to six years of age and found that its results correlated with other theory-of-mind tests, though the children found Heyes's test more difficult. Only half of those who passed the standard theory-of-mind tests reached a criterion of 75 percent on Heyes's experimental protocol. However, more recently Meltzoff (2007) ran a version of Heyes's experimental protocol with one-year-olds using two types of blindfolds (one with a viewing window cut into it and one without such a window) and received positive results.

10. It should not be assumed, however, that since researchers studying mindreading in animals take a realist view of animal minds and their mindreading capacities, mindreading animals do as well. This does not follow. It is quite possible, and not altogether implausible, to suppose that for mindreading animals, there is simply nothing more to another creature's having mental states than the fact that it tends to behaves as if it does. This is an empirical question, of course, but there are some data that suggest that it may be more than just a possibility. Claudia Uller (2004), for example, found that infant chimpanzees reliably anticipated the trajectory of a rectangle on a computer screen toward a circle only when the rectangle moved as if it had the goal to get to the circle in the most direct way possible. (This study shall be discussed in more detail in chapter 2.) On the assumption that the chimpanzees attribute such a goal to the rectangle, their simple conative state attribution is pretty clearly not underwritten by a realist interpretation of the mind. On any version of realism, rectangles on computer screens do not really have goals represented inside them, and there is no sound reason to think that infant chimpanzees would assume that they did. Moreover, it is quite plausible that the main purpose of mindreading in animals, insofar as it exists, is for predicting other creatures' behaviors. To this end, an animal need make no assumption about whether the attributed mental states are *internal causes* of other creatures' behaviors. Questions of internal causes come into play generally only when an attributor's interests move from being merely predictive to being explanatory (in a way that is not reducible to a type of prediction, such as retrodictive or postdictive explanations)—see Godfrey-Smith (2004). The latter goal, of course, is what interests empirical research-ers, and why, in general, they tend to adopt a realist view of mindreading in ani-mals—they seek to causally explain animals' anticipatory behaviors toward other agents in terms of their having beliefs (internal representations) about the other agents' mental states. It is far from clear that mindreading animals also seek to explain (in a way that is not just a type of prediction) the behaviors of other agents by attributing mental states to them. Thus, it should not be assumed that if animals are mindreaders, they must be thought to attribute inner causal states to other

agents in attributing mental states as some researchers seem to assume (Penn & Povinelli 2007). This issue will be examined more fully in chapter 3.

Chapter 2

1. Other animals that have been added to this list in recent years are dolphins (Tschudin 2001), goats (Kaminski et al. 2006), bee-eaters (Watve et al. 2002), elephants (Nissani 2004), and pigs (Held et al. 2001).

2. Povinelli and Vonk overstate the problem here a bit. It should not be assumed that a behavior-reading animal's prediction of another agent's behavior must involve only a single inferential step—a step from the observed behavioral/environmental cue to the predicted behavior. There is no reason why the behavior-reading animal could not engage in several inferential steps. The important point is that whatever further steps the animal may use, they will not involve the attribution of mental states.

3. As was shown in chapter 1, other researchers—most notably, Cecilia Heyes (1998)—are also credited with identifying the logical problem as a major issue in animal mindreading research. However, in the past ten years or so, due to his forceful arguments on its behalf, the logical problem has come to be associated with Daniel Povinelli. In fact, due to this association, some researchers now call it 'Povinelli's problem' (see Krachun 2008).

4. For a similar distinction along these line for human infants, see Lesie (1994).

5. Consider this analogy: Why do I anticipate my computer booting up when I press a particular button, despite having little (or no) appreciation of the intermediary internal states of the computer that causes the booting-up processes? Answer: because whatever reasoning or associative learning I use to make such a prediction, it is reliable (enough) for me to predict that the computer will boot up when I press the button.

6. Hare et al. (2006) and Bräuer et al. (2007) replicated Hare et al.'s (2000) initial findings. However, Karin-D'Arcy and Povinelli (2002) ran a similar study and received negative results. It appears that the distance between the barriers in the test is a critical variable: the closer the barriers are to each other, the less likely the subordinate chimpanzee discriminates between them. The barriers in Karin-D'Arcy and Povinelli's study were set closer together than those in the Hare and Bräuer studies, which may explain why the subordinate chimpanzees in Karin-D'Arcy and Povinelli's study behaved in the same way toward the barriers whether the food was placed behind them (and out of sight of the competing dominant) or out in front of the barriers (and, thus, visible to the dominant).

7. Since the opacity of barriers and media can come in degrees, a subject's line of gaze to an object can be more or less obstructed by such barriers and media and

hence more or less direct. This will be relevant for our discussion of Emery and Clayton's experiments on scrub jays below. However, this qualification is ignored in our discussion here since the barriers used in Hare and colleagues' experiments are either totally opaque or nearly totally transparent.

8. Or putting the negation outside, simply *not* observing such a barrier/medium between the subject's eyes or face and the object.

9. Or is disposed *not* to believe that Y is C*.

10. See Shillito et al. (2005) for a similar analogical-like inference explanation of (putative) perceptual state attribution by an orangutan in a transparent-barrier test.

11. This objection will be discussed further in chapter 3.

12. For gaze-following in great apes, see Bräuer et al. (2005); in ravens, see Bugnyar et al. (2004); in bee-eaters, see Watve et al. (2002); in starlings, see Carter et al. (2008); and in dolphins, see Pack and Herman (1995) and Tschudin (2001).

13. Gómez (2009) takes direct line of gaze to be an intentional relation. However, by 'intentional' he means an "external" relation between a subject and an existing distal object. On such a definition, Gómez acknowledges, intentionality does not function as a mark of the mental.

14. Of course, one's visual experience may represent an unobstructed line between an object and 'here' (i.e., where one's eyes or face are), as noted above, and one may even know by introspecting that it *appears* to one as if one has a direct line of gaze to an object, but neither of these is the same as knowing introspectively that one actually has a direct line of gaze to an object—for again, one cannot know introspectively whether there is such an object to which one appears to have a direct line of gaze.

15. The point here is not that subjects actually see such objects but merely fail to notice them. On any plausible account of seeing, subjects in such cases neither see nor notice the objects in their direct line of gaze. For a persuasive defense of this point, see Tye (2009).

16. See Heyes (1998) for a similar line of reasoning against such simplicity arguments.

17. One could add to this a study by Hostetter et al. (2001) that showed that chimpanzees tend to make more visible gestures to a seeing (eyes open and unoccluded) experimenter offering food but tended to make more audible gestures to an unseeing (eyes closed or occluded by experimenter's free hand) experimenter offering food.

18. See Call (2005) for a similar study with bonobos and gorillas, as well as Suda-King (2008) with orangutans. Both of these further studies yielded results that were consistent with Call and Carpenter's (2001) original study.

19. In fact, the data can be equally well explained by the hypothesis that chimpanzees simply tend to look for hidden items (e.g., food) when they know that the item is hidden but do not know (or have forgotten) where it is hidden. This hypothesis is neither a metacognitive nor the complementary behavior-reading hypothesis offered above. Too often in the literature on metacognition in animals researchers hastily move from the claim that an animal knows *when* it knows/doesn't know to the conclusion that the animal knows *that* it knows/doesn't know. The conclusion, of course, is unambiguously metacognitive, but its premise is not. 'Knowing when,' after all, admits of a cognitive-procedural ambiguity (similar to the distinction between 'knowing that' and 'knowing how'), and the premise can just as well be read as stating that the animal knows how to do certain things (e.g., look for hidden food) when it is in possession of certain first-order information about its physical environment (e.g., the information that food was hidden somewhere around here) but lacks other more specific first-order information (e.g., the information that the food was hidden right *there*) that would allow it to behave appropriately (e.g., to locate the food). Call and Carpenter appear to be guilty of such a hasty inference. They infer from the claim that the results of their study are "consistent with the hypothesis that [their apes] knew *when* [my emphasis] they did not know" to the conclusion that their apes had "metacognitive knowledge" (p. 218). However, the description, 'apes knew when they did not know,' is metacognitive only if one reads it as their knowing *that* they did not know, as opposed to reading it as their knowing *how* to act appropriately (e.g., looking into the tubes for the food) when they lacked specific first-order information about their environment (e.g., which tube the food was hidden in). The data, unfortunately, do not favor one of these readings over the other.

20. For meta-memory studies in animals, see Hampton (2009); for studies of meta-confidence judgments in animals, see Smith et al. (2009) and Son and Kornell (2005).

21. Dona, however, came to point to the key's new location before the helper began searching but only when the familiar hider was substituted for someone unfamiliar to Dona. When the hider was the old, familiar experimenter, Dona failed to point to the key's new location prior to the helper's searching for it. Gómez initially speculated that this change in Dona's tactic was due to her interpreting the unfamiliar hider's act of placing the key in a new location as an attempt to "deceive" the helper of the key's location. However, Zimmermann et al.'s (2009) study did not confirm this interpretation. When their apes were shown an experimenter placing the fork (the functional equivalent to the key) in a new location, and doing so in an overtly deceptive manner, the apes did not point to the fork's new location until after the helper had first failed to find the fork in the designated area. Thus, it may have been the mere unfamiliarity of the new hider that caused Dona to point to the key's new location before the helper began to search for it rather than Dona interpreting the unfamiliar hider's action as an attempt to deceive the helper. Based

on her experiences in the training trials, it is possible that Dona simply came to have a relatively high level of confidence that the helper would retrieve the key whenever it was placed in a location by a familiar human but a comparably low level of confidence that the helper would do the same were the key placed in a location by an unfamiliar human. Thus, given Dona's comparably low level of confidence that the helper would retrieved the key when it was hidden by the unfamiliar human, she may have decided to increase this level of confidence by indicating the location of the key in such trials.

22. Again, let me add that I am not here suggesting that there is no alternative account of Panzee's and Dona's respective performances other than in terms of the knowledge/ignorance hypothesis or the complementary behavior-reading hypothesis being proposed here. The point is merely that the latter hypothesis is no less plausible than the former, and, thus, the 'key' experiment alone cannot decide between them. See Heyes (1998, p. 140) for a possible alternative account of Dona's and Panzee's performances in terms of a brute associative learning model.

23. In fact it is quite possible that the storer jay's ability to track an observer's line of gaze to a particular distal object/event is reduced the longer the observer's line of gaze to the object/event is. For some independent support for this conjecture, see Michelon & Zacks (2006). Intuitively, it is more difficult (e.g., it takes longer and is more vulnerable to errors) to tell whether a far object/event is in a subject's line of gaze than it is to tell whether a close object/event is. Hence, it is quite possible that the storer jays were simply less able to determine whether the observer jay had a direct line of gaze to the caching event in the 'far' tray compared to their ability to determine whether the observer jay had a direct line of gaze to the caching event in the 'near' tray. This alone may account for the storer jays' differential caching/recaching performance in the test trials: They were simply less sure whether the observer had a direct line of gaze to the caching in the 'far' tray than they were that the observer had a direct line of gaze to the caching in the 'near' tray.

24. Emery and Clayton see their study as employing an experience-projection (EP) methodology. The general idea behind the EP methodology is to provide an animal with a novel cue for a type of mental state in itself (e.g., wearing blue goggles that allow the subject to see and red goggles that prevent the subject from seeing) and test whether the animal can predict the appropriate behavior of another subject (behavior, that is, that the animal has never observed correlated with the novel cue) by projecting that type of mental state onto the other subject when the novel cue is present (e.g., understanding that the other agent can see while wearing the blue goggles but not while wearing the red ones). As will become clear in the following chapters, I am quite sympathetic to the EP approach as a way to solve the logical problem, but I do not see that Emery and Clayton's present study employs it. For one, the observable cue that the jays purportedly use to project their own experience of stealing onto the observer jays is not novel in relation to the action of pilfering another jay's cache. The experienced and control jays, after all, have observed *in*

their own case a correlation between being present before another jay's cache (the cue) and stealing the food from it. And so they could just as well have taken this correlation between cue and pilfering observed in their own case as holding for other jays, too.

25. A similar complementary behavior-reading hypothesis can be given in other studies that have credited animals with attributing hearing to other agents (see Flombaum & Santos 2005; Melis et al. 2006).

26. In an attempt to avoid such skepticism, researchers routinely appeal to Searle's (1983) distinction between prior intentions (i.e., intentions the agent has before acting) and intentions-in-action (i.e., intentions the agent has at the time of the action, though not necessarily prior to it). It is the latter sort of intention that researchers claim animals are capable of attributing to others (see, e.g., Call & Tomasello 1998; Buttelmann et al. 2007). The motivation behind appealing to this distinction, according to the researchers, is that intentions-in-action are easier to detect in other agents (especially by means of nonverbal behavior) than prior intentions, which often require the interpretation of speech for their detection. Although this may be so, it does not avoid the above line of skepticism. For on the belief-based account of intentions, attributions of intentions-in-action, just as much as attributions of prior intentions, involve attributions of beliefs. If an agent does A with the intention-in-action to x, then, on the belief-based account, the agent must at least believe that his doing A stands a chance of leading to x. The way to remove the skepticism implied by the belief-based account, then, is not simply to appeal to the intention-in-action/prior intention distinction but to give an account of intention-in-action attribution that does not involve belief attribution. I have attempted to show above one way that this can be done.

27. In support of the possibility of simple conative state attribution in the absence of the capacity to attribute beliefs, it is relevant to note that autistic children, who are known to have difficulty with attributing beliefs, appear to be quite capable of attributing simple desires and goal-directed actions to themselves and others (see Tan & Harris 1991; Baron-Cohen 1991).

Chapter 3

1. See section 2.10 in the previous chapter for an argument that goal-directed/intentional-action attribution in animals does not require animals to understand simple cognitive states such as seeing and knowing.

2. See Povinelli and Vonk (2006) for replies to both sets of objections.

3. The point being made here is nearly identical to Whiten's (1996) intervening variable theory of mindreading, and Povinelli and colleagues (see Penn et al. 2008; Penn & Povinelli 2007) acknowledge the similarity. However, it should be noted that Whiten does not regard intervening variables as internal causes.

4. Or if it is plausible to suppose that s-type conditions followed by r-type behaviors is something that A knows innately, say as a result of its being a stereotypical behavior pattern of A's species. For ease of exposition this additional clause will be dropped from hereon.

5. Penn and Povinelli (2007) also endorse Heyes's EP protocol as a solution to the logical problem.

6. Throughout this chapter, I take attributions of seeing-as by animals to be equivalent to attributions of phenomenal appearing. If an animal thinks that another agent sees an object *as* red or *as* being in its direct line of gaze, for example, then the animal is taken to understand that the object phenomenally *looks* or *appears* red to the subject or phenomenally *looks* or *appears* to the subject to be in its direct line of gaze (see Chisholm 1957 and Jackson 1977 on this phenomenal sense of 'looks' distinct from its epistemic and comparative senses). There are, of course, nonphenomenal instances of seeing-as ascriptions (e.g., the Pope *sees* marriage *as* a sacred bond or Aurignacians were the first humans to *see* lines on a rock *as* bison; Davis 1986). Nonphenomenal ascriptions of seeing-as are generally taken to be instances of ascriptions of beliefs or belief-like states (e.g., to say that the Pope sees marriage as a sacred bond is just another way of saying that he *believes* marriage to be a sacred bond, and to say that Aurignacians were the first humans to see lines on a rock as bison is just to say that they were the first humans to *understand* or *believe* that such lines bore a resemblance to the shape or profile of a bison). Such nonphenomenal ascriptions of seeing-as are not what animals are here taken to attribute to other agents, however. In this chapter, seeing-as attributions are understood as attributions of phenomenal visual appearing. In chapter 4, I consider cases of nonphenomenal seeing-as attributions (i.e., perceptual belief attributions) in animals.

7. Of course, the complementary behavior-reading hypothesis here credits the chimpanzee with understanding which experimenter has a direct line of gaze to the baiting process without its having to observe the experimenters' eyes (since both types of goggles block this observation), and this is something that chimpanzees have not yet been shown to do. However, it should be kept in mind that something similar must be assumed even by the mindreading hypothesis under consideration. On the mindreading hypothesis, the chimpanzee is hypothesized to understand which experimenter can *see* the baiting process without the chimpanzeee observing the experimenters' eyes. And this too is something that chimpanzees have not yet been shown to do.

8. The Machiavellian intelligence hypothesis is typically interpreted as maintaining that mindreading evolved in animals for the purpose of enhanced predictability of *conspecifics'* behaviors. Expressed in this way, the hypothesis is, I believe, unnecessarily restrictive. Although it is plausible that mindreading within highly social species, such as apes and corvids, evolved for the purpose of enhanced predictability of conspecifics' behaviors, it does not follow that it evolved for predicting only

conspecifics' behaviors, or that it could not have evolved in nonsocial species for enhanced predictability of the behaviors of nonconspecific agents, such as predators and prey. The ARM theory makes no such restrictions on agent type. However, for the sake of simplifying the discussion, the predictability of conspecifics' behaviors will be the focus of discussion in the chapter.

9. A mindreading animal *may* be able to do things with its mindreading ability other than use it to predict other agents' behavior. It may, for example, use it to *explain* or *make sense* (in a manner that is not reducible to a type of prediction of) others' behaviors. However, it is difficult to see why such alternative uses of mindreading, though possible, might give animals any selective advantage if they could not be employed to predict and anticipate others' behaviors. After all, it is others' behaviors, not the mental states behind them, that directly affect a mindreading animal's state of well-being and chances of survival. In the words of Bernd Heinrich (1999), "[f]rom an ecological-evolutionary perspective, the effect [of others' behaviors] is critical and the intent [behind the behaviors] is irrelevant" (p. 135). Thus, as far as I can see, enhanced predictability of others' behaviors is the *primary* adaptive value of mindreading in the animal kingdom. Of course, the Machiavellian intelligence hypothesis *also* stresses the capacity to *manipulate* others' behaviors as a selective advantage that mindreading provides animals over behavior reading. This is evident from the emphasis that proponents of the hypothesis have placed on the existence of tactical deception in great apes—the hypothesized capacity of great apes to intentionally induce false beliefs in conspecifics (see Byrne 1995). However, the adaptive value of manipulating others' behaviors by means of tactical deception would be naught unless it led to the desired behavior that the mindreading animal *anticipated*. If the animal's conspecifics did not behave in the way that it desired and predicted they should when it tried to induce a false belief in them, it would be difficult to understand what value such a use of mindreading would have for the animal (cf. Byrne 1995, p. 146). The selective advantage of tactical deception, then, would seem to rest upon its providing an animal with an enhanced capacity to predict others' behaviors in certain situations.

10. I take introspection here to be a form of displaced perception, as opposed to a type of internal monitoring. More will be said in section 3.4 below on the nature of introspection in animals according to the ARM theory.

11. This is not to say, of course, that *only* by means of such introspective capacities could animals have evolved an ability to respond adaptively to illusory environments. Admittedly, some animals that lack such introspective capacities might nevertheless have evolved the ability to respond adaptively to illusory environments by, say, coming to acquire a disposition to act on their previously formed beliefs about the world (e.g., the belief that there is an insect on the leaf before me) rather than on their currently formed illusory percepts (e.g., the perception that there is just a leaf before me) when the content of the latter is inconsistent with the content of the former. (I owe this suggestion to Peter Carruthers.) This is certainly possible.

However, the point being made above is merely that in those animals that *have* the capacity to introspect their own perceptual states, this capacity is hypothesized to have been selected for enabling such animals to respond adaptively (or more adaptively) to illusory environments by distinguishing the way things perceptually appear from the way things really are. Just as hypothesizing that wings (with flight feathers) in birds were selected for aerial locomotion in these animals does not deny that aerial locomotion may have evolved in others animals without such wings (e.g., flying squirrels and flying fish, to name but two wingless fliers), hypothesizing that the capacity to introspect perceptual states evolved in animals with this capacity for the purpose of distinguishing appearance from reality does not deny that the ability to distinguish appearance from reality may have evolved in animals without such introspective capacities.

12. From here on, I drop the awkward qualification 'object/state of affairs' and use either 'object' or 'state of affairs' or 'event' as appropriate. On my view, an animal can bear the relations of *direct line of gaze* and *appearing to have a direct line of gaze* to both objects and states of affairs, as well as events (which are a type of state of affairs).

13. For data on the existence of temporal, spatial, quantitative, and probabilistic representations in a variety of animals, including invertebrates, see Gallistel (1990). For more recent data on the existence of temporal, quantitative, and exclusionary representations in corvids, primates, and canines, see Boysen (1997), Beran (2001), Correia et al. (2007), Aust et al. (2008), Hoffman et al. (2009), Beran (2010), Grodzinski and Clayton (2010).

14. It is quite likely, as Smith et al. (2008) note, that animals may employ exemplars in some case of categorization (e.g., where the number of particular exemplars is relatively low) and prototypes in other cases (e.g., where the number of particular exemplars is high and varied). Prototypes are typically understood as abstract representations resulting from an averaging together of all the various particular exemplars a subject has of a class. Now, since there is only one you, there cannot really be an averaging together of various exemplars of you. For this reason, I think that in the case of classifying others as like-minded, animals use a self-exemplar model of classification, rather than something like a self-prototype one.

15. F and G may be identical properties in some cases, such as in those instances where the animal does not suspect that it is subject to an illusion.

16. Alternatively, some of these generalizations may be innate folk psychological principles, as opposed to empirical generalizations as presented here. Moreover, it may even be possible to determine by empirical means whether some of the psychological principles that animals use to predict others' actions are empirically derived or innately known. For example, it seems rather intuitive that cognitive dissonance is no more a part of animal innate folk psychology than it is of our own (Stich & Nichols 1995). Nevertheless, animals are controlled by principles of

cognitive dissonance. Animals, for example, tend to favor otherwise identical positive stimuli if one of them is paired with or preceded by an aversive experience (Zentall et al. 2006). That is how animals actually behave, surprisingly. Assuming that animals have observed such patterns in other agents, do they anticipate other agents' behavior in accordance with such empirical facts or in accordance with some empirically false but innately known folk principle, such as the principle that other things being equal agents tend to favor those positive stimuli that are largely free of aversive experiences? Visit my homepage at (http://depthome.brooklyn.cuny .edu/philo/Lurz.htm) for a way to test this hypothesis which overcomes the logical problem.

17. It is relevant to note that the perceptual appearing representations that figure in these generalizations are very much like Ruth Millikan's (2006) "pushmi-pullyu" representations—they serve to indicate both how the world appears to an agent and how the agent is disposed to act as a result. Thus, these attributions can be thought to be a hybrid cognitive/conative state attribution. An animal, for example, that predicts that a conspecific will move to eat the object before it because, to the conspecific, the object visually appears to be a piece food is attributing a relational state to the conspecific (a state of perceptual appearing) that the animal takes to determine both how the world visually appears to the conspecific as well as how the conspecific is likely to behave as a result.

18. One thing that must be avoided in this phase of the experiment, however, is the chimpanzee coming to have a greater inclination toward retrieving yellow objects behind clear barriers than behind red barriers, for if the subordinate chimpanzee were a complementary behavior reader and came to have such a differential retrieval bias, it could, in the critical test (below), project this bias onto the dominant chimpanzee and thereby give the same prediction of the dominant chimpanzee's behavior as his mindreading counterpart is expected to. Measures can be taken here, however, that would eliminate the possibility of such a differential retrieval bias. First, before the chimpanzee is shown a yellow object placed behind the red barrier, he is encouraged and rewarded for retrieving orange objects placed behind the red barrier and orange and (particularly) yellow objects placed behind the clear barrier. The chimpanzee's level of inclination can be measured by the speed and alacrity with which he retrieves the objects. Once his speed and alacrity for retrieving the various yellow and orange objects behind the clear barrier matches or exceeds his speed and alacrity for retrieving the various orange objects behind the red barrier, he is then introduced to a yellow object behind the red barrier. To reinforce the likelihood that the chimpanzee will be initially inclined toward retrieving the object, we make sure the object is extremely attractive to the animal—perhaps, by making it a new toy with salient features. We can then measure his initial speed and alacrity here to make sure that it matches or exceeds the initial speed and alacrity with which he retrieved yellow objects behind the clear barrier. The chimpanzee is thereafter encouraged and rewarded for retrieving yellow objects placed

behind the red barrier. The chimpanzee is promoted to the critical test stage of the experiment only when his overall speed and alacrity for retrieving yellow objects behind the red barrier match or exceed his overall speed and alacrity for retrieving yellow objects behind the clear barrier. These measures (and perhaps others, as well) could be used to ensure that the chimpanzee is no less inclined, both initially and thereafter, toward retrieving yellow objects behind the red barrier than he is toward retrieving yellow objects behind the clear barrier. I see no reasons to think that a chimpanzee could not demonstrate clear signs of success on these measures.

19. For additional tests, see Lurz (2009a).

20. The reverse-contingency tests that Krachun and colleagues use in their study do not control for the image-tracking hypothesis since they do not test for whether the chimpanzees are able to use an image of a small grape to keep track of the container that contains the large grape.

21. In the next chapter, I provide what I believe to be a better test for a strict appearance–reality distinction in animals using amodal completion figures.

22. In conversation, Peter Carruthers has suggested an even weaker image-tracking hypothesis, one which does not credit the apes with *any* understanding of how objects *appear* to them, not even images on lenses. On this hypothesis, the apes simply come to understand that the small-grape image (or big-grape image) on the lens is a reliable indicator in the circumstance of a big grape (or small grape) behind the lens, without understanding anything about how these images *look* to them—for example, that the images look to be (but are not really) grapes of a certain size behind the lens. The data from Krachun and colleagues' study are consistent with this image-tracking hypothesis too, of course. However, the experimental protocol that I propose in this section is a way (and as far as I can see, the *only* way) of testing these two image-tracking hypotheses. For on Carruthers' hypothesis, chimpanzees are taken to have no understanding of how images look *to them,* and so they are not likely to have any understanding of how images look *to others.* Thus, on this hypothesis, chimpanzees are expected to fail the experimental protocol described in this section with size-distorting lenses. On the image-tracking hypothesis that I propose, however, it is quite conceivable that chimpanzees might understand how images on a lens look to others given that they understand how such images look to themselves. Thus, another important feature of the proposed protocol in this section is that it is a way (and perhaps the only way) of determining whether Krachun and colleagues' chimpanzees make an appearance–reality distinction *at all*—even if it is a nonstrict appearance–reality distinction about images rather than grapes.

23. As with the other experimental protocol, measures are taken in this phase of the experiment to guarantee that the subordinate does not learn that he is more likely to retrieve (or is initially more inclined to retrieve) objects placed behind the blue-trimmed (magnifying) barrier than he is to retrieve (or is initially inclined

to retrieve) objects placed behind the red-trimmed (minimizing) barrier. One can eliminate the possibility of such associations' being made by placing objects that are novel and salient to the chimpanzee behind the red-trimmer barrier and objects that are less interesting (but still interesting) to the chimpanzee behind the blue-trimmed barrier, as well as by introducing the chimpanzee to the blue-trimmed barrier after he has reached criterion for retrieving, without hesitation, objects behind the red-trimmed barrier. Again, I see no reason to think that chimpanzees could not show clear signs of passing these measures.

24. The term 'amodal completion' is from Kanizsa (1979). Kanizsa distinguished two kinds of filling-in illusions. In some instances, the visual system fills in the missing shape of an occluded object without filling in any other properties characteristic of the sense modality of vision, such as a color and brightness. In such cases, the missing part of the occluded object is said to be *a*modally filled in by the visual system. The triangle in figure 3.7c, for example, is seen as complete, but the visual system does not fill in the color or brightness of the occluded section of the triangle. In other instances of filling in, the color and brightness of the illusory shape are filled in as well. In such cases, the illusory object is completed with *all* of the properties (e.g., color, brightness, shape, etc.) associated with the modality of vision. The illusory object is thus described as being *modally* completed. Kanizsa's famous triangle (not shown here) is an example of modal completion.

25. The exception to this rule is in the case of food items (usually novel types of food) that are initially feared by the ravens (ravens are generally shy and cautious around new objects). In such cases, the dominant raven typically allows subordinates to feed first. When the subordinates have tested the new food, the dominant raven will then chase them off and begin to feed on its own (see Heinrich 1999).

26. This ability to learn the names of a large quantity of different items is not unique to Rico. Another border collie, named Betsy, has been shown to know the names of over 300 different items (Morell 2008).

27. What is more, Rico also showed signs of remembering the names of these new items. Ten minutes after being tested on a new word–new item task, his owner again requested the 'now-no-longer novel' item by its name. At this point, the item had been placed in the adjacent room along with a number of familiar items and some new novel items. Rico successfully retrieved the 'now-no-longer novel' item in 4 out of 6 of these test trials. Four weeks after the test trials, Rico was still able to remember the names of these 'now-no-longer novel' items at a rate of retention comparable to a three-year-old toddler. Rico appears to have the capacity to pick up a novel word–object pairing without special conditional training on the pairing and to remember this pairing for some time afterward.

28. A similar debate rages in developmental psychology, with Markman and colleagues (Markman & Wachtel 1988) arguing for a mutual exclusivity/whole object account of the disambiguation effect in young children and Clark (1990),

Bloom (2000), and Diesendruck and Markson (2001) arguing for a social-pragmatic account.

29. It is important to note that the issue that the following experimental protocol aims to addresses is not whether, as Paul Bloom (2004) writes, border collies understand fetching requests (e.g., "get the sock") as containing individual words ("sock") that refer to categories of objects in the world or whether they simply learn to "associate the word[s] spoken by [their] owner[s] with a specific behavior such as approaching a sock or fetching a sock" (p. 1605). The issue, rather, is whether emergent matching in these dogs is achieved by their understanding the communicative intention of their owners in the context of the utterance of the request (independently of whether they understand the request as containing referential words) or by some process of exclusion learning that does not involve their understanding their owners' intention.

30. It has been shown that some animals are more likely to see an occluded object as whole and continuous if the object is something familiar to the animal (Nagasaka et al. 2007). Thus, I use a fire hydrant here as an example of an object familiar to border collies—other familiar objects could be used instead. Using a familiar object may not be necessary in this case, however; it all depends upon whether border collies, like other animals, are aided in amodal completion tasks by using familiar objects. With this in mind, it may be suggested that for the raven experiment above, an occluded object that is more familiar to the birds than a triangle should be used.

31. To facilitate amputation in this case, the hydrant can be made out of plastic.

32. For additional experimental designs to test for perceptual appearing attribution in animals using deceptive amodal completion stimuli, see my home page (https://depthome.brooklyn.cuny.edu/philo/Lurz.htm).

Chapter 4

1. Davidson is also known for his arguments against *beliefs* in animals. These arguments, however, have been subjected to numerous criticisms over the years, and they are generally considered to be unpersuasive (see, e.g., Armstrong 1973; Routley 1984; Smith 1982; Tye 1997; Carruthers 2008). What is more, the question of whether animals *have* beliefs is orthogonal to whether they can *attribute* them, for even if animals are thought not to possess beliefs, it simply does not follow that they could not *represent* others as having them, provided that this mode of representation does not itself involve or require the possession of beliefs. And there is no reason why it *must*. Animals could, for instance, represent others as having beliefs by means of a distributed connectionist framework that does not encode belief states (see Ramsey et al. 1990 for an argument to this effect). Such a possibility would, in fact, be analogous to what eliminative materialists have longed argued is true in the case of humans beings (Churchland 1981). Thus, it is at least *possible*, though by no

means obligatory, that animals are in the same boat as humans, according to eliminative materialism: They lack beliefs but nevertheless represent others as having them by means of a representational system that does not support belief states. What this possibility shows is that the question of belief *attribution* in animals is not answered simply by settling the question of belief *possession* in animals. The former question, which is our interest here, must be examined directly.

2. These ideas have an obvious affinity to Wittgenstein's solution to the paradox of rule following (Wittgenstein 1953), to which Davidson states his indebtedness.

3. Quite apart from the question of language, it seems rather unlikely that animals would have such objectively normative ideas of truth and falsity. Animals, after all, are practical beings that are concerned with, and arguably only with, doing the right things (i.e., doing what will maximize their own well-being or fitness and perhaps that of their kin, too), not with doing the right thing for the objectively right (true) reasons. It is difficult to see how a distinction between a true belief and a subjectively useful one, or the idea of getting things right because one's belief is true, *period*, would have any value within the animal world. See Putnam (1992) for a similar argument.

4. The philosophical roots of this distinction can be traced back at least as far as Frege (1918/1977). According to the OED, the distinction in English can be traced back at least to the thirteenth century. Also see the entries on 'belief' and 'judgment' in Honderich (1995) as well as Thau (2002) for more contemporary uses of the distinction in philosophy.

5. We sometimes say, of course, that S *truly* or *falsely* believes that *p*, but this use of truth and falsity to qualify acts of believing is dependent on the use of these terms to qualify the object sense of belief. Whether or not S truly or falsely believes that *p* (except when the former merely means *strongly* or *sincerely* believes that *p*) depends upon whether the proposition that S is taken to believe (i.e., S's belief in the object sense) is true or false; however, whether the proposition that S believes is true or false does not dependent upon the truth or falsity of anything else—and especially not on S's subjective act of believing the proposition if the concept of truth applicable to belief is, as Davidson maintains, that of *objective* truth. Thus, insofar as beliefs in the act sense can be objectively true or false, they are so only in a derivative way: it is belief in the object sense that is the primary bearer of these values.

6. I follow the common practice in philosophy and linguistics of taking sentences to denote or be about the states of affairs that make them true. Thus, the sentence 'Tom is tall' denotes/is about Tom's being tall. That is why I interpret 'S/believes that/*p*' as expressing a two-place relation between S and the states of affairs denoted by the sentence '*p*.' Prior had a much more austere notion of denotation, reserving it only for names and nouns. For this reason, he preferred to read the expression '____ believes that____' not as a two-place relation but as a predicate-forming operator on sentences. According to this interpretation, once the right-hand slot in the

expression '____ believes that ____' is filled in with a sentence (e.g., '___ believes that p'), the expression becomes a monadic predicate that is predicable of an individual (e.g., S believes that p). Because of this difference, I call the model of animal belief attribution proposed here a Prior-*inspired* model rather than just Prior's model.

7. Of course, there are some types of belief attributions that animals would not be able to make on the Prior-inspired model. Belief attributions that quantify over propositions (e.g., S believes some truths/falsehoods) and belief attributions that make explicit reference to particular propositions and/or their truth values (e.g., S believes that the proposition that p is true/false) are two such examples. It is unlikely, however, that animals would be capable of these sorts of belief attributions on any account. Thus, such a limitation to the Prior-inspired model does not count against it as a viable model of belief attribution *in animals*.

8. Although I do not pursue the matter here, there are other possible accounts of belief attribution in animals that do not take them to be attributions of propositional attitudes. On one such account, for instance, belief attributions in animals could be understood as attributions of believing *in* states of affairs, rather than attributions of believing/*that* such-and-such states of affairs exist. Although it may be that the *state of mind* of believing in a state of affairs (e.g., the state of mind of believing in global warming) is the same as or is reducible to the *state of mind* of believing/that such state of affairs exists (e.g., the state of mind of believing/that global warming exists), Szabó (2003) has shown (rather persuasively to my lights) that the *concept* of believing in a state of affairs or object is not the same as or reducible to the *concept* of believing/that the state of affairs or object exists. Thus, it is conceivable that the concept of belief which animals employ in attributing beliefs to others is the two-place relational concept *believes-in*, which relates subjects to states of affairs, not propositions. On another possible account, which draws its inspiration from Bertrand Russell (1912), belief attributions in animals (in their simplest form) are understood as attributions of a *triadic* relation between a subject, an object, and a property. On this model, belief attributions in animals are similar to other types of triadic cognitive-state attributions, such as attributions of *attributes-to*, *ascribes*, and *classifies-as*. Just as the claim 'S attributes F to a' represents the subject S, the property F, and the individual a as linked together by the three-place relation ____ *attributes* ____ *to* ____, the claim 'S believes that a is F' is understood, on the triadic-relation model, as representing S, F, and a as linked together by the three-place relation ____ *believes* ____ *is* ____. On this model, when an animal represents that an agent, S, believes that a is F, it represents S, the property F, and the individual a as linked together by the triadic relation ____ *believes* ____ *is* ____. An interesting feature of the triadic-relation model is that some animals—most notably great apes (see Tomasello & Call 1997)—have been shown to understand other types of triadic relations, both in the social domain (e.g., understanding the triadic relation of being *between* individuals x and y in dominance rank) and in the domain of tool use (e.g., understanding the triadic tool-using relation that holds

among a demonstrator, a tool, and the object the tool is used to manipulate). On the triadic-relation model, belief attribution in these animals can be understood as an extension of their general ability to represent triadic relations in various domains. It should be noted that I take these alternative nonpropositional models of animal belief attribution here as being complementary to the Prior-inspired model presented above. Either one of them might be developed further to show how animals could be understood to attribute beliefs without attributing propositional attitudes. I have simply decided to do this with the Prior-inspired model.

9. See Hutto (2008, forthcoming) for a similar distinction between beliefs construed as propositional attitudes and beliefs construed as intentional relations to states of affairs.

10. I take events to be a species of states of affairs.

11. For such a theory, see Armstrong (1997).

12. It may be that on some accounts of belief attribution, what I am calling here 'states of affairs' are called 'propositions' (e.g., see Chisholm 1970, 1971). However, if these 'propositions' are in fact states of affairs, as I am using this term, then they are nonrepresentational entities that do not *aim* at the truth, and so they are no more bearers of objective truth and falsity than the things I call 'states of affairs.' Thus, even on such accounts of 'propositions' and 'propositional' attitudes, animals need not understand anything about the concepts of objective truth and falsity (or the object sense of belief) in order to attribute 'propositional' attitudes.

13. I am not here committing myself to the existence of negative states of affairs. The state of affairs that the negative sentence 'not-p' denotes is the actual state of affairs that makes the sentence 'not-p' true.

14. Recently Taylor et al. (2009) showed that New Caledonian crows succeeded on a similar string pulling problem but only when they were allowed to see that their string-pulling strategy was succeeding in bringing the food closer to them. The researchers took their results to suggest that spontaneous performance on insightful string-pulling tasks by crows and other corvids may be achieved through operant conditioning that is mediated by perceptual–motor feedback, not by insight (i.e., solving the problem in the mind before executing the proposed solution in behavior). However, it is not clear that Taylor and colleagues' operant-conditioning explanation is actually inconsistent with the insightful learning one, as the researchers claim. It may well be that the crows, like people, needed to see that their preconceived plan is working in order to be motivated to continue executing it.

15. Children younger than four years also seem to be introspectively unaware of their own *occurrent thoughts*. In a series of studies by Flavell and colleagues (1993, 1995), sixteen five-year-olds were presented with a problem while sitting in a particular location that required them to think of or make a judgment about a target object. Immediately after making their judgment, the children were asked to change

locations. While sitting in their new location, they were asked by the experimenter whether they had been thinking about anything (and if so, what) while they were sitting in the first location. Only 19 percent of the children, when asked this question, said they had been thinking about the target object. Similar results were achieved in the follow-up studies that were designed to eliminate confounding variables, such as memory constraints. From the results of their studies, Flavell and colleagues conclude that "preschoolers have very limited introspective skills" of their occurrent thoughts (Flavell et al. 1995, p. 76). If Flavell and colleagues are correct in what their studies show about normal five-year-olds, then it seem very unlikely that children of this age or younger are capable of entertaining thoughts/ states of affairs consciously, holding them in mind so as to consider and evaluate how they relate to each other logically and evidentially, as Bermúdez's model of belief attribution requires.

16. Gil Harman (1978) once made a similar point regarding Premack and Woodruff's (1978) original discriminatory mindreading tests, as mentioned in the preface.

17. Krachun and colleagues dismiss this possibility on the grounds that "chimpanzees almost always looked back and forth between the containers before making a choice, suggesting that they were not making an automatic, implusive decision" (p. 162). However, there is no reason to suppose that following the rule of choosing the colored cup based on the current contents of the yellow box would necessarily result in the chimpanzee's making an automatic, impulsive decision. After all, the chimpanzee would still need to (a) remember what the current content of the yellow box is and then (b) apply the discrimination rule to this remembered bit of information. It is surely not implausible to suppose that such an act of deliberation would naturally manifest itself in the chimpanzee's looking back and forth between the cups; perhaps doing so aids the animal in calling up the particular discrimination rule for each of the colored cups.

18. In a follow-up study by Tschudin, measures were taken to control for some of these potential confounds, though it did not control for the possibility that the dolphins were using their sonar abilities to detect small auditory differences between the sounds emitted from a tapped-empty box and those emitted from a tapped-baited box. This is unfortunate since dolphins are known for their ability to determine the presence and properties of distal objects by listening in ('eavesdropping') to the echoes bouncing off the object by other dolphins' sonar (see Xitco & Roitblat 1996). What is more, the one dolphin for which the follow-up study was designed failed to reach criterion on the initial training phase of the experiment, and, as a result, the study was terminated before test trials with these further controls could be run.

19. This is not actually true, as we saw. The dolphins did succeed in selecting the baited boxes under such conditions in the pilot study that was conducted prior to

the main study. However, since my interest here is whether the experiment *as such* can distinguish belief-attributing dolphins from their complementary behavior-reading counterparts, I bracket this concern for the sake of argument.

20. The dolphins may understand the action of tapping the baited box by the human communicator, as they seem to understand the purpose of indicative pointing by humans (see Herman et al. 1999; Herman 2006), on the model of their own use of echolocation to signal and indicate to conspecifics the presence of distal objects.

21. For a more thorough analysis of the epistemic sense of 'seeing-as,' 'looks,' and 'appears,' see Chisholm (1957) and Jackson (1977).

22. Obviously the distinction between perceptual-appearing- and perceptual-belief-attributing animals is not meant to be a strict, exclusive distinction. There are likely to be perceptual-appearing-attributing animals that fall somewhere in between.

23. The notion of 'revisability' here is similar to Jonathan Bennett's (1976) notion of 'educability' which he also took to be a mark of beliefs (as a kind) that distinguished them from perceptions (as a kind).

24. The AR task described here avoids some of the problems that we saw inherent in Krachun et al.'s (2009) AR task with magnifying/minimizing lenses, described in chapter 3. Unlike the latter, the AR task here does not involve the use of distorted images on the surface of lenses, and it is ecologically more plausible since chimpanzees (and their evolutionary ancestors) are more likely to have encountered amodal completion illusions in their natural habitats than perceptual illusions produced by magnifying/minimizing lenses.

25. In humans, amodal completion has been observed to occur between 200 and 400 ms after the onset of the stimulus (see Sekuler & Palmer 1992). I assume that something similar holds for chimpanzees, but this will need to be tested.

26. Such methods are routinely used by magicians to evoke surprise in their audience, as in Goldin's box sawing trick. Thus, one can think of the AR test that I am proposing here as a kind of magic trick for animals. It is not entirely surprising, then, that when I showed my three-year-old the actual video sequence illustrated in figure 4.5a, he exclaimed "Daddy, that's magic!"

27. Follow-up tests can be run using a set of different types of objects, both familiar and unfamiliar to the animal, as well as different types of occluders and settings (e.g., vertical as opposed to horizontal occluders, three-dimensional backgrounds as opposed to two-dimensional or blank backgrounds, as shown here).

28. Chimpanzees and other primates have been trained to use joysticks to manipulate objects on computer screens in a number of studies (see, e.g., Hopkins et al. 1996; Beran & Rumbaugh 2001).

29. If there is a concern that the test animal might not understand that when the video chimpanzee is offscreen it does not see what is happening onscreen, then a barrier can be placed between the entering video chimpanzee and the apparent whole banana, or the video chimpanzee can be onscreen with its back to the stimuli while the banana pieces are being aligned on the occluder. The video chimpanzee can then be shown to move around the barrier (or the barrier removed) or turn around and face the aligned banana pieces before moving toward the apparent whole banana or exiting the screen. This goes for the familiarization phase as well. See Surian et al. (2007) for a similar use of a barrier structure in their experiment.

30. Could the behavior-reading test animal mistakenly take the aligned banana pieces to be a whole occluded banana? After all, that is how they visually appear. Perhaps, it might be suggested, the test animal simply cannot discriminate between the way the aligned banana pieces look to it (as a whole occluded banana) and the way the stimulus really is (aligned banana pieces), taking the stimulus to be as it perceptually appears. However, if the test animal is incapable of making such an AR distinction with partially occluded objects, then it is unlikely to have passed the AR screening test described above, and if it didn't pass the AR screening test, it would not have been allowed to participate in the belief-attribution test here. Hence, the only behavior-reading test animal that would likely pass the AR test and, thus, participate in this belief-attribution test would be one that would likely take the video chimpanzee in test (II) to have a direct line of gaze to what is in fact (contrary to visual appearances) *banana pieces* aligned on top of a rectangle, and such a behavior-reading animal, as argued above, would be expected to predict that the video chimpanzee will leave the scene, which is different from what its belief-attributing counterpart is expected to predict.

31. Other sounds, even species-specific calls, can be used instead, of course.

32. Again, different auditory stimuli as well as different onscreen sound-emitting objects can be used.

33. Thompson and colleagues (1997) go further and interpret the success of their chimpanzees on such tasks as evidence that the animals judge the sameness/difference *of the relations* exemplified by the different object pairs. All that is being assumed above, however, is that the chimpanzees represent the abstract, second-order relations exemplified by each of the different pairs, not that they understand that the abstract relation exemplified in one pair of objects is numerically identical with/different from the abstract relation exemplified in the second pair of objects. On this point, it relevant to note that Penn et al. (2008) have argued that chimpanzees could pass such conceptual match-to-sample tests by simply representing the level of variability (entropy) existing between the items in a pair and by learning a conditional rule (to the effect) that if the between-items variability of the sample pair is low/high, then select the pair in the choice display that has a between-items variability that is also low/high. The chimpanzees, on such a view, are not neces-

sarily credited with understanding *relations about relations*—that the between-items variability relation exemplified in the sample pair is the very same relation exemplified in the choice pair. Nevertheless, the chimpanzees, on Penn and colleagues' analysis, are still credited with representing the between-items level of variability of the sample and choice pairs, which the researchers acknowledge is a representation of an abstract, second-order relation. Between-items variability is a determinable, higher-order property of a pair of items that is distinct from (though determined by) the items' determinate, first-order features (e.g., whether both items are square or whether one is square and the other is triangular). Thus, so far as I can see, Penn and colleagues' interpretation of the conceptual match-to-sample data with chimpanzees is quite consistent with the hypothesis that these animals are capable of representing abstract, second-order states of affairs.

34. See Murai et al. (2005) for a similar study that shows that infant chimpanzees are capable of representing abstract (global-level) categories, such as *mammal*, *furniture*, and *vehicle*.

35. Since right and left are sometimes difficult for animals to distinguish, the difference between the two paths can be made more salient to the test animal by placing a distinct type of object at the end of each, such as a man standing at one end and a woman at another. These distinguishing figures, moreover, could be pictures of human subjects, such as trainers or experimenters, that the test animal knows.

36. This is 'surprising' since the CGI figure did not see the placement of the stimuli and, thus, has no reason to believe that they are other than they appear—namely, as occluded stimuli that are congruent. Thus, given the CGI's behavior in the habituation videos in response to occluded stimuli that *looked* to be (and were) congruent, the CGI figure in this situation is expected to take the *right* path—at least, that is what a test animal should expect if it understands that the CGI figure believes that the occluded stimuli are congruent.

37. This is 'surprising' since the CGI figure did not see the placement of the stimuli and, thus, has no reason to believe that they are other than they appear—namely, as occluded stimuli that are incongruent. Thus, given the CGI's behavior in the habituation videos in response to occluded stimuli that *looked* to be (and were) incongruent, the CGI figure in this situation is expected to take the *left* path—at least, that is what a test animal should expect if it understands that the CGI figure believes that the occluded stimuli are incongruent.

References

Abend, L. (2008). "In Spain, human rights for apes." *Time* (July 18). Available at http://www.time.com/time/world/article/0,8599,1824206,00.html.

Adams, E., & Caldwell, R. (1990). Deceptive communication in asymmetric fights of the stomatopod crustacean *Gonodactylus bredini. Animal Behaviour, 4,* 706–716.

Anderson, J., & Vick, S.-J. (2008). Primates' use of others' gaze. In S. Itakura & K. Fujita (Eds.), *Origins of the social mind: Evolutionary and developmental views* (pp. 39–64). Tokyo: Springer.

Apperly, I., Samson, D., Carroll, N., Hussain, S., & Humphreys, G. (2006). Intact first- and second-order false belief reasoning in a patient with severely impaired grammar. *Social Neuroscience, 1,* 334–348.

Armstrong, D. (1973). *Belief, truth and knowledge.* Cambridge: Cambridge University Press.

Armstrong, D. (1997). *A world of states of affairs.* Cambridge: Cambridge University Press.

Astley, S., & Wasserman, E. (1992). Categorical discrimination and generalization in pigeons: all negative stimuli are not created equal. *Journal of Experimental Psychology. Animal Behavior Processes, 18,* 193–207.

Aust, U., Range, F., Steurer, M., & Huber, L. (2008). Inferential reasoning by exclusion in pigeons, dogs, and humans. *Animal Cognition, 11,* 587–597.

Aydin, A., & Pearce, J. (1994). Prototype effects in categorization by pigeons. *Journal of Experimental Psychology. Animal Behavior Processes, 20,* 264–277.

Baillargeon, R., Scott, R., & He, Z. (2010). False-belief understanding in infants. *Trends in Cognitive Science, 14,* 110–118.

Bania, A., Harris, S., Kinsley, H., & Boysen, S. (2009). Constructive and deconstructive tool modification by chimpanzees (*Pan troglodytes*). *Animal Cognition, 12,* 85–95.

Baron-Cohen, S. (1991). Do people with autism understand what causes emotion? *Child Development*, *19*, 579–600.

Bartsch, K., & Wellman, H. (1989). Young children's attribution of action to belief and desires. *Child Development*, *60*, 946–964.

Bekoff, M. (1977). Social communication in canids: evidence for the evolution of a stereotyped mammalian display. *Science*, *197*, 1097–1099.

Bekoff, M., Allen, C., & Burghardt, G. (2002). *The cognitive animal: Empirical and theoretical perspectives on animal cognition*. Cambridge, MA: MIT Press.

Bennett, J. (1976). *Linguistic behaviour*. Cambridge: Cambridge University Press.

Bennett, J. (1978). Some remarks about concepts. *Behavioral and Brain Sciences*, *4*, 557–560.

Bennett, J. (1990). How to read minds in behavior: a suggestion from a philosopher. In A. Whiten (Ed.), *The Emergence of mindreading* (pp. 97–108). Oxford: Oxford University Press.

Bennett, J. (1991). How is cognitive ethology possible? In C. Ristau (Ed.), *Cognitive ethology: The minds of other animals* (pp. 35–49). Hillsdale, NJ: Lawrence Erlbaum Associates.

Beran, M. (2001). Summation and numerousness judgments of sequentially presented sets of items by chimpanzees (*Pan troglodytes*). *Journal of Comparative Psychology*, *115*, 181–191.

Beran, M. (2010). Use of exclusion by a chimpanzee (*Pan troglodytes*) during speech perception and auditory–visual matching-to-sample. *Behavioural Processes*, *83*, 287–291.

Beran, M., & Rumbaugh, D. (2001). "Constructive" enumeration by chimpanzees (*Pan troglodytes*) on computerized task. *Animal Cognition*, *2*, 81–89.

Bermúdez, J. L. (2003). *Thinking without words*. Oxford: Oxford University Press.

Bermúdez, J. L. (2009). Mindreading in the animal kingdom. In R. Lurz (Ed.), *The philosophy of animal minds* (pp. 145–164). Cambridge: Cambridge University Press.

Bird, C., & Emery, N. (2009). Insightful problem solving and creative tool modification by captive nontool-using rooks. *Proceedings of the National Academy of Sciences of the United States of America*, *106*, 10370–10375.

Biro, D., & Matsuzawa, T. (1999). Numerical ordering in a chimpanzee (*Pan troglodytes*): planning, executing, and monitoring. *Journal of Comparative Psychology*, *113*, 178–185.

Block, N. (1978). Troubles with functionalism. In W. Savage (Ed.), *Perception and cognition: Minnesota studies in philosophy of science* (Vol. IX, pp. 261–325). Minneapolis, MN: University of Minnesota Press.

Bloom, P. (2000). *How children learn the meanings of words.* Cambridge, MA: MIT Press.

Bloom, P. (2004). Can a dog learn a word? *Science, 304,* 1605–1606.

Booth, J., Hall, W., Robinson, G., & Kim, S. Y. (1997). Acquisition of the mental state verb "know" by 2- and 5-year-old children. *Journal of Psycholinguistic Research, 26,* 581–603.

Bovet, D., & Vauclair, J. (2001). Judgment of conceptual identity in monkeys. *Psychonomic Bulletin & Review, 8,* 470–475.

Boysen, S. (1997). Representation of quantities by apes. *Advances in the Study of Behavior, 26,* 435–462.

Boysen, S., & Kuhlmeier, V. (2002). Representational capacities for pretense with scale models and photographs in chimpanzees (*Pan troglodytes*). In R. Mitchell (Ed.), *Pretending and imagination in animals and children* (pp. 210–228). Cambridge: Cambridge University Press.

Braaten, R., & Leary, J. (1999). Temporal induction of missing birdsong segments in European Starling. *Psychological Science, 10,* 162–166.

Bräuer, J., Call, J., & Tomasello, M. (2004). Visual perspective taking in dogs (*Canis familiaris*) in the presence of barriers. *Applied Animal Behaviour Science, 88,* 299–317.

Bräuer, J., Call, J., & Tomasello, M. (2005). All great ape species follow gaze to distant locations and around barriers. *Journal of Comparative Psychology, 119,* 145–154.

Bräuer, J., Call, J., & Tomasello, M. (2007). Chimpanzees really know what others can see in competitive situations. *Animal Cognition, 10,* 439–448.

Brooks, R., & Meltzoff, A. (2002). The importance of eyes: how infants interpret adult looking behavior. *Developmental Psychology, 38,* 958–966.

Broom, D., Sena, H., & Moynihan, K. (2009). Pigs learn what a mirror image represents and use it to obtain information. *Animal Behaviour, 78,* 1037–1041.

Bugnyar, T., & Heinrich, B. (2005). Ravens, *Corvus corax,* differentiate between knowledgeable and ignorant competitors. *Proceedings: Biological Sciences, 272,* 1641–1646.

Bugnyar, T., Stöwe, M., & Heinrich, B. (2004). Ravens (*Corvus corax*) follow gaze direction of humans around obstacles. *Proceedings of the Royal Society: Biological Sciences, 271,* 1331–1336.

Bulloch, M., Boysen, S., & Furlong, E. (2008). Visual attention and its relation to knowledge states in chimpanzees, *Pan troglodytes*. *Animal Behaviour, 76,* 1147–1155.

Burdyn, L., & Thomas, R. (1984). Conditional discrimination with conceptual simultaneous and successive cues in the squirrel monkey (*Saimiri sciureus*). *Journal of Comparative Psychology, 98,* 405–413.

Burge, T. (2009). Perceptual objectivity. *Philosophical Review, 118,* 285–324.

Burge, T. (2010). *Origins of Objectivity.* Oxford: Oxford University Press.

Buttelmann, D., Carpenter, M., Call, J., & Tomasello, M. (2007). Enculturated chimpanzees imitate rationally. *Developmental Science, 10,* 31–38.

Byrne, R. (1995). *The thinking ape.* Oxford: Oxford University Press.

Byrne, R., & Whiten, A. (1988). *Machiavellian intelligence: Social expertise and evolution of intellect in monkeys, apes, and humans.* Oxford: Clarendon Press.

Byrne, R. & Whiten, A. (1990). Tactical deception in primates: The 1990 database. *Primate Report, 27,* 1–101.

Cacchione, T., & Krist, H. (2004). Recognizing impossible object relations: intuitions about support in chimpanzees (*Pan troglodytes*). *Journal of Comparative Psychology, 118,* 140–148.

Call, J. (2001). Object permanence in orangutans (*Pongo pygmaeus*), chimpanzees (*Pan troglodytes*), and children (*Homo sapiens*). *Journal of Comparative Psychology, 115,* 159–171.

Call, J. (2004). Inferences about the location of food in the great apes (*Pan paniscus, Pan troglodytes, Gorilla gorilla*, and *Pongo pygmaeus*). *Journal of Comparative Psychology, 118,* 231–242.

Call, J. (2005). The self and other: a missing link in comparative social cognition. In H. Terrace & J. Metcalfe (Eds.), *The missing link in cognition: Origins of self-reflective consciousness* (pp. 321–341). Oxford: Oxford University Press.

Call, J., & Carpenter, M. (2001). Do apes and children know what they have seen? *Animal Cognition, 4,* 207–220.

Call, J., Bräuer, J., Kaminski, J., & Tomasello, M. (2003). Domestic dogs (*Canis familiaris*) are sensitive to the attentional states of humans. *Journal of Comparative Psychology, 117,* 257–263.

Call, J., Hare, B., Carpenter, M., & Tomasello, M. (2004). "Unwilling" versus "unable": chimpanzees' understanding of human intentional action. *Developmental Science, 7,* 488–498.

Call, J., & Tomasello, M. (1998). Distinguishing intentional from accidental actions in orangutan (*Pongo pygmaeus*), chimpanzees (*Pan troglodytes*), and human children (*Homo sapiens*). *Journal of Comparative Psychology, 112*, 192–206.

Call, J., & Tomasello, M. (1999). A nonverbal false belief task: the performance of children and great apes. *Child Development, 70*, 381–395.

Call, J., & Tomasello, M. (2008). Does the chimpanzee have a theory of mind? 30 years later. *Trends in Cognitive Sciences, 12*, 187–192.

Campbell, M., Carter, J., Proctor, D., Eisenberg, M., & de Wall, F. (2009). Computer animations stimulate contagious yawning in chimpanzees. *Proceedings: Biological Sciences, 276*, 4255–4259.

Carey, S., & Bartlett, E. (1978). Acquiring a single new word. *Language Development, 15*, 17–29.

Carruthers, P. (2000). *Phenomenal consciousness: A naturalistic theory.* Cambridge: Cambridge University Press.

Carruthers, P. (2004). On being simple minded. *American Philosophical Quarterly, 41*, 205–220.

Carruthers, P. (2006). *The architecture of the mind.* Oxford: Oxford University Press.

Carruthers, P. (2008). Meta-cognition in animals: a skeptical look. *Mind & Language, 23*, 58–89.

Carruthers, P. (2009). How we know our own minds: the relationship between mindreading and metacognition. *Behavioral and Brain Sciences, 32*, 121–138.

Carruthers, P., & Smith, P. (1996). *Theories of theories of mind.* Cambridge: Cambridge University Press.

Carter, J., Lyons, N., Cole, H., & Goldsmith, A. (2008). Subtle cues of predation risk: starlings respond to a predator's direction of eye-gaze. *Proceedings: Biological Sciences, 275*, 1709–1715.

Chandler, M., Fritz, A., & Hala, S. (1989). Small-scale deceit: deception as a marker of two-, three-, and four-year-olds' early theories of mind. *Child Development, 60*, 1263–1277.

Cheney, D., & Seyfarth, R. (1990). *How monkeys see the world.* Chicago: The Chicago University Press.

Chisholm, R. (1957). *Perceiving.* Ithaca: Cornell University Press.

Chisholm, R. (1970). Events and propositions. *Nous (Detroit, Mich.), 4*, 15–24.

Chisholm, R. (1971). States of affairs again. *Nous (Detroit, Mich.), 5*, 179–189.

Churchland, P. (1981). Eliminative materialism and the propositional attitudes. *Journal of Philosophy*, *78*, 67–90.

Clark, E. (1990). On the pragmatics of contrast. *Journal of Child Language*, *17*, 417–431.

Clayton, N., Griffiths, D., & Bennett, A. (1994). Storage of stones by jays *Garrulus glandarius*. *Ibis*, *136*, 331–334.

Clements, W., & Perner, J. (1994). Implicit understanding of belief. *Cognitive Development*, *9*, 377–395.

Collier-Baker, E., Davis, J., Nielsen, M., & Suddendorf, T. (2006). Do chimpanzees (*Pan troglodytes*) understand single invisible displacement? *Animal Cognition*, *9*, 55–61.

Corballis, M. (2003). Recursion as the key to the human mind. In K. Sterelny & J. Fitness (Eds.), *Mating to mentality: Evaluating evolutionary psychology* (pp. 155–171). New York: Psychology Press.

Corballis, M. (2007). The uniqueness of human recursive thinking. *American Scientist*, *95*, 240–248.

Correia, S., Dickinson, A., & Clayton, N. (2007). Western scrub-jays anticipate future needs independently of their current motivational state. *Current Biology*, *17*, 856–861.

Coussi-Korbel, S. (1994). Learning to outwit a competitor in mangabeys (*Cercocebus t. torquatus*). *Journal of Comparative Psychology*, *108*, 164–171.

Crystal, J., & Foote, A. (2009). Metacognition in animals. *Comparative Cognition & Behavior Reviews*, *4*, 1–16.

Csibra, G. (2008). Goal attribution to inanimate agents by 6.5-month-old infants. *Cognition*, *107*, 705–717.

Csibra, G., Gergely, G., Bíró, S., Koós, O., & Brockbank, M. (1999). Goal attribution without agency cues: the perception of "pure reason" in infancy. *Cognition*, *72*, 237–267.

Dally, J., Emery, N., & Clayton, N. (2004). Cache protection strategies by western scrub-jays (*Aphelocoma californica*): hiding food in the shade. *Proceedings of the Royal Society: Biological Letters*, *271*, 387–390.

Davidson, D. (1980). *Inquiries into truth and interpretation*. Oxford: Oxford University Press.

Davidson, D. (2001). *Subjective, intersubjective, and objective*. Oxford: Oxford University Press.

Davis, W. (1986). The origins of image making. *Current Anthropology*, *27*, 193–215.

de Waal, F. (1982). *Chimpanzee politics*. London: Jonathan Cape.

Dennett, D. (1978a). Beliefs about beliefs. *Behavioral and Brain Sciences, 4*, 568–570.

Dennett, D. (1978b). Conditions of personhood. Reprinted in *Brainstorms* (pp. 267–285). Cambridge, MA: MIT Press.

Dennett, D. (1987). *The intentional stance*. Cambridge, MA: MIT Press.

Diesendruck, G., & Markson, L. (2001). Children's avoidance of lexical overlap: a pragmatic account. *Developmental Psychology, 37*, 630–641.

Dretske, F. (1997). *Naturalizing the mind*. Cambridge, MA: MIT Press.

Dufour, V., & Sterck, E. H. M. (2008). Chimpanzees fail to plan in an exchange task but succeed in a tool-using procedure. *Behavioural Processes, 79*, 19–27.

Duhem, P. (1906). *La théorie physique, son objet et sa structure*. Paris: Chevalier et Rivière.

Dunbar, R. (1998). The social brain hypothesis. *Evolutionary Anthropology, 6*, 178–190.

Dunbar, R. (2007). Brain and cognition in evolutionary perspective. In S. Platek, J. Keenan, & T. Shackelford (Eds.), *Evolutionary cognitive neuroscience* (pp. 21–46). Cambridge, MA: MIT Press.

Emery, N., & Clayton, N. (2001). Effects of experience and social context on prospective caching strategies in scrub jays. *Nature, 414*, 443–446.

Emery, N., & Clayton, N. (2008). How to build a scrub-jay that reads minds. In S. Itakura & K. Fujita (Eds.), *Origins of the social minds* (pp. 65–97). Tokyo: Springer.

Emery, N., & Clayton, N. (2009). Comparative social cognition. *Annual Review of Psychology, 60*, 87–113.

Emery, N., Dally, J., & Clayton, N. (2004). Western scrub-jays (*Aphelocoma californica*) use cognitive strategies to protect their caches from thieving conspecifics. *Animal Cognition, 7*, 37–43.

Fagot, J., & Barbet, I. (2006). Amodal completion by baboons (*Papio papio*): contribution of background depth cues. *Primates, 47*, 145–150.

Fitzpatrick, S. (2009). The primate mindreading controversy: a case study in simplicity and methodology in animal psychology. In R. Lurz (Ed.), *The philosophy of animal minds* (pp. 258–276). Cambridge: Cambridge University Press.

Flavell, J., Green, F., & Flavell, E. (1993). Children's understanding of the stream of consciousness. *Child Development, 64*, 387–398.

Flavell, J., Green, F., & Flavell, E. (1995). Young children's knowledge about thinking. *Monographs of the Society for Research in Child Development, 60,* 1–95.

Flombaum, J., & Santos, L. (2005). Rhesus monkeys attribute perceptions to others. *Current Biology, 15,* 447–452.

Fodor, J. (1975). *The language of thought.* New York: Thomas Y. Crowell.

Fodor, J. (1983). *The modularity of mind.* Cambridge, MA: MIT Press.

Fogassi, L., Ferrari, P., Gesierich, B., Rozzi, S., Chersi, F., & Rizzolatti, G. (2005). Parietal lobe: from action organization to intention understanding. *Science, 308,* 662–667.

Frege, G. (1918/1977). Thoughts. Reprinted in P. Geach (Ed.), *Logical investigations* (pp. 1–30). New Haven: Yale University Press.

Fujita, K. (2006). Seeing what is not there: illusion, completion, and spatiotemporal boundary formation in comparative perspective. In E. Wasserman & T. Zentall (Eds.), *Comparative cognition: Experimental explorations of animal intelligence* (pp. 29–52). Oxford: Oxford University Press.

Fujita, K., & Giersch, A. (2005). What perceptual rules do capuchin monkeys (*Cebus Apella*) follow in completing partly occluded figures? *Journal of Experimental Psychology, 31,* 387–398.

Gallese, V. (2005). Embodied simulation: from neurons to phenomenal experience. *Phenomenology and the Cognitive Sciences, 4,* 23–48.

Gallese, V. (2007). Before and below "theory of mind": embodied simulation and the neural correlates of social cognition. *Philosophical Transaction of the Royal Society B, 362,* 659–669.

Gallese, V., Fadiga, L., Fogassi, L., & Rizzolatti, G. (1996). Action recognition in the premotor cortex. *Brain, 119,* 593–609.

Gallese, V., & Goldman, A. (1998). Mirror neurons and the simulation theory of mindreading. *Trends in Cognitive Sciences, 2,* 493–501.

Gallese, V., Keysers, C., & Rizzolatti, G. (2004). A unified view of the basis of social cognition. *Trends in Cognitive Sciences, 8,* 396–403.

Gallistel, C. R. (1990). *The organization of learning.* Cambridge, MA: MIT Press.

Gallup, G. (1982). Self-awareness and the emergence of mind in primates. *American Journal of Primatology, 2,* 237–248.

Gergely, G., & Csibra, G. (2003). Teleological reasoning in infancy: the naïve theory of rational action. *Trends in Cognitive Sciences, 7,* 287–292.

Gergely, G., Nadasdy, Z., Csibra, G., & Biro, S. (1995). Taking the intentional stance at 12 months of age. *Cognition, 56,* 165–193.

Godfrey-Smith, P. (2004). On folk psychology and mental representation. In H. Caplin, P. Staines, & P. Slezak (Eds.), *Representations in mind: New approaches to mental representation* (pp. 147–162). Amsterdam: Elsevier.

Goldman, A. (1993). The psychology of folk psychology. *Behavioral and Brain Sciences, 16*, 15–28.

Goldman, A. (2006). *Simulating minds: The philosophy, psychology, and neuroscience of mindreading*. Oxford: Oxford University Press.

Gómez, J. (2004). *Apes, monkeys, children, and the growth of mind*. Cambridge, MA: Harvard University Press.

Gómez, J. (2009). Embodying meaning: insights from primates, autism, and Brentano. *Neural Networks, 22*, 190–195.

Gómez, J., & Teixidor, P. (1992). "Theory of mind in an orangutan: a nonverbal test of false-belief appreciation?" Paper presented at *XIV Congress of the International Primatological Society* (August), Strasbourg.

Gopnik, A. (2009). *Philosophical baby*. New York: Farrar, Straus & Giroux.

Gopnik, A., & Graf, P. (1988). Knowing how you know: young children's ability to identify and remember the sources of their beliefs. *Child Development, 59*, 1366–1371.

Gordon, R. (1995). Simulation without introspection or inference from me to you. In T. Stone & M. Davies (Eds.), *Mental simulation* (pp. 53–67). Oxford: Blackwell.

Gordon, R. (1996). "Radical" simulationism. In P. Carruthers & P. Smith (Eds.), *Theories of theories of mind* (pp. 11–21). Cambridge: Cambridge University Press.

Graham, G. (1993). *Philosophy of mind*. Oxford: Blackwell.

Grice, H. P. (1971). Intention and uncertainty. *Proceedings of the British Academy, 57*, 267–279.

Griffin, D. (1992). *Animal minds: Beyond cognition to consciousness*. Chicago: University of Chicago Press.

Grodzinski, U., & Clayton, N. (2010). Problems faced by food-caching corvids and the evolution of cognitive solutions. *Philosophical Transactions of the Royal Society B, 365*, 977–987.

Hala, S., Chandler, M., & Frtiz, A. (1991). Fledgling theories of mind: deception as a marker of three-year-olds' understanding of false belief. *Child Development, 62*, 83–97.

Hampton, R. (2009). Multiple demonstrations of metacognition in nonhumans: converging evidence or multiple mechanisms? *Comparative Cognition & Behavior Reviews, 4*, 17–28.

Hanus, D., & Call, J. (2008). Chimpanzees infer the location of a reward based on the effect of its weight. *Current Biology, 18,* 370–372.

Hare, B. (2001). Can competitive paradigms increase the validity of experiments on primate social cognition? *Animal Cognition, 4,* 269–280.

Hare, B., Addessi, E., Call, J., Tomasello, M., & Visalberghi, E. (2003). Do capuchin monkeys, *Cebus paella,* know what conspecifics do and do not see? *Animal Behaviour, 65,* 131–142.

Hare, B., Brown, M., Williamson, C., & Tomasello, M. (2002). The domestication of social cognition in dogs. *Science, 298,* 1634–1636.

Hare, B., Call, J., Agnetta, B., & Tomasello, M. (2000). Chimpanzees know what conspecifics do and do not see. *Animal Behaviour, 59,* 771–785.

Hare, B., Call, J., & Tomasello, M. (2001). Do chimpanzees know what conspecifics know? *Animal Behaviour, 61,* 139–151.

Hare, B., Call, J., & Tomasello, M. (2006). Chimpanzees deceive a human competitor by hiding. *Cognition, 101,* 495–514.

Hare, B., & Tomasello, M. (2004). Chimpanzees are more skilful in competitive than in cooperative cognitive tasks. *Animal Behaviour, 68,* 571–581.

Harman, G. (1976). Practical reasoning. *Review of Metaphysics, 79,* 431–463.

Harman, G. (1978). Studying the chimpanzee's theory of mind. *Behavioral and Brain Sciences, 4,* 576–577.

Harman, G. (1990). The intrinsic quality of experience. *Philosophical Perspectives, 4,* 31–52.

Haun, D., & Call, J. (2009). Great apes' capacities to recognize relational similarity. *Cognition, 110,* 147–159.

Hauser, M., & Spaulding, B. (2006). Wild rhesus monkeys generate causal inferences about possible and impossible physical transformations in the absence of experience. *Proceedings of the National Academy of Sciences of the United States of America, 103,* 7181–7185.

Hauser, M., & Wood, J. (2010). Evolving the capacity to understand actions, intentions, and goals. *Annual Review of Psychology, 61,* 303–324.

Heider, F., & Simmel, M. (1944). An experimental study of apparent behavior. *American Journal of Psychology, 57,* 243–259.

Heinrich, B. (1995). An experimental investigation of insight in common ravens (*Corvus corax*). *Auk, 112,* 994–1003.

Heinrich, B. (1999). *Mind of the raven.* New York: Harper Collins.

Heinrich, B., & Bugnyar, B. (2005). Testing problem solving in ravens: string-pulling to reach food. *Ethology*, *111*, 962–976.

Held, S., Mendl, M., Devereux, C., & Byrne, R. (2001). Studies in social cognition: from primates to pigs. *Animal Welfare (South Mimms, England)*, *10*, 209–217.

Herman, L. (2006). Intelligence and rational behaviour in the bottlenose dolphin. In S. Hurley & M. Nudds (Eds.), *Rational animals?* (pp. 439–467). Oxford: Oxford University Press.

Herman, L., Abichandani, S., Elhajj, A., Herman, E., Sanchez, J., & Pack, A. (1999). Dolphins (*Tursiops truncatus*) comprehend the referential character of the human pointing gesture. *Journal of Comparative Psychology*, *113*, 1–18.

Herman, L., Richards, D., & Wolz, J. (1984). Comprehension of sentences by bottlenosed dolphins. *Cognition*, *16*, 129–219.

Heyes, C. (1993). Anecdotes, training, trapping and triangulating: do animals attribute mental states? *Animal Behaviour*, *46*, 177–188.

Heyes, C. (1994). Cues, convergence and a curmudgeon: a reply to Povinelli. *Animal Behaviour*, *48*, 242–244.

Heyes, C. (1998). Theory of mind in nonhuman primates. *Behavioral and Brain Sciences*, *21*, 101–148.

Heyes, C. (2001). Theory of mind and other domain-specific hypotheses. *Behavioral and Brain Sciences*, *24*, 1143–1144.

Hirata, S., & Matsuzawa, T. (2001). Tactics to obtain a hidden food item in chimpanzee pairs (*Pan troglodytes*). *Animal Cognition*, *4*, 285–295.

Hoffman, M., Beran, M., & Washburn, D. (2009). Memory for "what," "where," and "when" information in rhesus monkeys (*Macaca mulatta*). *Journal of Experimental Psychology*, *35*, 143–152.

Honderich, T. (1995). *The Oxford companion to philosophy*. Oxford: Oxford University Press.

Hopkins, W., Washburn, D., & Hyatt, C. (1996). Video-task acquisition in rhesus monkeys (*Macaca mulatta*) and chimpanzees (*Pan troglodytes*): a comparative analysis. *Primates*, *37*, 197–206.

Hostetter, A., Cantero, M., & Hopkins, W. (2001). Differential use of vocal and gestural communication by chimpanzees (*Pan troglodytes*) in response to the attentional status of a human (*Homo sapiens*). *Journal of Comparative Psychology*, *115*, 337–343.

Humphrey, N. (1976). The social function of intellect. In P. Bateson & R. Hinde (Eds.), *Growing points in ethology* (pp. 303–317). Cambridge: Cambridge University Press.

Hurley, S., & Nudds, M. (2006). *Rational animals?* Oxford: Oxford University Press.

Hutto, D. (2008). *Folk psychological narratives.* Cambridge, MA: MIT Press.

Hutto, D. (forthcoming). Elementary mind minding, enactivist-style. In A. Seemann (Ed.), *Joint attention: New developments in philosophy, psychology, and neuroscience.* Cambridge, MA: MIT Press.

Itakura, S. (2004). Gaze-following and joint visual attention in nonhuman animals. *Japanese Psychological Research, 46,* 216–226.

Jackson, F. (1977). *Perception.* Cambridge: Cambridge University Press.

Jacob, F. (1977). Evolution and tinkering. *Science, 196,* 1161–1166.

Jitsumori, M. (1996). A prototype effect and categorization of artificial polymorphous stimuli in pigeons. *Journal of Experimental Psychology. Animal Behavior Processes, 22,* 405–419.

Jolly, A. (1966). Lemur social behavior and primate intelligence. *Science, 153,* 501–506.

Kamar, D., & Olson, D. (1998). Theory of mind in young human primates: does Heyes's task measure it? *Behavioral and Brain Sciences, 21,* 122–123.

Kaminski, J., Call, J., & Fischer, J. (2004). Word learning in a domestic dog: evidence for "fast mapping." *Science, 304,* 1682–1683.

Kaminski, J., Call, J., & Tomasello, M. (2004). Body orientation and face orientation: two factors controlling apes' begging behavior from humans. *Animal Cognition, 7,* 216–223.

Kaminski, J., Call, J., & Tomasello, M. (2006). Goats' behaviour in a competitive food paradigm: evidence for perspective taking? *Behaviour, 143,* 1341–1356.

Kaminski, J., Call, J., & Tomasello, M. (2008). Chimpanzees know what others know, but not what they believe. *Cognition, 109,* 224–234.

Kanizsa, G. (1979). *Organization in vision: Essays on Gestalt perception.* New York: Praeger Publishers.

Kanizsa, G., Renzi, P., Conte, S., Compostela, C., & Guerani, L. (1993). Amodal completion in mouse vision. *Perception, 22,* 713–721.

Karin-D'Arcy, M., & Povinelli, D. (2002). Do chimpanzees know what each other see? A closer look. *International Journal of Comparative Psychology, 15,* 21–54.

Kohler, E., Keyser, C., Umiltà, A., Fogassi, L., Gallese, V., & Rizzolatti, G. (2002). Hearing sounds, understanding actions: action representation in mirror neurons. *Science, 297,* 846–848.

Köhler, W. (1927). *The mentality of apes.* New York: Harcourt Brace.

Krachun, C. (2008). *Mentalizing Capacities in Chimpanzees* (*Pan troglodytes*) (Unpublished doctoral dissertation). Carleton University, Ottawa.

Krachun, C., & Call, J. (2009). Chimpanzees (*Pan troglodytes*) know what can be seen from where. *Animal Cognition, 12,* 317–331.

Krachun, C., Call, J., & Tomasello, M. (2009). Can chimpanzees discriminate appearances from reality? *Cognition, 112,* 435–450.

Krachun, C., Carpenter, M., Call, J., & Tomasello, M. (2008). A competitive nonverbal false belief task for children and apes. *Developmental Science, 12,* 521–535.

Krachun, C., Carpenter, M., Call, J., & Tomasello, M. (2010). A new change-of-contents false belief test: children and chimpanzees compared. *International Journal of Comparative Psychology, 23,* 145–165.

Kuhlmeier, V., Wynn, K., & Bloom, P. (2003). Attribution of dispositional states by 12-month-olds. *Psychological Science, 14,* 402–408.

Kuroshima, H., Fujita, K., Adachi, I., Iwata, K., & Fuyuki, A. (2003). A capuchin monkey (*Cebus paella*) recognizes when people do and do not know the location of food. *Animal Cognition, 6,* 283–291.

Kuroshima, H., Fujita, K., Fuyuki, A., & Masuda, T. (2002). Understanding of the relationship between seeing and knowing by tufted capuchin monkeys (*Cebus apella*). *Animal Cognition, 5,* 41–48.

Leavens, D., Hostetter, A., Wesley, M., & Hopkins, W. (2004). Tactical use of unimodal and bimodal communication by chimpanzees, *Pan troglodytes. Animal Behaviour, 67,* 467–476.

Lesie, A. (1994). ToMM, ToBY, and agency: core architecture and domain specificity. In L. Hirschfeld & S. Gelman (Eds.), *Mapping the mind: Domain specificity in cognition and culture* (pp. 119–148). Cambridge: Cambridge University Press.

Lurz, R. (2001). How to solve the distinguishability problem. *Behavioral and Brain Sciences, 24,* 1142–1143.

Lurz, R. (2007). In defense of wordless thoughts about thoughts. *Mind & Language, 22,* 270–296.

Lurz, R. (2009a). If chimpanzees are mindreaders, could behavioral science tell? Toward a solution of the logical problem. *Philosophical Psychology, 22,* 305–328.

Lurz, R. (2009b). *The philosophy of animal minds.* Cambridge: Cambridge University Press.

Lurz, R. (2010). Belief attribution in animals: On how to move forward conceptually and empirically. *The Review of Philosophy and Psychology.*

Lurz, R. (2011). Can chimps attribute beliefs? A new approach to answering an old nettled question. In R. Mitchell and J. Smith (Eds.) *Minds of animals*. Columbia University Press.

Lurz, R. (forthcoming). The question of belief attribution in great apes: Its moral significance and epistemic problems. In K. Petrus & M. Wild (Eds.), *Animal minds and animal morals*. New York: Columbia University Press.

Lurz, R., & Krachun, C. (under review). How could we know whether nonhuman primates understand others' internal goals and intentions? Solving Povinelli's problem. *The Review of Philosophy and Psychology*.

Lycan, W. (1996). *Consciousness and experience*. Cambridge, MA: MIT Press.

Lyons, D., & Santos, L. (2006). Ecology, domain specificity, and the origins of the theory of mind: is competition the catalyst? *Philosophy Compass*, *1*, 481–492.

Malcolm, N. (1977). *Thought and knowledge*. Ithaca: Cornell University Press.

Mameli, M. (2001). Mindreading, mindshaping, and evolution. *Biology and Philosophy*, *16*, 597–628.

Mann, J., & Sargeant, B. (2003). Like mother, like calf: the ontogeny of foraging traditions in wild Indian Ocean bottlenose dolphins (*Tursiops sp.*). In D. Fragaszy & S. Perry (Eds.), *The Biology of traditions: Models and evidence* (pp. 236–266). Cambridge: Cambridge University Press.

Markman, E. (1979). Realizing that you don't understand: elementary school children's awareness of inconsistencies. *Child Development*, *50*, 643–655.

Markman, E., & Abelev, M. (2004). Word learning in dogs? *Trends in Cognitive Sciences*, *8*, 479–481.

Markman, E., & Wachtel, G. (1988). Children's use of mutual exclusivity to constrain the meanings of words. *Cognitive Psychology*, *20*, 121–157.

Martin-Ordas, G., Call, J., & Colmenares, F. (2008). Tubes, tables and traps: great apes solve two functionally equivalent trap tasks but show no evidence of transfer across tasks. *Animal Cognition*, *11*, 423–430.

Matsuno, T., & Fujita, K. (2009). A comparative psychophysical approach to visual perception in primates. *Primates*, *50*, 121–130.

McGinn, C. (1989). *Mental content*. Oxford: Blackwell.

Melis, A., Call, J., & Tomasello, M. (2006). Chimpanzees (*Pan troglodytes*) conceal visual and auditory information from others. *Journal of Comparative Psychology*, *120*, 154–162.

Meltzoff, A. (2007). "Like-me": a foundation for social cognition. *Developmental Science*, *10*, 126–134.

Meltzoff, A. (2009). Roots of social cognition: the like-me framework. In D. Cicchetti & M. Gunnar (Eds.), *Minnesota symposia on child psychology* (Vol. 35, pp. 29–58). Hoboken, NJ: John Wiley & Sons, Inc.

Menzel, E. (1974). A group of young chimpanzees in a one-acre field: leadership and communication. In A. Schrier & F. Stollnitz (Eds.), *Behavior of non-human primates* (pp. 83–153). New York: Academic Press.

Menzel, E., Savage-Rumbaugh, E., & Lawson, J. (1985). Chimpanzee (*Pan troglodytes*) spatial problem solving with the use of mirrors and televised equivalents of mirrors. *Journal of Comparative Psychology, 99,* 211–217.

Michelon, P., & Zacks, J. (2006). Two kinds of visual perspective taking. *Perception and Psychophysics, 68,* 327–337.

Miklósi, Á., Kubinyi, E., Topál, J., Gácsi, M., Virányi, Z., & Csányi, V. (2003). A simple reason for a big difference: wolves do not look back at humans, but dogs do. *Current Biology, 13,* 763–766.

Miller, C., Dibble, E., & Hauser, M. (2001). Amodal completion of acoustic signals by a nonhuman primate. *Nature Neuroscience, 4,* 783–784.

Millikan, R. (2006). Styles of rationality. In S. Hurley & M. Nudds (Eds.), *Rational animals?* (pp. 117–126). Oxford: Oxford University Press.

Mitchell, R. (1993). Humans, nonhumans and persons. In P. Cavalieri & P. Singer (Eds.), *The great ape project* (pp. 237–247). New York: St. Martin's Press.

Moll, H., & Tomasello, M. (2004). 12- and 18-month-old infants follow gaze to spaces behind barriers. *Developmental Science, 7,* 1–9.

Moll, H., & Tomasello, M. (2006). Level 1 perspective-taking at 24 months of age. *British Journal of Developmental Psychology, 24,* 603–613.

Morell, V. (2008). (March). "Minds of their own: animals are smarter than you think." *National Geographic.* Available at http://ngm.nationalgeographic.com/2008/03/animal-minds/virginia-morell-text.

Morris, A. (2000). Development of logical reasoning: children's ability to verbally explain the nature of the distinction between logical and nonlogical forms of argument. *Developmental Psychology, 36,* 741–758.

Moshman, D. (2004). From inference to reasoning: the construction of rationality. *Thinking & Reasoning, 10,* 221–239.

Moshman, D., & Franks, B. (1986). Development of the concept of inferential validity. *Child Development, 57,* 153–165.

Mulcahy, N., & Call, J. (2006). Apes save tools for future use. *Science, 312,* 1038–1049.

Muller, M., & Mitani, J. (2005). Conflict and cooperation in wild chimpanzees. *Advances in the Study of Behavior, 35*, 275–331.

Murai, C., Kosugi, D., Tomonaga, M., Tanaka, M., Matsuzawa, T., & Itakura, S. (2005). Can chimpanzee infants (*Pan troglodytes*) form categorical representations in the same manner as human infants (*Homo sapiens*)? *Developmental Science, 8*, 240–254.

Nagasaka, Y., Lazareva, O., & Wasserman, A. (2007). Prior experience affects amodal completion in pigeons. *Perception & Psychophysics, 69*, 596–605.

Nagel, T. (1974). What is it like to be a bat? *Philosophical Review, 83*, 435–450.

Nichols, S., & Stich, S. (2003). *Mindreading: An integrated account of pretence, self-awareness, and understanding of other minds.* Oxford: Oxford University Press.

Nieder, A. (2002). Seeing more than meets the eye: processing of illusory contours in animals. *Journal of Comparative Physiology. A, Neuroethology, Sensory, Neural, and Behavioral Physiology, 188*, 249–260.

Nisssani, M. (2004). Theory of mind and insight in chimpanzees, elephants, and other animals? In L. Rogers and G. Kaplan (Eds.), *Comparative vertebrate cognition: Are primates superior to non-primates?* (pp. 227–262). New York: Kluwer Academic.

O'Connell, S., & Dunbar, R. (2003). A test for comprehension for false belief in chimpanzees. *Evolution & Cognition, 9*, 131–140.

O'Neill, D., & Gopnik, A. (1991). Young children's ability to identify the sources of their beliefs. *Developmental Psychology, 27*, 390–397.

Oden, D., Thompson, R., & Premack, D. (1990). Infant chimpanzees spontaneously perceive both concrete and abstract same/different relations. *Child Development, 61*, 621–631.

Oden, D., Thompson, R., & Premack, D. (2001). Can an ape reason analogically? Comprehension and prediction of analogical problems by Sarah, a chimpanzee (*Pan troglodytes*). In D. Gentner, K. Holyoak, & B. Kokinov (Eds.), *The analogical mind* (pp. 471–498). Cambridge MA: MIT Press.

Okamoto-Barth, S., Call, J., & Tomasello, M. (2007). Great apes' understanding of other individuals' line of sight. *Psychological Science, 18*, 462–468.

Onishi, K., & Baillargeon, R. (2005). Do 15-month-old infants understand false beliefs? *Science, 308*, 255–258.

Osvath, M. (2009). Spontaneous planning for future stone throwing by a male chimpanzee. *Current Biology, 19*, 190–191.

Osvath, M., & Osvath, H. (2008). Chimpanzees (*Pan troglodytes*) and orangutan (*Pongo abelii*) forethought: self-control and pre-experience in the face of future tool use. *Animal Cognition, 11*, 661–674.

Pack, A., & Herman, L. (1995). Sensory integration in the bottlenose dolphin: immediate recognition of complex shapes across the senses of echolocation and vision. *Journal of the Acoustical Society of America, 98,* 722–733.

Pattison, K., Miller, H., Rayburn-Reeves, R. & Zentall, T. (2010). The case of the disappearing bone: dogs' understanding of the physical properties of objects. *Behavioral Processes, 85,* 278–282.

Penn, D., Holyoak, K., & Povinelli, D. (2008). Darwin's mistake: explaining the discontinuity between human and nonhuman minds. *Behavioral and Brain Sciences, 31,* 109–178.

Penn, D., & Povinelli, D. (2007). On the lack of evidence that nonhuman animals possess anything remotely resembling a "theory of mind." *Philosophical Transactions of the Royal Society B, 362,* 731–744.

Pepperberg, I. (2004). Insightful string-pulling in grey parrots (*Psittacus erithacus*) is affected by vocal competence. *Animal Cognition, 7,* 263–266.

Pepperberg, I., & Wilcox, S. (2000). Evidence for a form of mutual exclusivity during label acquisition by grey parrots (*Psittacus erithacus*)? *Journal of Comparative Psychology, 114,* 219–231.

Perner, J., & Ruffman, T. (2005). Infants' insight into the mind: how deep? *Science, 308,* 214–216.

Petkov, C., O'Connor, K., & Sutter, M. (2003). Illusory sound perception in macaque monkeys. *Journal of Neuroscience, 23,* 9155–9161.

Petkov, C., O'Connor, K., & Sutter, M. (2007). Encoding of illusory continuity in primary auditory cortex. *Neuron, 54,* 153–165.

Petkov, C., & Sutter, M. (forthcoming). Evolutionary conservation and neuronal mechanisms of auditory perceptual restoration. *Hearing Research.*

Pillow, B. (1999). Children's understanding of inferential knowledge. *Journal of Genetic Psychology, 160,* 419–428.

Pillow, B. (2002). Children's and adult's evaluation of certainty of deductive inference, inductive inference, and guesses. *Child Development, 73,* 779–792.

Poss, S., & Rochat, P. (2003). Referential understanding of videos in chimpanzees (*Pan troglodytes*), orangutans (*Pongo pygmaeus*), and children (*Homo sapiens*). *Journal of Comparative Psychology, 117,* 420–428.

Poti, P., & Saporiti, M. (2010). A capuchin monkey (*Cebus paella*) uses video to find food. *Folia Primatologica, 81,* 16–30.

Povinelli, D. (1996). Chimpanzee theory of mind? The long road to strong inference. In P. Carruthers & P. Smith (Eds.), *Theories of theories of mind* (pp. 293–329). Cambridge: Cambridge University Press.

Povinelli, D. (2000). *Folk physics for apes*. Oxford: Oxford University Press.

Povinelli, D., & Eddy, T. (1996). What young chimpanzees know about seeing. *Monographs of the Society for Research in Child Development, 61*, 1–189.

Povinelli, D., Nelson, K., & Boysen, S. (1990). Inferences about guessing and knowing by chimpanzees (*Pan troglodytes*). *Journal of Comparative Psychology, 104*, 203–210.

Povinelli, D., & Vonk, J. (2006). We don't need a microscope to explore the chimpanzee's mind. In S. Hurley & M. Nudds (Eds.), *Rational animals?* (pp. 385–412). Oxford: Oxford University Press.

Premack, D. (1983). The codes of man and beast. *Behavioral and Brain Sciences, 6*, 125–167.

Premack, D. (1988). "Does the chimpanzee have a theory of mind" revisited. In R. Byrne & A. Whiten (Eds.), *Machiavellian intelligence: social expertise and evolution of intelligence in monkeys, apes, and humans* (pp. 160–179). Oxford: Oxford University Press.

Premack, D. (2007). Human and animal cognition: continuity and discontinuity. *Proceedings of the National Academy of Sciences of the United States of America, 104*, 13861–13867.

Premack, D., & Premack, A. (1997). Motor competence as integral to attribution of goal. *Cognition, 63*, 235–242.

Premack, D., & Woodruff, G. (1978). Does the chimpanzee have a theory of mind? *Behavioral and Brain Sciences, 1*, 515–526.

Prior, A. (1971). *Objects of thought*. Oxford: Oxford University Press.

Proust, J. (2009). The representational basis of brute metacognition: a proposal. In R. Lurz (Ed.), *The philosophy of animal minds* (pp. 165–183). Cambridge: Cambridge University Press.

Putnam, H. (1992). *Renewing philosophy*. Cambridge, MA: Harvard University Press.

Pylyshyn, Z. (1999). Is vision continuous with cognition? The case for cognitive impenetrability of visual perception. *Behavioral and Brain Sciences, 22*, 341–365.

Quine, W. V. (1953). Two dogmas of empiricism. Reprinted in *From a logical point of view* (pp. 20–46). Cambridge, MA: Harvard University Press.

Ramsey, W., Stich, S., & Garon, J. (1990). Connectionism, eliminativism, and the future of folk psychology. *Philosophical Perspectives, 4*, 449–533.

Reaux, J., Theall, L., & Povinelli, D. (1999). A longitudinal investigation of chimpanzees' understanding of visual perception. *Child Development, 70*, 215–290.

Regolin, L., & Vallortigara, G. (1995). Perception of partly occluded objects by young chicks. *Perception & Psychophysics, 57*, 971–976.

Reid, P. (2009). Adapting to the human world: dogs' responsiveness to our social cues. *Behavioural Processes, 80*, 325–333.

Ristau, C. (1991). *Cognitive ethology: The minds of other animals*. Hillsdale, NJ: Lawrence Erlbaum Associates.

Rizzolatti, G., Fadiga, L., Gallese, V., & Fogasi, L. (1996). Premotor cortex and the recognition of motor action. *Brain Research. Cognitive Brain Research, 3*, 131–141.

Rosati, A., & Hare, B. (2009). Looking past the model species: diversity in gaze-following skills across primates. *Current Opinion in Neurobiology, 19*, 45–51.

Routley, R. (1984). Alleged problems in attributing beliefs, and intentionality, to animals. *Inquiry, 24*, 385–417.

Ruffman, T., & Perner, J. (2005). Do infants really understand false beliefs? *Trends in Cognitive Sciences, 9*, 462–463.

Russell, B. (1912). *The problems of philosophy*. Oxford: Oxford University Press.

Salwiczek, L., Emery, N., Schlinger, B., & Clayton, N. (2009). The development of caching and object permanence in Western scrub-jays (*Aphelocoma californica*): which emerges first? *Journal of Comparative Psychology, 123*, 295–303.

Santos, L., Flombaum, J., & Webb, P. (2007). The evolution of human mindreading: how nonhuman primates can inform social cognitive neuroscience. In S. Platek, J. Keenan, & T. Shackelford (Eds.), *Evolutionary cognitive neuroscience* (pp. 433–456). Cambridge, MA: MIT Press.

Santos, L., Nissen, A., & Ferrugia, J. (2006). Rhesus monkeys, *Macaca mulatta*, know what others can and cannot hear. *Animal Behaviour, 71*, 1175–1181.

Sargeant, B., & Mann, J. (2009). Developmental evidence for foraging traditions in wild bottlenose dolphins. *Animal Behaviour, 78*, 715–721.

Sato, A., Kanazawa, S., & Fujita, K. (1997). Perception of object unity in chimpanzees (*Pan troglodytes*). *Japanese Psychological Research, 39*, 191–199.

Savage-Rumbaugh, S., Rumbaugh, D., & Boysen, S. (1978). Sarah's problems in comprehension. *Behavioral and Brain Sciences, 1*, 555–557.

Schusterman, R., Kastak, C., & Kastak, D. (2002). The cognitive sea lion: meaning and memory in the laboratory and in nature. In M. Bekoff, C. Allen, & M. Burghardt (Eds.), *The cognitive animal* (pp. 217–228). Cambridge, MA: MIT Press.

Scott, R., & Baillargeon, R. (2009). Which penguin is this? Attributing false beliefs about object identity at 18 months. *Child Development, 80*, 1172–1196.

Searle, J. (1983). *Intentionality*. Cambridge: Cambridge University Press.

Seeba, F., & Klump, G. (2009). Stimulus familiarity affects perceptual restoration in the European starling (*Sturnus vulgaris*). *PLoS ONE, 4,* e5974.

Seed, A., Tebbich, S., Emery, N., & Clayton, N. (2006). Investigating physical cognition in rooks (*Corvus frugilegus*). *Current Biology, 16,* 697–701.

Sekuler, A. & Palmer, S. (1992). Perception of partly occluded objects: A microgenetic analysis. *Journal of Experimental Psychology, 121,* 95–111.

Shatz, M., Wellman, H., & Silber, S. (1983). The acquisition of mental verbs: a systematic investigation of the first reference to mental state. *Cognition, 14,* 301–321.

Shettleworth, S. (1998). *Cognition, evolution, and behavior.* Oxford: Oxford University Press.

Shields, W., Smith, D., Guttmannova, K., & Washburn, D. (2005). Confidence judgments by humans and rhesus monkeys. *Journal of General Psychology, 132,* 165–186.

Shillito, D., Shumaker, R., Gallup, G., & Beck, B. (2005). Understanding visual barriers for level 1 perspective taking in an orangutan, *Pongo pygmaeus. Animal Behaviour, 69,* 679–687.

Shoemaker, S. (1996). *The first-person perspective and other essays.* Cambridge: Cambridge University Press.

Slocombe, K., Kaller, T., Call, J., & Zuberbühler, K. (2010). Chimpanzees extract social information from agonistic screams. *PLoS ONE, 5,* e11473.

Smith, D., Beran, M., Couchman, J., Coutinho, V., & Boomer, J. (2009). Animal metacognition: problems and prospects. *Comparative Cognition & Behavior Reviews, 4,* 40–53.

Smith, D., Redford, J., & Haas, S. (2008). Prototype abstraction by monkeys (*Macaca mulatta*). *Journal of Experimental Psychology. General, 137,* 390–401.

Smith, P. (1982). On animal beliefs. *Southern Journal of Philosophy, 20,* 503–512.

Sober, E. (1998). Black box inference: when should intervening variables be postulated? *British Journal for the Philosophy of Science, 49,* 469–498.

Son, L., & Kornell, N. (2005). Metaconfidence judgments in rhesus macaques: explicit versus implicit mechanisms. In H. Terrace & J. Metcalfe (Eds.), *The missing link in cognition: Origins of self-reflective consciousness* (pp. 296–320). Oxford: Oxford University Press.

Song, H., & Baillargeon, R. (2008). Infants' reasoning about others' false perceptions. *Developmental Psychology, 44,* 1789–1795.

Southgate, V., Senju, A., & Csibra, G. (2007). Action anticipation through attribution of false belief by 2-year-olds. *Psychological Science, 18,* 587–592.

Sovrano, A., & Bisazza, A. (2008). Recognition of partly occluded objects by fish. *Animal Cognition, 11,* 161–166.

Sterelny, K. (2003). *Thought in a hostile world.* Oxford: Blackwell.

Stich, S., & Nichols, S. (1995). Folk psychology: simulation or tacit theory? In M. Davies & T. Stone (Eds.), *Folk psychology* (pp. 123–158). Oxford: Blackwell.

Strawson, P. (1959). *Individuals.* London: Methuen.

Stulp, G., Emery, N., Verhulst, S., & Clayton, N. (2009). Western scrub-jays conceal auditory information when competitors can hear but cannot see. *Biology Letters, 5,* 583–585.

Suda-King, C. (2008). Do orangutans (*Pongo pygmaeus*) know when they do not remember? *Animal Cognition, 11,* 21–42.

Sugita, Y. (1997). Neuronal correlates of auditory induction in the cat cortex. *Neuroreport, 8,* 1155–1159.

Surian, L., Caldi, S., & Sperber, D. (2007). Attribution of beliefs by 13-month-old infants. *Psychological Science, 18,* 580–586.

Szabó, Z. G. (2003). Believing in things. *Philosophy and Phenomenological Research, 66,* 584–611.

Tan, J., & Harris, P. (1991). Autistic children understand seeing and wanting. *Development and Psychopathology, 3,* 163–174.

Taylor, A., Hunt, G., Medina, F., & Gray, R. (2009). Do New Caledonian crows solve physical problems through causal reasoning? *Proceedings: Biological Sciences, 276,* 247–254.

Taylor, A., Medina, F., Holzhaider, J., Hearne, L., Hunt, G., & Russell, H. (2010). An investigation into the cognition behind spontaneous string pulling in New Caledonian crows. *PLoS ONE, 5,* e9345.

Tebbich, S., Seed, A., Emery, N., & Clayton, N. (2007). Non-tool-using rooks, *Corvus frugilegus,* solve the trap-tube problem. *Animal Cognition, 10,* 225–231.

Thau, M. (2002). *Consciousness and cognition.* Oxford: Oxford University Press.

Theall, L., & Povinelli, D. (1999). Do chimpanzees tailor their gestural signals to fit the attentional states of others? *Animal Cognition, 2,* 207–214.

Thompson, R., Boysen, S., & Oden, D. (1997). Language-naïve chimpanzees (*Pan troglodytes*) judge relations between relations in a conceptual matching-to-sample task. *Journal of Experimental Psychology, 23,* 31–43.

Thompson, R., & Flemming, T. (2008). Analogical apes and paleological monkeys revisited. *Behavioral and Brain Sciences, 31,* 149–150.

Thompson, R., & Oden, D. (1993). "Language training" and its role in the expression of tacit propositional knowledge in chimpanzees (*Pan troglodytes*). In H. Roitblat, L. Herman, & P. Nachtigall (Eds.), *Language and communication: Comparative perspectives* (pp. 265–384). Hillsdale, NJ: Lawrence Erlbaum Associates.

Thompson, R., & Oden, D. (1996). A profound disparity revisited: perception and judgment of abstract identity relations by chimpanzees, human infants, and monkeys. *Behavioural Processes, 35,* 149–161.

Thompson, R., & Oden, D. (2000). Categorical perception and conceptual judgments by nonhuman primates: the paleological monkey and the analogical ape. *Cognitive Science, 24,* 363–396.

Tomasello, M., & Call, J. (1997). *Primate cognition.* Oxford: Oxford University Press.

Tomasello, M., & Call, J. (2006). Do chimpanzees know what other see—or only what they are looking at? In S. Hurley & M. Nudds (Eds.), *Rational animals?* (pp. 371–384). Oxford: Oxford University Press.

Topál, J., Erdőhegyi, Á., Mányik, R., & Miklósi, A. (2006). Mindreading in a dog: an adaptation of a primate mental attribution study. *International Journal of Psychology & Psychological Therapy, 6,* 365–379.

Tschudin, A. (2001). "Mind-reading" mammals: attribution of belief task with dolphins. *Animal Welfare (South Mimms, England), 10,* 119–127.

Tschudin, A. (2006). Belief attribution tasks with dolphins: what social minds can reveal about animal rationality. In S. Hurley & M. Nudds (Eds.), *Rational animals?* (pp. 413–436). Oxford: Oxford University Press.

Tvardíková, K., & Fuchs, R. (2010). Tits use amodal completion in predator recognition: a field experiment. *Animal Cognition, 13,* 609–615.

Tye, M. (1995). *Ten problems of consciousness.* Cambridge, MA: MIT Press.

Tye, M. (1997). The problem of simple minds: is there anything it is like to be a honey bee? *Philosophical Studies, 88,* 289–317.

Tye, M. (2009). *Consciousness revisited: Materialism without phenomenal concepts.* Cambridge, MA: MIT Press.

Tyrrell, D., Stauffer, L., & Snowman, L. (1991). Perception of abstract identity/ difference relationships by infants. *Infant Behavior and Development, 14,* 125–129.

Uller, C. (2004). Disposition to recognize goals in infant chimpanzees. *Animal Cognition, 7,* 154–161.

Uller, C. (2008). Developmental and evolutionary considerations of numerical cognition: a review. *Journal of Evolutionary Psychology (Budapest)*, *6*, 237–253.

Vallortigara, G. (2006). The cognitive chicken: visual and spatial cognition in a nonmammalian brain. In E. Wasserman & T. Zentall (Eds.), *Comparative cognition: Experimental explorations of animal intelligence* (pp. 53–70). Oxford: Oxford University Press.

Visalberghi, E., & Limongelli, L. (1994). Lack of comprehension of cause–effect relations in tool-using capuchin monkeys (*Cebus apella*). *Journal of Comparative Psychology*, *108*, 15–22.

Vogels, R. (1999). Categorization of complex visual images by rhesus monkeys. Part 1: behavioral study. *European Journal of Neuroscience*, *11*, 1223–1238.

Vonk, J. (2003). Gorilla (*Gorilla gorilla gorilla*) and orangutan (*Pongo abelii*) understanding of first- and second-order relations. *Animal Cognition*, *6*, 77–86.

Vonk, J., & Povinelli, D. (2006). Similarity and difference in the conceptual systems of primates: the unobservability hypothesis. In E. Wasserman & T. Zentall (Eds.), *Comparative cognition: Experimental exploration of animal intelligence* (pp. 363–387). Oxford: Oxford University Press.

Walker, S. (1983). *Animal thought*. London: Routledge & Kegan Paul.

Watve, M., Thakar, J., Puntambekar, A., Shaikh, I., Jog, K., & Paranjape, S. (2002). Bee-eaters (*Merops orientalis*) respond to what a predator can see. *Animal Cognition*, *5*, 253–259.

Welker, D. (1988). On the necessity of bodies. *Erkenntnis*, *28*, 363–385.

Wellman, H. (1990). *Young children's theory of mind*. Cambridge, MA: MIT Press.

Werner, C., & Rehkämper, R. (2001). Categorization of multidimensional geometrical figures by chickens (*Gallus gallus f. domestica*): fit of basic assumptions from exemplar, feature and prototype theory. *Animal Cognition*, *4*, 37–48.

West, R., & Young, R. (2002). Do domestic dogs show any evidence of being able to count? *Animal Cognition*, *5*, 183–186.

Whiten, A. (1996). When does smart behaviour-reading become mind-reading? In P. Carruthers & P. Smith (Eds.), *Theories of theories of mind* (pp. 277–292). Cambridge: Cambridge University Press.

Whiten, A. (2000). Chimpanzee cognition and the question of mental re-representation. In D. Sperber (Ed.), *Metarepresentations: A multidisciplinary perspective* (pp. 139–170). Oxford: Oxford University Press.

Whiten, A., & Byrne, R. (1997). *Machiavellian intelligence II: Extensions and evaluations*. Cambridge: Cambridge University Press.

Wilkinson, K., Dube, W., & McIlvane, W. (1998). Fast mapping and exclusion (emergent matching) in developmental language, behavior analysis, and animal cognition research. *Psychological Record*, *48*, 407–425.

Wimmer, H., & Perner, J. (1983). Beliefs about beliefs: representation and constraining function of wrong beliefs in young children's understanding of deception. *Cognition*, *13*, 103–125.

Wittgenstein, L. (1953). *Philosophical investigations*. New York: MacMillan.

Wood, J., & Hauser, M. (2008). Action comprehension in nonhuman animals: motor simulation or inferential reasoning? *Trends in Cognitive Sciences*, *12*, 461–465.

Wood, J., Glynn, D., Phillips, B., & Hauser, M. (2007). The perception of rational, goal-directed action in nonhuman primates. *Science*, *317*, 1402–1405.

Wood, J., Hauser, M., & Glynn, D. (2008). Rhesus monkeys' understanding of actions and goals. *Social Neuroscience*, *3*, 60–68.

Xitco, M., & Roitblat, H. (1996). Object recognition through eavesdropping: passive echolocation in bottlenose dolphins. *Animal Learning & Behavior*, *24*, 355–365.

Zentall, T., Clement, T., Friedrich, A., & DiGian, K. (2006). Stimuli signaling rewards that follow a less-preferred event are themselves preferred: implications for cognitive dissonance. In E. Wasserman & T. Zentall (Eds.), *Comparative cognition: Experimental explorations of animal intelligence* (pp. 651–667). Oxford: Oxford University Press.

Zimmermann, F., Zemke, F., Call, J., & Gómez, J. (2009). Orangutan (*Pongo pygmaeus*) and bonobos (*Pan paniscus*) point to inform a human about the location of a tool. *Animal Cognition*, *12*, 347–358.

Index